THE
DIRTY TRICKS
DEPARTMENT

THE
DIRTY TRICKS
DEPARTMENT

STANLEY LOVELL, THE OSS, AND
THE MASTERMINDS OF WORLD WAR II
SECRET WARFARE

JOHN LISLE

St. Martin's Press
New York

First published in the United States by St. Martin's Press, an imprint of
St. Martin's Publishing Group

www.stmartins.com

Design by Meryl Sussman Levavi
Endpapers designed by Rob Grom
Endpaper art: Hi-Standard HDM silenced .22 pistol silhouette © Carl
Miller/Alamy

Library of Congress Cataloging-in-Publication Data

Names: Lisle, John, author.
Title: The dirty tricks department : Stanley Lovell, the OSS, and the masterminds
    of World War II secret warfare / John Lisle.
Other titles: Stanley Lovell, the OSS, and the masterminds of World War II
    secret warfare
Description: First edition. | New York : St. Martin's Press, 2023. |
    Includes bibliographical references and index. |
Identifiers: LCCN 2022039367 | ISBN 9781250280244 (hardcover) |
    ISBN 9781250280251 (ebook)
Subjects: LCSH: United States. Office of Strategic Services. Research and
    Development Branch—History. | Lovell, Stanley P.—Influence. | United States.
    Office of Strategic Services—Officials and employees—Biography. | Intelligence
    service—United States—History—20th century. | United States. Central
    Intelligence Agency—History—20th century. | Espionage, American—History—
    20th century. | Project MKULTRA.
Classification: LCC D810.S7 .L57 2023 | DDC 940.54/8673—dc23/
    eng/20220902
LC record available at https://lccn.loc.gov/2022039367

Our books may be purchased in bulk for promotional, educational, or business
use. Please contact your local bookseller or the Macmillan Corporate and
Premium Sales Department at 1-800-221-7945, extension 5442, or by email at
MacmillanSpecialMarkets@macmillan.com.

First Edition: 2023

10 9 8 7 6 5 4 3 2 1

To my parents

Yea, stranger engines for the brunt of war,
Than was the fiery keel at Antwerp's bridge
I'll make my servile spirits to invent.

—Christopher Marlowe, *Doctor Faustus*

Oh, what a tangled web we weave,
When first we practice to deceive!

—Sir Walter Scott, *Marmion*

Contents

THE
DIRTY TRICKS
DEPARTMENT

1
Donovan's Dragoons

"Wild Bill" Donovan didn't fear the hellish circumstances of war. Instead, the thrill of combat excited him "like a youngster at Halloween," he wrote home to his wife. He had been fighting along the Western Front for less than a year, but in that short time he had already taken shrapnel to his leg, survived a poison gas attack, and rescued Allied soldiers buried under debris, for which the French awarded him the Croix de Guerre medal.

On October 15, 1918, Donovan and his men of the U.S. Army's 69th Infantry Regiment, the "Fighting Irish," found themselves bunkered down in shell holes while an onslaught of German bullets grazed the ground. They were supposed to make an advance behind an escort of tanks, but the tanks never showed up. They started anyway.

Donovan leapt out of his muddy hole to lead the advance. As he cleared the ledge, a machine-gun bullet ripped through his right knee, destroying his tibia. He later said that it "felt as if somebody had hit me on the back of the leg with a spiked club." Although nauseated from the pain, he continued to yell orders at his men. And despite his injury, none of them dared to disobey. He was known to sock them in the jaw for less, a punch that one soldier said carried enough force to rival a kick from a mule.

While Donovan lay in the crimson-tinted mud with a mangled leg, a German artillery shell exploded in the hole beside him. Three of the men whom he had been yelling at were instantly blown apart. Donovan was "showered with the remnants of their bodies." Then, he said, "Gas was thrown at us, thick and nasty." He inhaled the noxious fumes. His mind became groggy. His body slumped over.

Five hours later, during a lull in the action, a group of soldiers put Donovan in a blanket and carried him more than a mile through exploding shells and whizzing bullets—one soldier was hit in the process—to a makeshift hospital. They arrived to find a harrowing scene. One officer had been shot through the stomach and was bleeding out on the floor. Two more had undergone surgery and were begging their nurse to hold their hands and smooth their brows. Another man died while crying for his wife and children.

Donovan survived his injuries, but he ultimately lost half his regiment, a fact that would weigh heavily on his conscience for years to come. Nevertheless, despite the mental and physical anguish that he had endured, and despite the men whom he had lost, when he returned home from Europe, he hungered for another taste of combat.

In 1923, Donovan was awarded the Medal of Honor for his heroic actions in World War I, making him the most decorated officer in the entire U.S. military. At an emotional ceremony in front of a crowd of four thousand veterans, he unfastened the medal from his neck and gave it to his regiment. Tears welled up in his piercing blue-gray eyes. "It doesn't belong with me," he said. "It belongs to the boys who are not here, the boys who are resting under the white crosses in France or in the cemeteries of New York, also to the boys who were lucky enough to come through."

Bill Donovan was a star athlete from a tough, working-class neighborhood in Buffalo, New York. He had graduated from Columbia Law School in 1907, the same year that classmate Franklin Roosevelt had dropped out after passing the New York bar exam. The two men differed greatly in their politics and social circles—one was a Republican of humble Irish ancestry, the other a Democrat from the upper class—but they shared a common character defined by bravery, energy, and optimism that would unite them in the years to come.

After World War I, Donovan worked in the Department of Justice as an attorney for the Western District of New York and enforced Prohibition with a vigor that rivaled his appetite for war. He once launched a liquor raid on the famous Saturn Club, a swanky social club in Buffalo to which he himself belonged. Afterward, he told the angry members who called to complain, "The law is the law and I have sworn to uphold it."

Donovan himself never drank. Only once did his acquaintance Carleton Coon ever see him hold a glass of amber-tinted liquid, and even then, he never took a sip. "Nor did he smoke," Coon added.

During the 1928 presidential election, Donovan campaigned and wrote speeches for Republican candidate Herbert Hoover, who promised to make Donovan the attorney general if he won. Hoover did win, but he reneged on the promise under pressure from a group of anti-Catholic Southerners. A contemptuous

Donovan thereafter resigned from the Department of Justice and opened a private law firm. He then ran to succeed Franklin Roosevelt as governor of New York, but he lost the election—in part because of grudges held over from the Saturn Club raid.

Although Donovan was a Republican, he wasn't against co-operating with the Democrats across the aisle. When Franklin Roosevelt defeated Hoover for the presidency in the midst of the Great Depression, he sent Donovan on a series of trips to Europe to gather information on the state of international affairs (and to gather rare stamps for Roosevelt's private collection). On one of these trips, Donovan spoke with high-ranking members of the Nazi Party and sensed that their authoritarian calls to restore Germany's pride, rebuild its military, and appropriate land from others would inevitably lead to another world war.

Given this prospect, Donovan urged President Roosevelt to create a centralized intelligence organization to oversee the collection of intelligence abroad. Ideally, this organization would rise above the bureaucratic rivalries that stymied other intelligence organizations—the Federal Bureau of Investigation, the Army's Military Intelligence Division, the Office of Naval Intelligence—and provide the president with the most accurate and up-to-date information possible. Donovan also wanted this centralized intelligence organization to engage in espionage, sabotage, propaganda, and disinformation campaigns against America's enemies. "Modern war operates on more fronts than battle fronts," he explained to Secretary of the Navy Frank Knox. "Each combatant seeks to dominate the whole field of communications. No defense system is effective unless it recognizes and deals with this fact."

For thousands of years, humans had fought by land and sea. In the early twentieth century, they had added aerial combat to the mix. Now, Donovan reasoned, the United States needed to officially expand its arsenal to include a fourth domain: "Underground."

On September 1, 1939, a blitzkrieg of German tanks, planes, and soldiers poured east into neighboring Poland, initiating World War II. Donovan's plea to Roosevelt to create a centralized intelligence organization grew louder, and Roosevelt grew more receptive. He confided in a letter to Secretary Knox, "Bill Donovan is an old friend of mine—we were in law school together—and frankly, I should like to have him in the Cabinet, not only for his own ability, but also to repair in a sense the very great injustice done him by President Hoover."

But before Roosevelt could create the organization, another great injustice struck Donovan. In 1940, his twenty-three-year-old daughter, Patricia, skidded her car on a wet highway and crashed into a tree. A passing motorist found her lying unconscious on the side of the road. She was rushed to a hospital, but she died before Donovan could reach her. The emotional toll on him was so great, it was said, that his hair turned gray overnight.

As the conflict in Europe escalated—Germany soon invaded Norway, Denmark, the Netherlands, Belgium, Luxembourg, and France—President Roosevelt sent Donovan on two more trips to Europe, during which he met with King George, Queen Mary, and Winston Churchill, and visited the British and Mediterranean coasts to gauge their preparedness for a potential German invasion. Churchill made sure that Donovan received full British cooperation because, he said, Donovan had "great influence with the President." On returning to the United States, Donovan's message to Roosevelt was simple: The British needed American support, and the United States needed a centralized intelligence organization.

Roosevelt finally relented to Donovan's plea. On July 11, 1941, he named Donovan to the new position of Coordinator of Information (COI). The COI was essentially responsible for collecting any intelligence related to national security and performing other "supplementary activities"—a euphemism for espionage, sabotage, propaganda, and disinformation—as necessary. Roosevelt, paralyzed from the waist down due to what was diagnosed as a late case of polio, began referring to Donovan as "my secret legs."

In September 1941, Donovan moved COI headquarters to a three-story limestone building near the Potomac River in the Foggy Bottom district of Washington, D.C., a quarter mile north of the Lincoln Memorial. The dreary neighborhood contained a skating rink, a row of dilapidated warehouses, and a brick brewery with a green copper roof that emitted the telltale stench of fermenting yeast. Little about the area invited attention except, once the COI moved in, the armed guard who stood beneath the building's ionic colonnade.

The COI headquarters had previously been occupied by the National Institutes of Health, and signs of the former tenant were apparent. When Donovan first arrived, the windows were barred, and the third floor still contained caged animals—test subjects for syphilis research—that were destined for the incinerator. German radio joked that the building contained a zoo of "fifty professors, twenty monkeys, ten goats, twelve guinea pigs, and staff of Jewish scribblers."

In reality, the building mostly contained cubbyhole offices filled with filing cabinets, walls plastered with maps of Europe and Asia, desks stacked with piles of paper that only grew taller over time, and COI workers who were "as unromantic as their surroundings," one employee said. There were analysts and anthropologists, forgers and foreign language experts, safe-crackers and scientists. The different species of animal test subjects had been replaced by their human counterparts.

Donovan's organization quickly came to resemble his own restless personality. James Aswell, a recruit, wrote in a letter to his superiors that he felt as if he were working in a "meat grinder turned by a maniac." Army intelligence officer Edwin Sibert visited the new COI headquarters and similarly said that it "closely resembled a cat house in Laredo on a Saturday night, with rivalries, jealousies, mad schemes, and everyone trying to get the ear of the director."

As chaotic as the COI was, it nevertheless projected an intimidating aura. Three months after its creation, a German newspaper announced that "a secret bureau" had been formed in Washington "to which very few have entrée." The paper said that Donovan had first come to Germany's attention when Roosevelt had sent him as his "special envoy" to Europe "in order to incite the people of those countries to rebellion against Germany." The paper further claimed that "a second and *more monstrous meddling* is at present underway, and as usual under the leadership of Colonel Donovan. Roosevelt has named the Colonel Coordinator of Information. Hiding behind this title he is brewing a Jewish-Democratic crisis which is directed at all of Europe. Donovan has unlimited power. He can spend any sum of money he desires. He can have as many assistants as he chooses. And he can get any information he desires." Donovan delighted in reading the Nazi rant against him. Ironically, disinformation was spreading about the COI before he even had a chance to spread it himself.

On December 7, 1941, Donovan joined 55,050 fellow spectators at the Polo Grounds stadium in Upper Manhattan to watch a rivalry game between the New York Giants and Brooklyn Dodgers football teams. According to the next day's *New York Times*, the Giants looked like "dismal cellar tenants" compared to the nimble Dodgers, in part because of the injuries that the Giants sustained on the gridiron. Ben Sohn sprained his ankle. Frank Cope bruised his shoulder. George Franck fractured his pelvis. Orville Tuttle split open his big toe. Lou DeFilippo took a shot to his nose, then "flattened" Dodger Jim Sivell in a fist fight. Mel Hein, the Giants' center, nicknamed "Old Indestructible," broke his nose and suffered a concussion, forcing him to leave a game for the first time in eleven years. A cleat ripped open Nello Falaschi's leg, laying bare his right shin bone, "and the rest of the Giants were as cut and torn by cleats as if they had gone through a meat chopper." In an upset, the Dodgers won 21–7.

In the middle of the game, as the crowded spectators cheered from the stands, a curious announcement came over the loud-speaker: "Attention, please! Attention! Here is an urgent message. Will Colonel William J. Donovan call operator nineteen in Washington, D.C." Donovan, surprised, walked to a nearby phone booth. He called the operator, who patched him through to James Roosevelt, President Roosevelt's son and an early member of the COI. The exchange was short and to the point. Donovan was informed that at that very moment, six time zones to the west, Japanese aircraft were attacking the U.S. Pacific Fleet at the Pearl Harbor naval base in Hawaii. President Roosevelt wanted him back in Washington immediately.

Eleven hours later, at a few minutes past midnight, Donovan entered Roosevelt's private study. Roosevelt sat behind his desk, his face illuminated by a small lamp, obviously exhausted from the torrent of generals, admirals, and aides who had been vying for his attention all day. He nibbled on a sandwich and sipped a beer. His stamp album, which he had been working on when he first learned of the surprise attack on Pearl Harbor, had been moved to a far corner of the room, and on his desk sat the latest damage report from Hawaii. The death toll ultimately amounted to 2,403 Americans. The Japanese had destroyed 350 planes and damaged or sunk nearly two dozen Navy vessels, including five battleships. Roosevelt glanced at the report, then up at Donovan. "They caught our ships like lame ducks! Lame ducks, Bill! . . . It's a good thing you got me started on this [intelligence business]. They caught our planes on the ground—on the ground!"

The next day, Roosevelt addressed a joint session of Congress to ask for a formal declaration of war on Japan. Steel braces locked his knees in place so that he could deliver the speech standing up. He gripped the lectern to steady himself. All nine justices of the Supreme Court were on his left; all ten cabinet secretaries were on his right. He began, "Yesterday, December 7, 1941, a date which will live in infamy . . ." In his most rousing statement, Roosevelt vowed in a resonant cadence, "No matter how long it may take us to overcome this premeditated invasion, the American people in their righteous might will win through to absolute victory." Before he could even finish the last of these words, a deafening chorus of cheers filled the chamber. Congress passed the war declaration within an hour. The United States had entered World War II.

By the beginning of 1942, the COI's payroll included six hundred personnel, known among old-line military men as "Donovan's Dragoons." The organization generated a slew of additional epithets around Washington, D.C. Some called it the "Bad Eyes Brigade" or "Draft Dodger Heaven" because many of its personnel escaped deployment. The COI, one saying went, handed out "cellophane commissions," so-called because they were see-through and kept the Draft off. Others called it a group of "East Coast Faggots." Donovan preferred the nickname "League of Gentlemen," and gentlemen there were in the COI, but not without a relatively high proportion of women in administrative roles and serving as undercover agents overseas where they were less likely to arouse suspicion when traveling alone.

Donovan bitterly defended his organization against the insults. At one formal dinner party, Admiral Horace Schmahl called the COI "a Tinker Toy outfit, spying on spies." Donovan overheard the slight and said, "I don't know, Admiral, I think that we could get your secret files and blow up your ammunition dump on the other side of the river before midnight." Schmahl laughed, thinking the suggestion outrageous. Donovan then excused himself from the table and called COI headquarters with an urgent request. Within an hour, a group of agents broke into Schmahl's office at the Navy Building. They cracked his safe, removed the secret documents, and sped them over to Donovan. Next, they snuck into the ammunition dump and planted fake dynamite. At the end of the dinner party, Donovan walked up to Schmahl and handed him the contents of his own safe. He then informed the slack-jawed admiral where to find the dummy dynamite.

In the wake of Pearl Harbor, the COI grew too fast to remain a White House operation. On June 13, 1942, President Roosevelt signed an order establishing the Office of Strategic Services (OSS), the successor to the COI and the precursor to the Central Intelligence Agency. The order placed the OSS under the purview of the Joint Chiefs of Staff, a group composed of the highest-ranking members of the military branches. Donovan remained its director.

Despite the name change, the epithets kept coming. One popular quip was that "OSS" stood for "Oh So Social." Being a secretive organization by definition, the OSS cast an aura of exclusivity that struck many as elitist and snobbish. Nor did the OSS help its uppity reputation by hiring members of many of the wealthiest families in the United States: DuPont, Mellon, Morgan, and Vanderbilt among them.

Austine Cassini, a columnist for the *Washington Times-Herald*, visited OSS headquarters and commented on its composition:

> If you should by chance wander in the labyrinth of the OSS you'd behold ex-polo players, millionaires, Russian princes, society gambol boys, scientists and dilettante detectives. All of them are now at the OSS, where they used to be allocated between New York, Palm Beach, Long Island, Newport and other meccas frequented by the blue-bloods of democracy. And the girls! The prettiest, best-born, snappiest girls who used to graduate from debutantedom to boredom now bend their blonde and brunette locks, or their colorful hats, over work in the OSS, the super-ultra-intelligence-counter-espionage outfit that is headed by brilliant "Wild Bill" Donovan.

As the OSS grew in size and ambition, it sprouted differentiated branches to carry out its mission. The Special Operations Branch organized foreign resistance groups. The Foreign Information Service broadcast anti-Axis radio programs in Europe. The Secret Intelligence Branch sent spies abroad to report back on the locations of enemy troops, bridges, tunnels, searchlights, roadblocks, airfields, minefields, and coastal gun emplacements. The Morale Operations Branch "brewed a slow poison" of disinformation "to be injected in the Nazi blood-stream," said one officer. It spread rumors, distributed leaflets, issued fake reports, and ran subversive radio stations in enemy territory. The Research and Analysis Branch hired the brightest intellectuals—economists, historians, anthropologists, political scientists—that Donovan could coax from their academic posts at American museums, laboratories, and universities to evaluate the flood of information that came pouring in from OSS agents and contacts abroad.

The OSS hired hundreds of new recruits to staff these branches. But before they became full-fledged members of the organization, they attended a training school where they learned the ins and outs of espionage, including lock-picking, secret writing, parachute jumping, radio transmission, discreet letter-opening, and other tricks of the trade. As a capstone to their education, they took one final, hands-on test. They were told to steal classified material from American defense plants and other sensitive targets. If they stole the material without getting arrested, they passed training school. The FBI constantly complained about these tests, but the OSS considered it good practice for both organizations.

Roger Hall never forgot his final test—few did. He targeted a factory in Philadelphia that made circuit breakers and radar equipment. His plan was to interview for a job, get a tour of the factory, gather whatever classified information he could, and disappear. To ensure that he would be taken seriously as a job candidate, he developed an elaborate cover story and forged what he called "the clincher," several glowing letters of recommendation that were guaranteed to impress anyone who read them.

Hall was interviewed by a "naïve and extremely impressionable" young lady, he later recalled. He won her over with his cover story, a heroic war tale casting himself in the lead role. He then gave her the letters of recommendation, "icing on the well-baked cake." She immediately arranged for him to meet with the company's vice president—her father—the next morning for a final interview. In the meantime, she asked, "Would you care to have a look around?"

"I'd like that very much," Hall said. "Would it be all right?"

"I'll give you the deluxe guided tour."

On the tour, Hall learned the layout of the factory, who the workers were, what they made, and how they made it. His mission was practically complete. But he nevertheless decided to return for the interview with the vice president. If he could land a security-sensitive position at the company, nobody in the OSS would ever question his skills.

The next day, Hall met with the vice president for what turned out to be the easiest interview of his life. The two of them got along famously, especially after Hall learned that the vice president had a particular passion for Army-Navy football games. The son of a Navy grad, Hall had seen every one of those games for the past twenty years. By the end of the interview, the enchanted vice president insisted that they have lunch together. That sounded perfectly fine to Hall, who later said that he "had thoughts of stuffing my craw with expensive delicacies and necking with his lovely heiress between courses."

Lunch was in the factory cafeteria, not at a fancy restaurant as Hall had hoped. At least, he said, "it still meant the heiress." He and the vice president entered the cafeteria to the sound of several thousand workers belting out "God Bless America." To Hall's surprise, and soon to his dismay, there was a war bond rally taking place that day.

Without warning, the vice president walked to a stage in front of the cheering crowd and announced, "This gathering is honored by the presence of one of the boys back from over there, a former captain in the paratroopers, wounded in action and honorably discharged. Let's show him how we feel about it, and maybe we can get him up here to say a few words. Fellow workers, meet Captain Robert Hawthorne of the United States Parachute Infantry!" Robert Hawthorne was Hall's cover name.

Hall nervously walked to the stage while a mob of workers sang a rendition of "Dixie." Halfway there, he began limping to account for the injury that he had supposedly received in battle. In an improvised speech, he told the workers to buy war bonds until it hurt. He urged them to donate to the blood banks. He asked them to write letters to the soldiers overseas because, he lied, "I was in a tough outfit, but I've seen men walk away from mail call empty-handed with tears in their eyes."

At the end of the performance, Hall limped off the stage to a standing ovation. "There wasn't a dry eye in the house," he recalled with pride. The vice president shook his right hand while the heiress clung to his left. His speech made such a stir that a local newspaper ran a story about him in their morning issue. War bonds saw a spike in sales overnight. "Robert Hawthorne" was offered a job starting the next Monday, but he never showed up. Hall had passed his test.

The various branches of the OSS had been created to spy on the enemy, spread disinformation, and analyze the mountains of intelligence gathered abroad, but something was still missing. Donovan needed another branch, the most underhanded of them all, to *destroy* the enemy. He needed a branch that could equip an undercover agent with a fighting knife to slit a guard's throat, an incendiary device to set a building on fire, a camouflaged explosive to blow apart a locomotive's boiler, or a cyanide pill to kill themselves with before being captured alive. He needed a branch that could develop and deploy all of the dirty tricks that were needed to win the greatest war in history. And he needed a scientist, a "Professor Moriarty," in his words, to oversee it.

2
Professor Moriarty

Stanley Lovell experienced one of the more formative events of his life when he read German historian Oswald Spengler's two-volume book *The Decline of the West*. In it, Spengler argues that the rise and fall of "high cultures" follows a predictable, cyclical pattern and that Western high culture was quickly coming to its inevitable end. Lovell, an obscure New England chemist—a "salty little Yankee inventor," in the words of one colleague—wrote a letter to Spengler saying that there was an apparent contradiction in the book: "The glorification of war in one volume, the vituperation of war in the next." Spengler, intrigued by the observation, invited Lovell to Munich for a discussion.

Lovell accepted the invitation to meet "that great German savant," as he called Spengler in a newspaper article describing his trip. He arrived in Germany on June 30, 1934, the Night of the Long Knives when Adolf Hitler purged the Nazi Party to consolidate his power. "Military motorcycles screeched through the streets, calling families to their doorways and killing them in cold blood," Lovell wrote. "More than six hundred were so assassinated, and all the time I was in Dr. Spengler's enormous apartment on the bank of the Green Isar river."

The chemist and the historian talked in rapt attention until midnight. During their conversation, Spengler made a number of grave predictions about the future of the United States. He told Lovell, a Cape Cod Republican, that President Franklin Roosevelt was leading the American people down the road to dictatorship; that, in the midst of the Great Depression, the United States was becoming a welfare state, which would bankrupt the country; and that Americans could no longer rely on a buffer of oceans to separate them from world events—isolationism was over.

In his most ominous prediction of all, Spengler said that two future world wars would occur, each a generation apart. One would begin in five years, 1939, itself coming a generation after World War I. Another would begin around 1964. The wars would be fought over one issue: dictatorship versus democracy. Although Lovell wasn't religious, he received Spengler's prophecy as if from on high. If Spengler was right and another world war began in 1939, Lovell pledged to defend democracy.

Stanley Lovell thought that his ancestors had fled England in the seventeenth century to escape religious persecution. They had sailed across the Atlantic to Boston Harbor, paid the captain under the table for a boat to row ashore, and paddled to Cape Cod, thereby avoiding certain capture in Boston. This, he thought, explained why the Lovells of Osterville, Massachusetts, were sailors. Then again, he knew how to spin a good yarn.

Stanley's own father was indeed a sailor from Osterville. Gustavus Lovell grew up sailing packets between Boston to New

York. In 1849, at the age of fifteen, his captain decided to sail around South America's Cape Horn to San Francisco. When they arrived, most of the crew abandoned ship to try their fortunes prospecting in the California Gold Rush. The captain, desperate for sailors, pleaded for Gustavus to stay with the ship in exchange for support for his own captain's papers. Gustavus accepted the deal, became a captain as promised, and established a lucrative sailing route between San Francisco and Shanghai, exchanging his cargo of dried fruit for young Chinese agricultural workers.

When Gustavus's first wife, Ellen, became ill with an unknown disease, he took her to the healing springs in northern Vermont, but the waters failed to cure her. Two years after her death, Gustavus met and married Ella May Platt, the daughter of a Vermont farmer. The couple moved to Brockton, Massachusetts, and had two children: a daughter, Nellie, and a younger son, Stanley, who was born on August 29, 1890.

When Nellie was seventeen and Stanley ten, a flu epidemic struck Massachusetts. Ella May left Brockton to take care of her sick parents. On the trip, she developed a severe case of pneumonia and died before returning. Gustavus, already in his midsixties, died two years later.

None of the extended Lovell family wanted to adopt the two orphaned children, a point made painfully clear one day when Nellie and Stanley hid behind a couch and eavesdropped on their adult relatives arguing back and forth, "No, no, I don't want them, do you want them?" The children were enraged and embarrassed. They jumped out from behind the couch, yelling, "We don't care, we don't want any of you! We're going to take off on our own!"

And for the most part they did. Nellie became a seamstress and supported her younger brother, a star student, until 1907 when he left for college at Dartmouth. A year later, he transferred to Cornell.

Behind Stanley Lovell's slight frame and solemn features—dark, penetrating eyes and slicked-back brown hair—was a sharp sense of humor and, one friend said, "a strong belief that the impossible only took a bit longer." The Cornell yearbook similarly noted his resolve. On his past, it said that he was raised near Boston in a culture of "bad English." On his future, it said, "He will move mountains."

At Cornell, Lovell edited the student newspaper and developed an ear for witty turns of phrase. He also led a muckraking campaign against the substandard living conditions in the student boarding houses. In an article that was covered in *The New York Times*, he brought particular attention to their unsanitary food practices. "The practice of 'shifting' is almost universal," he wrote. "Shifting consists in transferring from a plate returned to the kitchen, to an outgoing dish, those pieces of meat, potato, and so forth, that have not yet been consumed." The food itself was "neither clean, wholesome nor varied." The owner of one boarding house threatened to sue Lovell because of the story, though nothing came of it.

Lovell had a flair for the dramatic, but he found himself increasingly drawn to the rationality of the sciences. And to his delight, if ever there was a period in the history of science filled with drama, it was during his formative years. Within the two short decades of his life, Wilhelm Röntgen had discovered X-rays, Henri Becquerel had discovered radioactivity, Marie and Pierre Curie had discovered new elements, J. J. Thomson had discovered the electron, Max Planck had laid the foundations for quantum mechanics, Albert Einstein had published his special theory of relativity, and Ernest Rutherford had discovered the atomic nucleus. The next great discovery seemed just around the corner, and Lovell wanted to find it.

In particular, Lovell was drawn to the field of chemistry, which he viewed as a form of modern-day magic. He was amazed that chemists could, for example, create new and useful substances out of literal thin air. In fact, while Lovell was at Cornell, German chemist Fritz Haber actually invented a process whereby nitrogen could be harnessed straight from the air, thus enabling the large-scale production of explosives and fertilizers. Haber later won the 1918 Nobel Prize in Chemistry for this work, though the award was tinged with controversy because, in the intervening time, he had spearheaded Germany's effort to develop and deploy chemical weapons during World War I.

In time, Lovell would similarly face the moral dilemma of whether to develop and deploy controversial weapons. As a scientist, he felt a Hippocratic obligation to do no harm. But as an American, he felt a patriotic obligation to defend the country that had allowed a poor boy with nothing but his sister's meager support to receive a world-class education.

Lovell's scientific worldview clashed with, and ultimately eroded, his religious faith. He was agnostic. And rather than keep quiet about his beliefs, or lack thereof, he openly criticized organized religion, going so far as to confront people who freely expressed their faith-based views.

In 1911, Lovell graduated from Cornell with a bachelor's degree in chemistry. He spent the next year working on a graduate degree, but he never finished it. Instead, his priorities shifted when he met a calm and quiet-mannered Latin teacher named

Mabel Bigney. The two quickly fell in love. Mabel adored Lovell and his eccentricities even though her face always flushed red with embarrassment whenever he debated religion in public. The couple married in June 1915. Four years later, they had their first and only child, a son named Richard.

Over the next two decades, Lovell worked as an industrial chemist for four different shoe and leather companies, a thriving industry around Boston. At the George E. Keith Company, he earned the nickname "The Moth Ball King" for inventing cunning ways of turning the company's industrial waste into profitable products. Besides the nickname, his inventions also earned him an ingenious reputation, both among his peers and, little did he know, among a handful of influential government scientists who were looking for a clever chemist to join their ranks.

In May 1942, five months after the United States entered World War II, Lovell was walking across Boston Common when Karl Compton, the president of the Massachusetts Institute of Technology, stopped him mid-stride. The two only had a nodding acquaintance, making this forced interaction unusual. Compton wanted to know whether Lovell had heard of the National Defense Research Committee (NDRC), a government organization led by James Conant, the president of Harvard University, that had been created two years earlier to coordinate wartime scientific research and to devise new weapons for defeating the Axis powers.

"Aren't they a group of college professors?" Lovell asked.

"Exactly," Compton said, "but they are all snarled up with businessmen, with whom they are placing big contracts. Neither seems to understand one another."

The professors and the businessmen weren't seeing eye to

eye. They didn't speak the same language. Compton realized that Lovell had both scientific training and business experience. Perhaps he could help the NDRC bridge the gap between the two worlds. "Come down to Washington and help us."

The day after his chance encounter with Compton, Lovell spoke with a colleague who told him that he would always regret it if he refused Uncle Sam now. Lovell had promised himself that if the day ever came, he would defend democracy against dictatorship. He felt obligated to stand behind his convictions. Within a week, he was at NDRC headquarters in Washington, D.C. His stated reason for leaving the shoe and leather company that he worked at: "War."

In the hullabaloo of wartime Washington, Lovell was assigned to work in the Quartermaster Corps, which manages the general supplies of the Army, instead of as a liaison between NDRC scientists and businessmen like Compton had promised. Lovell later described some of the "prosaic" problems that he faced in his new job: "How to make a grommet from plastics rather than metal and thus save so many pounds of steel or tin; how to redesign the Army canteen; how to make mold-proof tents, shoes, leggings, etc." Despite his lack of enthusiasm for the work, there were accidental moments of excitement. Once, when Lovell gave a presentation to a group about the types of garments used in desert fighting, he asked with a cigarette between his lips, "What can we do about thermal armor?" A voice from the back rang out, "Shoot the son-of-a-bitch!" One perturbed Republican had mistakenly heard "Thurman Arnold," a New Deal trustbuster in President Roosevelt's administration.

Vannevar Bush saved Lovell from further banal work by taking him on as an aide. Bush, a scrawny man with a long face and large, pointed ears, was a fellow salty Yankee inventor. Moreover, he was an electrical engineer who had done pioneering work with computers, co-founded the defense contractor Raytheon, and was obsessed with coordinating scientific research. Bush believed that with focused effort, scientists could develop the tools and weapons to win World War II.

It was Bush who, within the course of a ten-minute meeting and equipped with a single sheet of paper, had persuaded President Franklin Roosevelt to create the NDRC. Later, he helped persuade Roosevelt to develop the atomic bomb, resulting in the Manhattan Project. In essence, Bush was Roosevelt's unofficial science advisor and the government's official science coordinator. As head of the Office of Scientific Research and Development, which subsumed the NDRC, he oversaw the American efforts to develop radar, proximity fuses, and the atomic bomb itself. Jonathan Lovell, Stanley Lovell's grandson, said that his grandfather "probably had the highest regard for Vannevar Bush of all the people that he talked about." Lovell "was in awe of Vannevar Bush," who he thought "was just a genius."

Bush took a liking to Lovell. He admired his New England tenacity, or what Bush called the "pioneering spirit of the old fellows who built the clipper ships and made a profit out of them, the old chaps who traded with China, the chaps that ran miners around to the Pacific coast after '49 and made a good profit out of their needs." Bush and Lovell had both descended from sailors and inherited this "pioneering spirit." They would make good use of it during the war.

Bush occasionally tested his aides with thought experiments to keep their minds sharp and, Lovell would soon learn, to evaluate them for secret positions. One thought experiment went as follows: "You are about to land at dead of night in a rubber raft on a German-held coast. Your mission is to destroy a vital enemy wireless installation that is defended by armed guards, dogs and searchlights. You can have with you any one weapon you can imagine. Describe this weapon." Lovell sunk his teeth into the challenge. He walked the streets at night contemplating the perfect answer, his mind withdrawn from the external world. "I was imagining myself wading ashore a hundred times," he recalled, "but with what?" After "soul-searching for a week," he submitted his final answer to Bush: "I want a completely silent, flashless gun—a Colt automatic or a submachine gun—or both. I can pick off the first sentry with no sound or flash to explain his collapse, so the next sentry will come to him instead of sounding an alarm. Then, one by one, I'll pick them off and command the wireless station."

Lovell's answer took first prize among all of Bush's aides. And soon after submitting the winning entry, he received a mysterious order to report to a building that he had never been to before. His answer had apparently caught someone's attention.

The sun was setting when a taxi dropped Lovell off in front of a limestone building in the Foggy Bottom district of Washington, D.C. The smell of fermenting yeast lingered in the air.

Lovell walked past the building's imposing colonnade and through the front door. He found himself in a narrow lobby, which in a few dozen feet intersected a hallway. He walked across the creaky wooden floor to the confluence of the two, looked left and right, and saw nobody. During the day, the place would have been filled with the sight of scurrying workers and the sound of clanking typewriters, but at this late hour it was still and silent.

Lovell suddenly felt a hand touch his shoulder. He jumped away in terror. When he turned around, he saw a security guard standing behind him. "Follow me," said the guard without explanation. Lovell was spooked, but he allowed the guard to lead him to a small, plain room with two chairs. The lone picture on the walls of the room showed an antiquated map of the world, most of which was labeled "Terra Incognita." How appropriate, Lovell thought. That's where he felt like he was.

Lovell grew apprehensive waiting for something to happen. Where was he? Why was he there? Who was he meeting? How long was he supposed to wait? His stomach rumbled in the quiet room—he hadn't eaten all day—though at the moment he was too anxious to feel hungry.

After a disconcerting amount of time, Lovell heard footsteps approaching in the hallway. Then the door opened. An imposing figure dressed in a gray suit and gray tie, with gray hair and blue-gray eyes to match, finally entered the room and sat in the other chair. The sheer size of the man, at least compared to Lovell, was intimidating enough on its own, never mind the mysterious context of the encounter or the Medal of Honor lapel pin that the man wore on his chest.

"I'm Colonel Donovan," said the man. "You know your Sherlock Holmes, of course. Professor Moriarty is the man I want for my staff here at O.S.S. I think you're it."

Lovell called to mind what he knew of Professor Moriarty, Sherlock Holmes's brilliant nemesis. Little of it was flattering. For instance, in the short story "The Final Problem," Holmes calls Moriarty "the Napoleon of crime" and someone with "hereditary tendencies of the most diabolical kind."

Lovell asked Donovan, "Do I look to be as evil a character as Conan Doyle made him in his stories?"

"I don't give a damn how you look," Donovan said. "I need

every subtle device and every underhanded trick to use against the Germans and the Japanese." He paused, then gave Lovell his first order: "You have to invent all of them, Lovell, because you're going to be my man. Come with me."

The two men could hardly have been more different from one another. Donovan was Catholic, impulsive, a fearless war hero. Lovell was agnostic, calculated, an unassuming chemist. But despite their differences, they were both patriots. Lovell accepted the job.

Lovell became the director of the embryonic OSS Research and Development Branch, which was officially established on October 17, 1942. The founding mandate gave the R&D Branch responsibility "for the invention, development, and testing of all secret and other devices, material and equipment." In essence, the R&D Branch was responsible for equipping undercover agents with anything that they needed in their line of work, ranging from deadly weapons to forged documents to flawless disguises. If Lovell was the equivalent of Sherlock Holmes's criminal mastermind Professor Moriarty, the R&D Branch was the equivalent of James Bond's legendary Q Division, the fictional organization that created the superspy's most ingenious gadgets, from X-ray glasses to a bagpipe flamethrower.

At first, the chemist in Lovell found it difficult to harmonize the scientific spirit of open collaboration with his new mandate to devise secret dirty tricks. Science had been an indisputable force for good in his own life and, he thought, in the world. Scientists had produced vaccines, electricity, modern agriculture, communication systems, and new understandings of the universe. How could he now harness it to produce weapons of war? What does a man do when asked to commit a small evil in the name of a greater good?

Lovell visited Donovan at his fourteen-room Georgetown home to discuss his moral dilemma. When he walked in, Donovan poured him some sherry—but none for himself—to calm Lovell's nerves. Lovell began the conversation: "The American people are a nation of extroverts. We tell everything and rather glory in it. A Professor Moriarty is as un-American as sin is unpopular at a revival meeting."

Donovan was having none of it. "Don't be so goddam naïve," he said. "P. T. Barnum is still a basic hero because he fooled so many people. They will applaud someone who can outfox the Nazis and the Japs."

Lovell wasn't so sure.

In the beginning, Lovell's R&D Branch was inexperienced and unsophisticated. Lovell and three colleagues therefore traveled to England to learn a few tips and tricks from the Special Operations Executive (SOE), the British counterpart to the OSS that British prime minister Winston Churchill had created in July 1940 with a mission to "go out and set Europe ablaze!" And set Europe ablaze the SOE and OSS would do, on some occasions quite literally.

While abroad for their lessons in skulduggery, the four Americans visited SOE laboratories and training camps and held discussions with British scientists on the art of developing "special" weapons. "Ah, those first OSS arrivals in London!" said British intelligence officer Malcolm Muggeridge. "How well I remember them like *jeune filles en fleur* straight from finishing school, all fresh and innocent to start work in our frowsty old intelligence brothel.

All too soon they were ravished and corrupted, becoming indistinguishable from seasoned pros who had been in the game for a quarter century or more."

OSS officer Frank Gleason made a similar trip to England and elaborated on the types of dirty tricks that OSS personnel gleaned from the SOE. "What they teach you at sabotage school will blow your mind," he said. "Six or seven people that are properly trained can cripple a good-sized city. It's as easy as can be. . . . We learned how to operate and destroy locomotives and power plants, the turbines in power plants, communication systems, and telephones. We also learned how to make people sick by poisoning a city's water supply. Shitty stuff like that—we were taught how to fight dirty." Despite Lovell's initial moral reservations, the R&D Branch would soon take fighting dirty to heart.

While Lovell was organizing the R&D Branch, he learned that Vannevar Bush and Bill Donovan had never met in person. Lovell assumed that this was because Bush thought of the OSS as nothing more than a social club, "a bundle of playboys who accomplish nothing," as Bush would later say. Bush had, in part, originally forwarded Lovell's name to Donovan because he thought that Lovell might help reform the "highly undisciplined" culture of the OSS. Lovell wanted the two men to get along because he needed the scientists working under Bush to help him create weapons for the R&D Branch, the kinds of weapons that Wild Bill Donovan expected from his Professor Moriarty.

One evening, Lovell invited both men to dinner at the Carlton Hotel, a ritzy hangout for government officials in Washington. The conversation was cordial enough, but none of them spoke much about their work. Bush was overseeing the Manhattan Project and worried about accidentally disclosing classified information; Donovan was overseeing OSS operations abroad and worried about doing the same. Afterward, Donovan told Lovell, "Stanley, I'm so glad to have met Dr. Bush. He's a great man—but did you notice he began every single sentence with 'I'? Quite an egoist, wouldn't you say?" The next morning, Lovell attended a meeting with Bush, who told him, "I didn't have a chance to thank you adequately last night for the fine dinner, Stan. You know it was rather noticeable, I thought, that Bill Donovan talked so much about himself. I couldn't get a word in edgewise." When reflecting on the incident, Lovell said, "The humble may inherit the earth, but the egoists own it right now."

Although Bush was skeptical of the OSS, he respected Donovan and saw merit in the R&D Branch. He granted Lovell's request and allowed his scientists to help the R&D Branch with its unorthodox projects, saying, "If they want to make a fountain pen that does things no self-respecting fountain pen would ever do, we will make one." Ever the salty little Yankee inventor, Lovell told Donovan that his message to the new recruits would be simple: "Throw all your normal law-abiding concepts out the window. Here's a chance to raise merry hell. Come, help me raise it."

Under Lovell's leadership, and with the help of Bush's scientists, the R&D Branch created a secret division to develop all of the weapons that a spy or saboteur could possibly need in their line of work. The division was officially named NDRC Division 19, though it was really an arm of the R&D Branch, itself an arm of the OSS. Informally, Division 19 was referred to as the "Sandeman Club" because of the "secrecy in which it moved" and "the frequently bizarre tasks it was asked to perform," said one member.

Lovell appointed Harris Chadwell, a chemistry professor at Tufts University, to head Division 19. On the surface, everything about Chadwell was intimidating. He was uncommonly large, barrel-chested, and had thick jowls that pulled down the edges of his mouth into a permanent frown. But in actual countenance he was mild-mannered and soft-spoken. Bush characterized him as "one of the last chaps in the world that you'd think of as being involved in various types of skulduggery."

Little has ever been written about the inner machinations of the R&D Branch or its Division 19. In 1946, historian James Baxter wrote a Pulitzer Prize–winning history of American wartime scientific research, *Scientists Against Time*, but he left out any discussion of the two groups because, Chadwell told Bush in a letter, they "should be brought to the attention of a minimum number of people." Fortunately, the government has since declassified a trove of wartime reports, letters, memoranda, and minutes of meetings that allow for a full description of the devious work that these secret groups engaged in.

3
The Sandeman Club

As a first order of business, Stanley Lovell and Harris Chad-well sought to establish a permanent laboratory where Division 19 could build its "special" weapons. They needed somewhere that was spacious enough to test the weapons and secluded enough to avoid drawing any suspicion from the public. As fate would have it, in April 1943, the OSS commandeered the four-hundred-acre Congressional Country Club in Maryland, a perfect location for a secret laboratory.

The founders of the Congressional had included a Hearst, a DuPont, two Rockefellers, and Charlie Chaplin. Presidents William Howard Taft, Woodrow Wilson, Warren Harding, Calvin Coolidge, and Herbert Hoover were all lifetime members of the prestigious country club. Its manicured fields had once hosted society's elite. Now they hosted the OSS, a fitting location for an organization mocked as "Oh So Social."

During World War II, the Congressional's picturesque golf course was transformed into a hazardous wartime training ground.

The pond full of stray golf balls became a site for underwater explosives demonstrations. The sandy bunkers lining the holes became targets for grenade practice, as did the putting greens for mortars. The driving range, formerly used by golfers to practice their shots, became a rifle range for troops to practice theirs. The smooth fairways became a field where agents-in-training crawled on their bellies amid an onslaught of live machine-gun fire to accustom their nerves to the sights and sounds of war.

"We literally just blew the place up," said OSS veteran Al Johnson. "Back then, it would have been hard just finding the greens. And we left some divots that no golfer could have gotten out of in less than three shots." (The OSS promised to repair the damages after the war.) Alex MacDonald, another OSS veteran, nicknamed the place "Malice in Wonderland." He said of his training there, "It was the 10 Commandments in reverse: lie and steal, kill, maim, spy."

Code-named Area F, the Congressional also served as a reallocation center for OSS personnel who were on furlough, returning from overseas, or waiting for an assignment. Upon arrival, they were given a short welcome booklet describing what life was like at their new accommodations. For exercise, they could play baseball, volleyball, basketball, or touch football, or go on "long brisk hikes" in the countryside. For leisure, there was pool, chess, card games, the shooting range, and half a dozen tables for ping-pong, as well as classes in carpentry, printing, and photography. The booklet also hints at another diversion that was sure to occupy the minds of the young men: girls. "We realize that you may have in mind some pastime for which F is unequipped. So if you want to go to Washington of an evening you can." Another section of the booklet was less subtle: "It has been mentioned that some of the OSS gents have a pretty rough idea of how to be charming. Take it easy, or you'll queer the deal for everybody."

The booklet concludes by noting that "a certain section of the club house is closed to all of us. It is being used by a group of scientists engaged in laboratory research. Don't try to enter. It is Out of Bounds." In the basement of the four-story Italianate clubhouse—a space that had previously held a barber shop, a bowling alley, an indoor swimming pool, and a ladies' locker room—the scientists of Division 19 installed barometers, pycnometers, thermometers, potentiometers, a vacuum pump, a hydraulic press, a steam generator, corrosion chambers, vibration tables, and humidity cabinets for experiments. Dubbed the Maryland Research Laboratory, this unorthodox space served as a fitting location for the development of even more unorthodox weapons.

Lovell and Chadwell now had a laboratory, but they still didn't know what weapons to develop. Nobody, not even Bill Donovan, knew what "special" weapons were needed for the war since no organization in U.S. history had ever engaged in such unconventional warfare. Lovell was without direction, a fact made clear when he asked Colonel David Bruce, Donovan's right-hand man and the OSS director of European operations, "Just what is my job?" Bruce responded with a piece of advice that guided Lovell's work for the rest of the war: "It's whatever you can make of it. Colonel Donovan is a lawyer, not a scientist or inventor. Never ask him what to do. Do it and show him what you have done." Donovan respected those who were bold. Better to ask for forgiveness than permission.

On Bruce's advice, Lovell, Chadwell, and the rest of the "cloak and dagger boys" of Division 19, as Lovell called them, began developing weapons straight from their imaginations. Their initial efforts were akin to "a pianist, improvising his melodies and rhythms," Lovell said. "The chords had to be found and the dissonances corrected or ignored."

Roger Hall, the OSS recruit who had delivered the improvised speech in the factory cafeteria, witnessed firsthand how the scientists of Division 19 improvised their own work. One day while touring the Congressional, he and fellow agent Malcolm MacKenzie stumbled upon the Maryland Research Laboratory in the basement of the clubhouse. Hall remembered seeing a group of "wild-eyed" scientists resembling "cartoon characters." He asked MacKenzie, "What in the world are they doing here?"

"Supposed to be developing something or other," MacKenzie said.

"What?"

"I haven't the vaguest idea."

"Have they?"

"I doubt it."

Right then a door flung open. Hall saw a "tweed-suited string-bean with the face of an intelligent squirrel" poke his face out the door and politely ask, "Do either of you gentlemen have a match which I might borrow?" Hall did, for smokes, but he handed it to him anyway. The scientist graciously took the match and scurried back in the room. "Seconds later," Hall said, "while we were walking down the hall, there was a muffled explosion followed by some triumphant whoops."

Lovell soon had plenty to show for the improvisational effort. In a 1943 report to Donovan, David Bruce wrote that Lovell had recently told him tales of new inventions that "made my hair stand on end."

One of the first weapons that Division 19 made was a time pencil. With a time pencil, a saboteur could plant an explosive

on a target—a warehouse, power station, ammunition dump—
and delay the detonation from anywhere between ten minutes
to fourteen hours, plenty of time for the saboteur to establish
an alibi across town. To activate the time pencil, the saboteur
would break a glass ampule containing acid, which ate through
a restraining wire. Once the wire snapped, it released a spring,
which drove a striker into a matchhead and ignited the fuel,
causing an explosion.

The time pencil was a simple enough device, but according
to the minutes of an early Division 19 meeting, it took "one
of the great universities of this country" several months to develop a satisfactory restraining wire. The name of the university
was purposely kept off the record. The members of Division
19 agreed that their contractors "will be secret, and are to be
covered with ambiguous titles" to mask any association between
them and the OSS. Nevertheless, it's still sometimes possible to
identify the contractors. (In the case of the time pencil, it was
Columbia University.)

The time pencil was often used in conjunction with other
Division 19 weapons. One of the most common and effective
was the limpet mine, a small box of explosives that attached
to the hull of a metal ship with six magnets. A saboteur would
set the time pencil, quietly attach the limpet to a ship—ideally
below the water line to avoid detection—and flee before the
contraption exploded. For metal ships that were overrun with
barnacles, and for wooden ships in general, there was a "Pin-up
Girl" limpet with a hardened steel nail that could be driven into
the hull.

On one maritime mission in the Gironde Estuary in western
France, British Royal Marines Bill Sparks and Henry Hasler used
limpets to sink four German freighters carrying radar equipment bound for Japan. Under cover of night, Sparks sat in a

canoe with a stash of limpets while Hasler swam underwater and attached them to the ships. In the middle of the operation, a German sentry heard a clanking noise and pointed his flashlight down toward the water. Sparks quickly huddled over the limpets in the canoe. Out of the corner of his eye, he watched the yellow orb of light move closer toward him, then pass directly across his back. He was sure that he had been caught, but for some reason—bad eyesight, sympathy for the Allies—the sentry never sounded the alarm.

Meanwhile, Hasler was still underwater. He had attached a limpet and was just about to surface when he saw the light penetrate the water beside him. All he could do was wait. Any noise or movement might get him killed. His diaphragm involuntarily contracted for lack of oxygen, but he refused to surface until the light flickered off. When it finally did, he waited a few extra seconds for good measure, delicately breached the water's surface, and gasped for breath as quietly as possible. After attaching a few more limpets, the two saboteurs paddled nonstop away from the estuary until, hours later, they heard the satisfying sound of distant booms echo across the water.

Time pencils were also used in conjunction with small incendiary devices to start fires. Lovell recruited Harvard chemist Louis Fieser to develop these incendiaries for Division 19, and for good reason. Fieser had been Harris Chadwell's former roommate and therefore came with a good recommendation. More importantly, he was a professional arsonist.

In 1942, Fieser had been the first person to create napalm, a highly flammable form of jellied gasoline that burns at 2,100 degrees Fahrenheit and sticks to everything that it touches. Some of his first detonation tests with napalm bombs had taken place on the Harvard soccer field, prompting a Navy captain to chastise him for endangering the health of the students, but more so for hogging the soccer field, which the captain needed for drill instruction. When Lovell heard about Fieser and his rogue napalm tests, he knew that he had found a kindred spirit to join the ranks of Division 19.

Fieser often came home from work covered in ash, "looking like a blackface comedian," he said. His first product for Division 19, known as the pocket incendiary, used a time pencil to ignite a wallet-size reservoir of napalm. The idea was to have multiple saboteurs set multiple pocket incendiaries throughout an enemy city, thus overwhelming the local fire department. If done correctly, the city would become an ash heap without the need for a costly bomber raid.

Fieser nearly got into big trouble after finishing the first few pocket incendiaries for Division 19. He shipped them to Washington, D.C., for testing, and along the way they accidentally set fire to a Boston train station. Only charred bits of the packaging survived, one of which bore Fieser's name. He soon received an anonymous phone call questioning him about the incident, likely as part of an FBI investigation. He told the caller that he was working on a secret government project and couldn't say anything more for fear of breaching national security. He then cleverly insinuated that any further questioning would be seen as an attempt to steal government secrets. There were no further questions.

Fieser also built a device for Division 19 that could set fire to oil slicks floating atop the ocean. Earlier in the war, a considerable portion of the Italian Navy had been trapped in an Adriatic harbor surrounded by loose oil. The British bombed the oil slick, thinking that it would catch fire and destroy the Italian fleet, but the oil failed to ignite. Maybe, Fieser thought, a modified pocket incendiary could do the trick. His final design for the device consisted of a water-tight box filled with napalm and its own supply of oxygen. Lovell named it the "City Slicker."

On June 10, 1944, the Coast Guard let Fieser dump a thousand gallons of Navy Special Fuel Oil into Virginia's Little Beach Cove to test the City Slicker. Ships full of military spectators, and even a blimp, gathered around to watch. As soon as the device hit the water, the oil slick ignited and gave rise to fifty-foot flames. The inferno burned for seven minutes, after which the awestruck spectators, eager for an encore, dumped several reserve barrels of fuel and accompanying City Slickers into the water. "Everyone was happy," Fieser noted, "and we had a gay party of celebration in the evening."

Not all the ideas for Division 19's weapons originated with the members of Division 19 themselves. During the war, OSS leader Bill Donovan led a crowdsourcing effort that urged ordinary Americans to submit their ideas for new military technologies to the National Inventors Council, a committee of technical experts who would vet the ideas and send the best ones to the R&D Branch, its Division 19, or to the relevant military branch.

Hundreds of thousands of submissions were made. Most of them were bizarre and impractical. As the administrative history of the National Inventors Council admits, "many of these, although extremely amusing or fantastic, were worthless," such as flying cars, shells filled with sneezing powder, or a "spherical tank for both land and water operations having a diameter of 300 feet."

Donovan nonetheless kept an open mind. When Adlai Stevenson forwarded to him, as a joke, an outlandish plan to establish clandestine air bases behind Japanese lines in China, he responded, "I ignore nothing—you can never tell."

Few of these ideas ever made it to production. The "chaps out in the woods somewhere," as Vannevar Bush called the amateur inventors making these submissions, lacked a broad understanding of the military and, in many cases, a basic understanding of the science underpinning their own ideas. At least six separate people submitted designs for a mythical "death ray." Two of them even claimed to have killed a total of five ducks with the device, but Richard Tolman, the head of an NDRC division for armor and ordnance, suspected that they had shot the ducks with strychnine pellets, "a favored stunt of self-styled death ray inventors."

Many of these inventors simply *knew* that they had developed the next great weapon and would stop at nothing to make sure the government knew about it. One earnest man learned that Vannevar Bush coordinated the country's wartime scientific research and followed him around Washington waiting for a chance to pitch his idea. Bush kept brushing him off, but the man kept appearing outside of buildings asking for a moment of his time. Bush grew so concerned for his own safety that he notified members of the Secret Service, who interviewed the man and concluded that he was "just a simple-minded fellow." Bush gave him a ten-minute interview, listened to his nonsensical idea, and sent him packing.

On another occasion, a man drove hundreds of miles to tell Bush about an idea that would surely win the war. This time, instead of playing a prolonged game of cat-and-mouse, Bush sat down with the man as soon as he could. He let the man explain his idea, then turned him away with an ingenious tactic. He looked the man in the eye and said, "Now look. You must understand the situation in which I'm placed. If this idea was already in the hands of the military, if it was worked on intensively, it would be made very secret, so that the enemy wouldn't learn anything about it. I couldn't tell you anything about what's going on, because of the regulations on secrecy. I'm not saying that this is the case; I'm merely saying that if it was the case, I couldn't tell you about it." The man, now convinced that the military was already pursuing his idea, hopped into his car and drove home.

Stanley Lovell never forgot the crazy idea that one supposed feline expert—"whose name I happily forget"—submitted to the National Inventors Council. Lovell summarized the concept: "Everyone knows that a cat always lands on her feet. Everyone knows that a cat hates water. Ha! Here we have the idea that will help win the war. Simply sling a cat, feet down, in a harness below an aerial bomb with mechanism so set that the cat's every move will guide the vanes of the free-falling bomb." The cat would somehow avoid the dreaded water and steer the bomb to fall on an enemy ship.

The "Cat Bomb" idea would have fallen by the wayside had not Senator Kenneth McKellar, the chairman of the Appropriations Committee, given it his enthusiastic support. Lovell was forced to run an experiment to satisfy McKellar's curiosity. Things went poorly, as expected. The cat became unconscious within the first fifty feet of the fall and, Lovell said, "had no control of the bomb's direction, even if kitty tried."

Lytle Adams's idea received more attention than all the rest. An eccentric dentist and amateur inventor who bore an uncanny resemblance to Santa Claus, Adams had already convinced the government to pursue an idea of his once before. Throughout the 1930s, he had developed an air mail delivery system to bring rapid mail service to isolated "flyover" communities. In Adams's system, a pilot would descend to just fifty feet above the ground, lower a dangling hook from the plane, and snag a line on the ground that was tied to a mail package. The crew would then pull the package into the fuselage for sorting, thus eliminating the need to land the plane. The system was only ever implemented on a small scale, but Adams somehow managed to give a personal demonstration to First Lady Eleanor Roosevelt.

On December 7, 1941, Adams was driving home from a vacation in New Mexico when he turned on his car radio and learned of the Japanese attack on Pearl Harbor. Like many other Americans, he was stunned, angry, and eager for revenge. The United States would now enter World War II, and he wondered how he might contribute to the effort.

During his vacation, Adams had visited Carlsbad Caverns, an enormous underground cave system near the Texas–New Mexico border that harbors a colony of millions of Mexican free-tailed bats. What if, Adams thought on his drive, the military captured bats from Carlsbad, strapped them with time-delayed incendiary devices, and dropped them over Japanese cities? Once free in enemy territory, the bats would roost in attics, factories, lumber piles, and munition dumps, the incendiaries would explode, and the resulting fires would wreak havoc on Japan's high concentration of wooden buildings.

Adams feverishly wrote a proposal for his "Bat Bomb" idea. It began, "The millions of bats that have for ages inhabited our belfries, tunnels and caverns were placed there by God to await this hour to play their part in the scheme of free human existence, and to frustrate any attempt of those who dare desecrate our way of life." While Adams considered bats "lowly" creatures, he wrote, "If the use of bats in this all out war can rid us of the

Japanese pests, we will, as the Mormons did for the gull at Salt Lake City, erect a monument to their everlasting memory." In his view, the United States needed to launch a crusade against an inferior Japanese race, with the Bat Bomb as an opening salvo.

Adams's proposal would have been dead on arrival had he not had an important ally interceding on his behalf: Eleanor Roosevelt. Perhaps because she considered Adams a personal friend after the demonstration of his air mail delivery system, she agreed to deliver the proposal directly to her husband.

President Franklin Roosevelt was intrigued by the idea of a Bat Bomb. He passed it along to Bill Donovan with a short cover note explaining, "This man is *not* a nut. It sounds like a perfectly wild idea but is worth your time looking into." Wild Bill Donovan certainly wasn't one to dismiss a wild idea. And despite Lovell's objections that the Bat Bomb was silly and impractical, Donovan assigned the project to the one OSS branch capable of pulling it off, Lovell's R&D Branch, which in turn assigned it to Division 19.

To bring the Bat Bomb to life, Harris Chadwell, the head of Division 19, enlisted the help of Harvard zoology professor Donald Griffin, the foremost bat expert in the country. Unlike Lovell, Griffin saw promise in the Bat Bomb. In a letter to the NDRC and the National Inventors Council, he said that while America's military commanders would ultimately be the ones to decide whether to use the weapon, "it is suicidal folly" not to at least give them the option. Jack von Bloeker, a bat expert from California, reached the same conclusion. "As wild as it seems," he said, "the idea's got something going for it. Fanciful, yes. Yet the individual elements, crazy as they are, make fundamental sense."

Lovell and the other skeptics weren't so easily swayed. How

would they secretly capture thousands, if not millions, of bats? How would they attach the incendiary bombs? How would they transport the bats halfway across the world? How would they release the bats? Could bats fly while encumbered with an incendiary bomb? Would the bats seek out the desired targets in Japan? These and a hundred other questions threatened to ground the Bat Bomb for good.

Griffin set about answering the questions to quiet the critics. In late 1942, he traveled to Carlsbad Caverns and, with the permission of the National Park Service, caught three hundred bats to see whether he could cool their body temperatures to the point where they would enter a state of hibernation, his best idea for how to transport them to Japan. The test was only partially successful, but that was good enough for Griffin. It wasn't known until later that Mexican free-tailed bats don't hibernate but rather migrate south for the winter.

Chadwell next enlisted the help of his former roommate, professional arsonist Louis Fieser, to develop the miniscule incendiary bombs that the bats would carry. Fieser confessed to his diary, "The project seems silly," but over time he gained faith in the underlying concept.

Fieser visited the bat expert von Bloeker in California to determine how much weight a bat could carry. Von Bloeker, a chain smoker, eased into the subject carefully, knowing that the answer would upset his guest. "Female red bats carry their young in flight until they're nearly grown, that's at least a third of their own weight. And sometimes they have twins and triplets. Quadruplets are not unknown. In that case, they carry more than their own weight in flight."

"So how much does a bat weigh?" Fieser asked.

"There's a lot of variety over the world in different species," von Bloeker said. "There's a tropical bat, the flying fox, that'll go two or three pounds. But the one we're probably stuck with . . . is the Mexican free-tail. It weighs . . . what? Maybe ten, eleven grams."

"Grams?" Fieser said in disbelief. "Or ounces?"

"Grams, I'm afraid."

"Jesus!"

Fieser was discouraged, but he had no choice but to make the lightest incendiaries possible.

Meanwhile, Lytle Adams, the portly dentist who had first proposed the Bat Bomb idea, was having problems securing funding for the project. He told von Bloeker that he had heard "the damnedest thing while I was in D.C. Some general I met regarding appropriations confused our secret project with another secret project that's apparently going on somewhere [in New Mexico]. It's the silliest nonsense you ever heard of."

Von Bloeker nodded in sympathy through a haze of smoke, a cigarette limply held between his pursed lips.

"This general practically threw me out of his office," Adams said, "he was so enraged at the waste of time and money. 'Don't tell me you're the one promoting that crazy notion of making bombs out of atoms?' I had a hell of a time convincing him that I had nothing to do with that kind of fraud." Adams ended the conversation with a touch of humor and a dollop of irony: "We got a sure thing like the bat bomb going, something that could really win the war, and they're jerking off with tiny little atoms. It makes me want to cry."

The first test of the Bat Bomb occurred on May 19, 1943, at the Muroc Dry Lake, a flat expanse of hard white clay in California's Mojave Desert. To capture the bats, a handful of von Bloeker's assistants flew to Carlsbad Caverns and swung around giant nets in the underground chambers. When the crates of shrieking bats arrived in California, they were placed in a refrigerated truck to induce the hibernation state. Next, Louis Fieser clipped the incendiaries to their limp bodies. Instead of containing napalm, the incendiaries for this test contained highly visible red phosphorous smoke to make it easier for the observers to track the bats against the white background of the dry lake bed.

The bats were loaded into cardboard canisters, put aboard a bomber plane, and flown to a low altitude of two thousand feet. The plan was for a parachute to slow the descent of the canisters and allow the bats to fly away, but things didn't go according to plan. As soon as the canisters were tossed out of the fuselage, they got caught in the bomber's slipstream and ripped apart. Hundreds of groggy bats plummeted toward the earth. A ground crew kept their eyes peeled for the telltale sign of red phosphorous smoke. When the crew spotted a patch of red in the distance, they sped their jeeps across the desert floor. To their dismay, the color came as much from blood and guts as it did from the phosphorous smoke. Apparently, the refrigerated truck had been too efficient. Most of the bats had failed to wake on the descent, and the few that did had broken their wings in the slipstream and fell to their deaths.

Despite the setback, or perhaps because of it, another test was scheduled for a month later at an Army air base near Carlsbad, New Mexico, closer to the source of the bats. This time, the bats were strapped with fake incendiaries, packed into sturdier metal canisters, and flown to a higher altitude to give them more time to wake on the descent. Fieser, von Bloeker, and their assistants watched the B-25 through binoculars. When the canisters finally emerged from the belly of the plane, Fieser shouted, "Bombs away!"

The onlookers breathed a sigh of relief when the parachutes

deployed, and they openly cheered when tiny specks of brown fluttered away from the dangling canisters. A slight wind was carrying the bats northward, so the ground crew jumped in their jeeps and raced toward them "with white knuckles," said von Bloeker's assistant Jack Couffer, "dodging around larger bushes, plowing through smaller ones head-on."

The chase led them down a lonely dirt road, across a series of cattle guards, and through the front gate of a private ranch. A grizzled cowboy stood on the porch of the main house. Bobby Herold, another assistant, got out of the jeep and approached him with caution.

"Good morning, sir," Herold said.

The stoic cowboy nodded. "Mornin'."

"Ah, did you see anything, ah, that you might call unusual flying around here?" Herold didn't want to reveal any more than was necessary about the secret project.

"I see a noisy airplane," the cowboy said.

"I don't mean that. Something, ah, smaller."

The cowboy eyed the intruders. "Maybe."

"We're conducting experiments," Herold said as he looked around nervously. "We're from the air base. You know, over there." He gestured in its direction.

The cowboy nodded.

"The United States Air Force. Experiments with, ah—well, highly secret experiments. We didn't expect them, that is, anything, to come this far. Probably didn't. But if they did, ah, well . . . I hope we can depend on you to keep the confidentiality. You know, under your hat."

The cowboy shifted his weight but otherwise let the words linger in the air.

Herold filled the silence. "As I said—asked, that is—Did you see anything . . . ? Unusual?"

The cowboy finally let out a slow drawl of words, "Like bats flyin' 'round in broad daylight? Unusual like that? What'd you give 'em? No-Doz?"

"Yes. No. You saw them, then . . . ? Bats?"

"Like that one?" The cowboy gestured to the rafters overhead.

"Yeah. Just like." Herold then asked the cowboy for his discretion.

"Listen here, young feller," the cowboy said, letting down his guard. "I got two sons somewhere in Europe fightin' the Hun. If you tell me that what yer doin', however damned fool as it looks to me, is a military secret, nobody's goin' to get me to say peep even by puttin' bamboo splinters under my fingernails and alightin' fire to 'em. . . . But I do wish you'd tell that blessed airplane to fly away and stop spookin' my livestock."

The crew captured the rogue bats and returned to the air base, relieved that nothing worse had happened. Fieser, however, felt the urge to conduct one last test. So far, he hadn't had a chance to see whether his tiny napalm-filled incendiaries worked as planned. He decided to detonate a few complete Bat Bombs—time pencils, incendiaries, and live bats—to make sure that everything functioned properly together.

Fieser placed six lethargic bats on top of a sagebrush and set the ten-minute time pencils. The rest of the crew ran behind another sagebrush for cover. A photographer readied his camera for the fateful moment. As they counted down the seconds, Fieser noticed the bats begin to stir. "Hey!" he shouted, "Hey! They're becoming hyperactive. Somebody! Quick! Bring a net!" But it was too late. The bats had already flown away.

Ten minutes later, the group noticed smoke coming from the administration building. Then the control tower and an adjacent barracks burst into flames, sending up pillars of black smoke.

Without firefighters standing by—they had been deemed a threat to secrecy—both structures were completely destroyed. Fieser later described the remnants of the tower as "a mesh of twisted steel girders." Afterward, a bulldozer pulverized the wreckage to remove any evidence of cremated bats.

The test hadn't gone the way that Fieser had intended, but in a strange way, it proved that the Bat Bomb was an effective weapon. On September 14, Fieser wrote a letter to Warren Lothrop, another scientist in Division 19, saying that the Bat Bomb had a promising future. But others disagreed, especially in the wake of these embarrassing tests. Harris Chadwell responded to Fieser's letter on Lothrop's behalf: "Upon receipt of your letter I checked with Mr. Allen Abrams, in the absence of Stanley Lovell, in OSS, and was informed that so far as he knows there is no further interest in OSS on the Adams Bat problem." By this point, Lovell and Chadwell had grown weary of the Bat Bomb, and their judgment won out.

Division 19 turned over the Bat Bomb to the Marine Corps, where it was rechristened Project X-Ray. The Marines conducted another full-scale test, this time on a replica Japanese village constructed for the occasion at the Dugway Proving Grounds, an Army biological and chemical weapons testing facility eighty miles west of Salt Lake City. The replica village reminded Jack Couffer of an abandoned movie set. "I was very glad I was seeing it this way, without people," he said. "I could watch our little incendiaries do their dirty work without hearing the screams, the cries of pain, the yells of hysteria, the clanging of the fire carts, the roar of burning paper and wood, the sobs of mothers and fathers and sons and daughters."

Fieser attached live incendiaries to the bats and released them by hand inside the Japanese houses. When they exploded, the houses quickly caught fire, just as intended. Two fire trucks then extinguished the flames before the blaze could spread beyond control (Fieser had learned his lesson in Carlsbad). Based on the damage, Fieser concluded that 3,720 pounds of Bat Bombs could start 4,768 fires, whereas the same amount of M69 incendiary bombs could start only 160 fires.

Fieser could hardly contain his excitement, though it didn't last long. The Marine Corps soon scrapped the project. Chadwell, who had kept in touch with the Marines, assured Fieser that it was because of "uncertainties involved in the behavior of the animal, rather than the behavior of the technical units [incendiaries]." However, in a letter to Warren Lothrop, Chadwell admitted that he didn't think it was possible to produce enough incendiaries in time for the Bat Bomb to affect the outcome of the war. It turns out, those other scientists "jerking off with tiny little atoms" in New Mexico were making significant progress on a different weapon that was even more devastating.

4
Division 19 Destruction

Wild Bill Donovan found the courage—he always did—to perform a bold experiment. He walked over to the White House with a bag of sand in his hand and a silenced, flashless .22 automatic pistol hanging in his shoulder holster. Stanley Lovell had earlier submitted the idea for this weapon as a solution to Vannevar Bush's thought experiment, which in turn had led Donovan to recruit Lovell as his Professor Moriarty. Now that Division 19 had produced the weapon (in conjunction with the manufacturer High Standard), Donovan wanted to show it to the president. It never hurt to have friends in high places, or to keep those friends in high places in high spirits.

As Donovan approached the door to Roosevelt's office, Edwin "Pa" Watson, Roosevelt's senior aide, gave him a once-over with his eyes and waved him inside. Donovan dropped the bag of sand in the corner of the room and crept toward the back of the paralyzed president. Roosevelt sat in his wheelchair, unaware of Donovan's presence, dictating a letter to his secretary.

Quietly, Donovan raised the pistol, aimed the barrel at the bag, and squeezed the trigger ten times in quick succession.

A few seconds later, Roosevelt caught a whiff of burnt gunpowder. He looked up with wide eyes and saw Donovan standing behind him with a smoking gun in his hand. Roosevelt was shocked to realize that Donovan had fired off the full clip. Donovan later told Lovell, "If he could, physically, have jumped to his feet, he would have." Donovan then wrapped the heated muzzle in a handkerchief and presented it to the president. Roosevelt eagerly accepted the gift, joking that Donovan was the only Republican whom he would ever allow in his office with a gun.

When remembering the incident, Lovell made a poignant remark about the perks of power: "Security is often a one-way street. The gabby stenographer who lets slip some mildly classified trivia at a cocktail party is sent packing to her home in disgrace, but higher authority is above such discipline. Who makes the rules may break them with impunity."

Such a stunt was typical of Donovan. On another occasion, Lovell joined him in the back seat of a car that lacked a barrier separating them from the driver. Donovan began discussing the exact date and location of Operation Dragoon, the Allied invasion of southern France. Lovell gestured toward the driver, indicating that they should speak with caution, but Donovan brushed it off, "Oh, Harry's all right, aren't you, Harry?"

"If you say so, Boss," Harry replied.

Given that Donovan was the head of the OSS, an intelligence organization dedicated to spying, sabotage, and subterfuge, Lovell later said, "I cannot rationalize his often flagrant breaching of security and secrecy."

In the case of the silenced .22, perhaps Donovan was emboldened because Dr. Robert King of Division 19 had already performed a similar impromptu experiment to wide acclaim. Ac-cording to the minutes of an April 29, 1943, meeting of Division 19, King "loaded and brandished the weapon to the consternation of the group." He then fired it into a "bucket of sand, using long cartridges." His "nervous audience" was "impressed by the excel-lent performance of the device."

The silenced .22 was only one of a number of guns that the scientists of Division 19 either made or modified. They also produced the "Stinger," a small, easily concealable pistol; the "En-Pen," a single-shot pistol disguised as a pocket pen (other vari-ants were disguised as cigarettes, cigars, and pipes); and a silenced barrel for the M3 .45-caliber submachine gun, which transformed the weapon's resonant booms into something that one OSS officer described as sounding "more like a giant typewriter."

Furthermore, the "Hold-up" was a device that fastened a forward-facing pistol to the side of a person's body. By expand-ing the chest, the wearer could fire the pistol without having to touch it. That way, if they were ever caught and forced to put their hands up, all that they had to do to escape was face their captor and take a deep breath. In testing, the Hold-up proved to be less practical than intended. During a day-long trial in which a test subject wore a cocked but unloaded pistol in the Hold-up, it accidentally fired four times (when the subject was sitting down, leaning forward, lifting weights, and jumping over a row of hedges). An OSS evaluation committee concluded, "This is emphatically not a weapon for general issue."

Al Polson, a twenty-four-year-old scientist in Division 19, led the effort to develop an umbrella gun, a staple of any spy organization. The idea was first suggested to him by a secret agent who "was sent off to assassinate people," Polson said. "So we took a couple of umbrellas and we figured out how to put the gun into the handle of the umbrella. You could have it under your arm and just turn it half a turn and it would go off. The way they would kill people was by putting it right up against a guy's kidney and bam it was gone. If you don't have a kidney—you're gone."

In addition to stealing classified information from defense plants across the country, OSS recruits had to give a ten-minute demonstration of their mastery with one of these weapons in order to graduate training school. For added realism, the guns held live ammunition. Rather than dread the demonstrations, OSS agent William Morgan suspected that many of the recruits secretly enjoyed them because, for the first time, they had their superior officers at their mercy. A few of the recruits intentionally fumbled their guns at crucial moments in their demonstrations to keep their hostage audience on edge. Other times, the audience came to the rescue of a flustered recruit. When one recruit held a Stinger pistol facing the wrong direction, Morgan said to him, "Wait a minute. Are you sure you are holding it right?" The recruit realized his mistake before accidentally sending a round into his own abdomen.

Al Polson also led the development of a new type of hand grenade. Lovell had been eager to replace the traditional "Mills bomb" ever since he had learned about a group of OSS agents in Yugoslavia who had lobbed several of them at a German convoy only to have them bounce off the automobiles and explode harmlessly in a roadside ditch. The Germans, thus alerted to the ambush, sprayed the agents with machine-gun fire.

Lovell wanted the new grenade to explode on impact rather than a certain number of seconds after the pin was pulled. He also insisted that Polson ditch the Mills's pineapple shape for something more spherical, reasoning that every American boy could throw a baseball. The result was the "Beano" grenade. According to Polson, "The way it killed people was that it stunned first and then sent little pieces of steel into their internal organs such as kidneys and heart and they would die. We loaded the Beano with TNT, which packed about twice the explosive force of a typical grenade."

Unfortunately, during final testing at the Aberdeen Proving Ground, nobody briefed an Army civilian engineer on how the Beano worked. "To the horror of us all," Lovell said, the young engineer lobbed a Beano skyward and, as it fell back down, attempted to catch it. "He was blown apart by the explosion," Polson recalled.

Division 19 ultimately produced safer explosives—at least for the saboteur—than the Beano. These were, with Lovell's colorful commentary, booby traps that activated with pressure, "You sit down in a chair and go boom!"; booby traps that activated when pressure was released, "You pick up a book but never live to read it"; and the pull type, "where a wire you trip over ends that trip for you."

OSS officer Edward Hymoff oversaw the transport of these deadly weapons to Europe. When the pilots who flew the cargo planes learned that their inventory contained explosives, they asked him, "You're sure this stuff won't go up?" Hymoff couldn't resist having a little fun at their expense. "Don't worry," he told them, "you won't ever hear the bang."

The most famous Division 19 weapon sounds the most innocuous: pancake mix. "Aunt Jemima" was an explosive compound camouflaged as flour. Lovell had come up with the idea while trying to think of an easy way to sneak explosives into enemy territory.

Chemist George Kistiakowsky developed the recipe for Aunt Jemima. It was essentially 80 percent HMX explosive and 20 percent flour. When mixed with water, it formed a dough that could be baked into bread, biscuits, or cookies. Aside from a slight grittiness in texture, most people could hardly tell a difference from the real thing. Kistiakowsky even took a tray of Aunt Jemima cookies to a high-level meeting at the War Department "and ate them in front of all those characters to show them what a wonderful invention it was," he said. "All you had to do was attach a powerful detonator, and it exploded with the force of dynamite."

In theory, Aunt Jemima would enable the OSS to conduct imaginative new schemes that would have been difficult to conduct with conventional explosives. For example, in a scheme known as "The Disappearing Donkey," one OSS agent proposed loading the saddle bags of a donkey with Aunt Jemima. A little boy would be hired to lead the donkey into a German camp, tie it up, set the charge, and run away. If any German soldiers got curious and looked inside the bags before the explosion occurred, they wouldn't suspect a thing.

Harris Chadwell gave the scientists in Division 19 blanket approval to conduct Aunt Jemima detonation tests. One group naturally shot .50-caliber incendiary bullets at the doughy target. To their surprise, it failed to detonate. They concluded, "Aunt Jemima doughs probably are the safest available high explosive."

John Jeffries, an officer in the R&D Branch, conducted an Aunt Jemima detonation test on a much larger scale. He dumped one hundred pounds of it into a tub of water and carefully stirred the mixture for ten minutes with a wooden paddle. The resulting dough filled ten assault canteens, which he hauled to the Aberdeen Proving Ground for a day of excitement. But to his disappointment, the water content was too high and the dough again failed to detonate.

Stanley Lovell's own troubles with Aunt Jemima began when he had one hundred pounds of it sitting in his office that he wanted gone. He called an unnamed scientist who had helped develop Aunt Jemima and asked him to come take it away, but the scientist told Lovell that there was no need, he could flush it down the toilet instead. Lovell and his assistant, Allen Abrams, did just that.

The phone was ringing when Lovell returned to his office. It was another scientist, the boss of the first one. "Don't flush that explosive down the toilet," he said. "The organic matter in the sewer will react with it and blow the whole Washington sewer system sky-high." Lovell, feigning calmness, lied and said that he would do no such thing.

Lovell set the phone down and went into a full panic. He realized that the sewer's trajectory followed 16th Street, adjacent to the White House. His career at the OSS, and indeed the entire OSS organization, would come to a crashing halt if worse came to worst.

For hours, Lovell and Abrams nervously waited to receive another phone call telling them that they had been fired. On the way to dinner at the Cosmos Club, they jumped at every door that slammed and car that backfired on the street. Even worse, while they were gulping down drinks for courage, a waiter dropped a tray of dishes beside their table. Lovell had to go walk outside to calm his nerves.

His anxiety gradually subsided throughout the night. By sunrise, he was relieved to know that the White House remained standing. He knew because he walked over to see it himself, just to make sure.

Lovell experienced another close call with Aunt Jemima during a series of weapons tests held at the Congressional Country Club. Bill Donovan had recently been promoted to brigadier general and hoped that the tests would legitimize both himself and the OSS in the eyes of the other high-ranking military figures in attendance. Lovell understood the gravity of the situation. He could allow nothing to go wrong. He made sure that his best men prepared each test.

While John Jeffries was preparing a lump of Aunt Jemima for detonation, a general from Army Ordnance asked him if he could lay a steel plate of armor on top of it to see what would happen. Both Jeffries and Lovell were hesitant, but who were they to deny a general's request, especially in the company of other military personnel? Jeffries stuck a short time pencil in the dough, placed the plate of armor on top, and told everyone to move back a considerable distance.

When the dough exploded, the steel plate was launched through the air like shrapnel. One chunk flew just a few feet above Donovan's head, nearly decapitating him, and lodged itself in a nearby tree trunk. Another piece pierced the windshield of General George Marshall's parked car. Lovell was horrified. After all, it was—figuratively—his neck on the line for any and all mishaps. Donovan, on the other hand, "had not flickered an eyelash," Lovell said, "while I was trembling like an aspen leaf." In characteristic style, an unfazed Donovan turned to Lovell and, without even mentioning the near-death experience, nonchalantly asked, "What's next on the program?"

On August 28, 1943, Lovell and a newly minted General Donovan shared a similar experience at a meeting of the Joint Chiefs of Staff. As usual, Donovan, the most decorated American officer from World War I, wore only his Medal of Honor pin on his uniform while the Joint Chiefs "were covered from collarbone to breastbone with 'fruit salad'—except for the Medal of Honor," said OSS officer John Beaudouin.

During the meeting, Lovell was supposed to explain the mechanisms behind some of his special weapons. To liven up the presentation, he and Donovan had decided beforehand to secretly detonate a "Hedy," a Division 19 device that simulated the screech of a falling bomb. Surely, they thought, it wouldn't hurt to impress the bosses with a show. After all, hadn't President Roosevelt been impressed by the silenced .22?

Lovell had gotten the idea to make the Hedy when an OSS spy told him that he had once been trapped inside the Adlon luxury hotel in Berlin and "would have given anything if I could have created a panic in that lobby" as a diversion for his escape. The Hedy consisted of a small tube filled with pressed gallic acid and potassium chlorate. When the chemicals burned together, they formed an enormous volume of gas that was forced through a narrow aperture to produce a shrill screech. The name "Hedy" referred to actress Hedy Lamarr, whose unrivaled beauty "created panic wherever she went," Lovell said.

While describing Division 19's booby traps and incendiary devices to the Joint Chiefs, Lovell surreptitiously pulled a small wire loop to activate a Hedy and dropped the device in a metal trashcan. A few seconds later, it "interrupted me by suddenly shrieking and howling with an ear-piercing wail." The acoustics of the room amplified the noise far beyond what Lovell had expected. "To my surprise," he said, "I saw two- and three-star Generals clawing and climbing to get out through the room's single door." The demonstration was a success, at least in grabbing the audience's attention, if not in giving them psychological trauma.

When it was over, Donovan pulled Lovell aside and told him in businesslike manner, "Professor Moriarty, we overdid that one, I think." They were never again asked to give a presentation to the Joint Chiefs.

For the most part, though, Lovell's presentations left a more positive, if not a longer lasting, impression. Once when Elizabeth MacDonald, a strategist for the OSS Morale Operations Branch, accidentally opened the door to a room in OSS headquarters where Lovell was describing limpets, time pencils, the silenced .22, and the Hedy, the audience barely acknowledged her existence. As she slowly backed out of the room, she recalled, "The group had gone back to their searching examinations of the weapons with all the ardor of a small boy over his first electric train set."

Now that Division 19 had a handful of successful weapons in its arsenal, Lovell next set his sights on the more difficult task of sabotaging trains, motivated by the fact that the American military struggled to derail German trains in Europe. Traditionally, to derail a train, a saboteur would place an explosive on the side of the rail to blow the train off its tracks. But that often failed to bruise the hearty locomotives. A request was made to the OSS, which got passed on to the R&D Branch, which got passed on to Division 19, to develop a more effective derailment method. After consulting with the American Railroad Association and the American Society of Civil Engineers, the scheming scientists thought that they had found a solution. Simply remove small portions of the rail, perhaps only a few feet long, and the train would derail.

John Jeffries was tasked with testing this new method. He

bought a dilapidated engine for its scrap value and took it to Camp Claiborne, a U.S. Army basic training camp in central Louisiana with fifty miles of railroad track. Jeffries wasn't one to do anything halfheartedly. Instead of removing a couple of feet of rail as recommended, he removed thirteen feet.

Jeffries watched with anticipation as the engine chugged along at twenty-five miles per hour toward its assured doom. But to his dismay, it simply jumped the gap without derailing. Frustrated and eager to blow off some steam of his own, Jeffries decided to conduct an impromptu experiment. He figured that if he placed an explosive beneath the rail instead of beside it, not only could he blow a gap in the rail, but the blast might also form a crater into which the engine would fall.

Jeffries set up the new experiment with the same old engine. And to his delight, the method worked spectacularly, though not because of the crater. By placing the explosive beneath the rail, the blast fractured the rail and bent it upward. The bent rail impaled the approaching engine, greatly increasing the method's effectiveness. Word was immediately sent to OSS headquarters and from there to saboteurs in the field. Afterward, successful train derailments in German-occupied Europe increased from 50 to 90 percent. The OSS was unaware of *any* failure to derail a train when the new method was properly executed.

OSS agent Angelo Lygizos was part of a team in Greece that derailed a German troop train with the new method. He watched as the explosion caused fifty jumbled railcars to grind to a halt, the deafening wail of rending steel ringing out like a victory bell heralding his team's success. But the team wasn't done. Another agent fired a bazooka at the immobilized train, "which scored a direct hit on the engine's boiler creating a big explosion and a lot of steam," Lygizos recalled. The rest of the team then lit up the wrecked railcars with their weapons, "spraying everything that moved for about ten minutes, turning the train into Swiss cheese." Better safe than sorry, they reckoned.

Division 19 developed several other clever ways to sabotage trains. The "Mole" was a light-sensitive contraption that attached to the inside of a train's wheel well with magnets, similar to how a limpet attached to a ship's hull. Whenever the Mole detected a sudden shift from light to dark, such as when a train entered a tunnel, it detonated. If everything worked according to plan, the train would derail and plug the tunnel, preventing other trains from traveling along the same route. To prevent German soldiers from removing the Mole, a label was attached to each one that read, "This is a Car Movement Control Device. Removal or tampering is strictly forbidden under heaviest penalties by the Third Reich Railroad Consortium. Heil Hitler." Lovell speculated that few Moles were ever removed because, "We guessed, the German soldier was regimented to let Berlin think for him."

One of the most cunning methods for sabotaging trains involved filling hollow lumps of fake coal with high-explosive Pentolite. A saboteur would toss this "Black Joe" into an enemy's coal reserves and hope that it eventually got shoveled into a boiler. During preliminary tests, a three-pound chunk of Black Joe was placed in the fireplace of a test house. According to a summary report, "The Joe exploded lifting the roof and blowing out several windows." The interior partitions of the house were blown down, "the one exterior wall of the central room was shattered, the ceiling was shattered and sagging and the porch was loosened from the house."

Black Joe saw plenty of use in the field. Elizabeth MacDonald once delivered a piece of Black Joe to a Chinese saboteur who used it to blow up a Japanese train. He threw it into the boiler and jumped to safety just moments before the train crossed over a tall bridge. The resulting fireball ripped apart the bridge's supporting trestle, causing a string of railcars full of Japanese soldiers to plummet to the ground. MacDonald felt guilty about her role in causing so many deaths, but over time she forgave herself, saying, "I was just the one who handed it to the guy who did the job."

Division 19 developed ways to sabotage vehicles of all types, not just trains. For example, the "Odometer" exploded after a vehicle traveled a certain distance. The "Speedometer" exploded after a vehicle reached a certain speed. The "Anerometer" exploded after a vehicle reached a certain altitude. And the "Firefly" exploded after sitting in a vehicle's gasoline tank for a certain amount of time. If the gasoline caught fire, the driver "would be sitting over a very hot seat indeed," Lovell said. The vehicle "would become a carapace in which he would be cremated along with his gunner and companions."

Lovell attributed the success of Operation Dragoon, the Allied invasion of southern France, in part to the Firefly. Resistance soldiers working undercover as gas attendants sabotaged two German divisions that were headed to the beaches for battle. "Along the highways," Lovell said, "off in fields or smack in the roadway, there were the two tank division vehicles, abandoned if the driver kept moving and leaving a trail of burning gasoline behind him, but crematoriums if he stopped. Before anyone could escape through the tank hatch, the fumes of the gasoline burning under the tank had asphyxiated the tank personnel."

Destroying armored tanks apparently wasn't too difficult, at least if the saboteur was crafty. In occupied France, one OSS agent disguised as a French peasant walked up to a tank and yelled in German, "Mail!" When the lid opened, he tossed in two grenades. That was that.

But fires and explosions weren't the only ways to destroy vehicles. Lovell gave the nickname "Turtle Egg" to a small rubber sack filled with abrasive material that could be placed in an oil intake pipe and cause an internal combustion engine to malfunction. Others jokingly called it "Caccolube." Depending on the target, the abrasive material ranged from flash powder to cashew nut shell oil. (The most effective material was sulfur chloride, but it was abandoned because its strong odor betrayed its presence.) The cashew nut shell oil had the additional benefit of provoking allergic reactions among the German mechanics who were assigned to fix the busted engines. In fact, one American mechanic performing tests with Turtle Eggs was hospitalized for two weeks upon learning a bit too late that he was severely allergic to cashews.

In certain cases, Division 19 even created maritime devices. These included a collapsible kayak, a one-man submarine, a two-man inflatable motorized raft called the "Surfboard," and the Lambertsen Dive Unit, which provided oxygen to an underwater diver without leaving a noticeable trail of bubbles behind. Christian Lambertsen had originally developed the unit for the Navy, but after they rejected it—"We got submarines and torpedoes to sink enemy ships. We don't want no human torpedoes!"—he approached the OSS and successfully demonstrated the device in the swimming pool of the Shoreham Hotel. (Lambertsen later coined the acronym SCUBA, standing for Self-Contained Underwater Breathing Apparatus.)

One OSS maritime group performed a training exercise with the new equipment against U.S. defenses at Guantanamo

Bay, Cuba. "Using the Lambertsen Units," said member John Booth, "we swam underwater and penetrated the sub nets, no problem. We could have swum in and destroyed everything in there. They had an old barge in the harbor that the Navy didn't want so we placed live charges on it, blew it up, and got out of there."

The OSS rarely used divers on actual combat missions, unlike the Japanese. According to an OSS report, the Japanese deployed "human mine suicide swimmers" to destroy transports, landing craft, and cargo ships.

During one of the few OSS maritime missions in the Philippines, divers wearing long johns as wetsuits helped American ships avoid pockets of coral on the sea floor while mortars, machine-gun fire, and even the occasional kamikaze plane rained down from above. Diver Les Bodine remembered a mortar landing beside him as he swam toward the beach. "A concussion from the mortar forced me to the bottom. I went about 10 feet underwater.... When you get hit by an explosion like that water goes into every orifice: the ears, nose, rectum, and tears things up a bit. I was spitting blood and blacked out." Someone—Bodine never learned who—inflated his artificial bladder and towed him back to a ship. The onboard doctor gave him a shot of whiskey to recover. Walter Mess, another diver, remembered fondly, "I mean you are *alive*. I think it was the most fun I had in my life."

The most ingenious maritime project that Division 19 ever pursued was "Javaman." OSS officer John Shaheen conceived the idea while contemplating the best way to destroy the warehouses, shipyards, and oil depots that lined enemy harbors. Traditional air raids weren't effective against these targets because of antiaircraft guns and barrage balloons. Nor would a traditional naval approach work because of enemy ships, mines, and submarines.

Shaheen knew that local fishing vessels often penetrated these coastal defenses. He realized that if he loaded a motorboat with explosives and camouflaged it to look like a local fishing vessel, it could slip through the defenses. But the real genius of Javaman came next. Instead of sending a crew aboard the boat on a suicide mission, Shaheen wondered if an operator sitting safely in a B-17 bomber could watch a television screen that showed a live video feed from a camera mounted on the front of the unmanned boat and steer it via radio signal.

General Donovan, never one to ignore a wild idea, told Shaheen to coordinate the Javaman project with Lovell and to make sure that "technical development be carried out under his direction." The resulting motorboat "missiles" were thirty-four feet long, traveled up to forty-five miles per hour, and could carry eight thousand pounds of explosives. The engines were muffled, and an onboard loudspeaker played the sounds of native engines. Life-size human dummies were stationed at the helm, their hands fastened to the tiller. A few City Slickers were tossed in the hulls for good measure since each blast would create an oil slick in the harbor.

In April 1944, the OSS conducted the first remote control steering test of a Javaman missile off the Virginia coast. An operator sat in the Little Creek military base in Virginia, watched a television screen, and occasionally adjusted the direction of the boat via radio signal. Everything went as planned. No design modifications were necessary.

The first full test of a Javaman missile, including 3,485 pounds of explosives, occurred four months later in the Gulf of Mexico near Pensacola, Florida. The target was the *San Pablo*, a decommissioned banana freighter that had been damaged in a German torpedo attack. When the missile rammed into the *San Pablo*, the explosion ripped a sixty-foot-wide hole in its side and sent a column of water six hundred feet into the air. The *San Pablo* sank in less than two minutes.

Donovan and several other senior OSS officers soon attended another successful demonstration of the missiles. Afterward, Donovan wrote to the Javaman team, "I am grateful to each of you for the contribution you have made and for the fine spirit you have shown." Two months later, an NDRC review of the project concluded, "Equipment and training of personnel has reached a point near maximum efficiency. The unit is ready for combat."

But like the Bat Bomb, these boat bombs were never deployed. By the time that Division 19 had finished camouflaging them as Cantonese harbor craft and Irrawaddy river steamers, the atomic bomb was nearing completion and Javaman was liquidated.

Regardless, Javaman, as well as the rest of Division 19's devices, impacted Stanley Lovell in a profound way. With the creation of each new dirty trick, the moral qualms that he had once felt about his work gradually diminished, as did those of the other scientists in Division 19. An internal report on "New O.S.S. Weapons" explains their developing mindset: "Any means which hastens the conclusion of the war by only one day, will pay off in the lives saved and casualties prevented." In fact, before long, the callousness with which Lovell began advocating for waging unconventional warfare would give Donovan, Vannevar Bush, and a number of the military's top generals pause.

5
Kill or Be Killed

Division 19 created the explosives and incendiaries that the OSS used to destroy enemy buildings, vehicles, and personnel, but there was also a need for other devices that were far more discreet. Secret agents, after all, need to keep a low profile. Beyond the raucous weapons of Division 19, Stanley Lovell and his underlings in the R&D Branch developed an entire catalog of illicit items. Among them were crossbows, tire spikes, matchbox cameras, tear gas pencils, invisible inks, CO_2 dart guns, and a "Dog Drag" that masked a person's body odor to confuse any search dogs in pursuit.

And even without these devices, the OSS taught its agents how to sabotage enemy targets with nothing but ingenuity. A declassified OSS field manual on "Simple Sabotage" lists several inventive tricks for the unarmed agent. To ruin warehouse equipment, it says, tap the automatic sprinkler system with a hammer or hold a match under a sprinkler head to set it off. To ruin a building's sewage system, flush a compact sponge down the toilet; it will expand in the water and block the pipes. To ruin a building's doors, "Jam paper, bits of wood, hairpins, and anything else that will fit into the locks of all unguarded entrances to public buildings." To cause wear on a machine, uncover the filter system and poke holes in the mesh. And strangest—or perhaps most brilliant—of all, to ruin a showing of an enemy propaganda film, "Put two or three large moths in a paper bag. Take the bag to the movies with you, put it on the floor of an empty section of the theater as you go in and leave it open. The moths will fly out and climb into the projector beam, so that the film will be obscured by fluttering shadows."

The R&D Branch shared many of its devices with the British SOE, but the exchange went both ways. An R&D Branch memo from 1944 notes, "Our British associates were most cooperative in making their devices available and did not ask questions as to their use." One item that the SOE developed was an itching powder made from the needle-like hairs on the seedpods of the mucuna plant. On one occasion, a worker in a French clothing factory sprinkled liberal quantities of the powder on vests that were destined for the German Navy. Soon afterward, a German U-boat returned to port when its crew complained of a mysterious epidemic that had broken out among them. Another time, the itching powder was put inside German condoms. Local hospitals soon noted an uptick in reports of painful irritation during sex. And as an added bonus, the condoms had been sold for a handsome profit.

The SOE also famously developed a "Rat Bomb." Workers cut open one hundred dead rats, removed their organs, filled their hollow carcasses with plastic explosives, and sewed them shut. The idea was to place these Trojan rats in German coal reserves in hopes that the Germans would shovel them into their boilers, similar to Black Joe. The Germans, however, intercepted the only shipment of Rat Bombs ever sent to the field, foiling the plan. But in an odd twist, this actually worked to the Allies' advantage. Once the Germans learned that Rat Bombs existed, they wasted precious time and effort searching through their coal reserves looking for stuffed rat carcasses. The SOE concluded, "The trouble caused to them was a much greater success to us than if the rats had actually been used."

The British weren't the only ones swapping tricks with the Americans. So did the Soviets—or at least they almost did. The Soviet Union and United States had distinct desires, economic systems, and forms of government, but during World War II, they found themselves aligned against a common enemy. General Bill Donovan was a staunch anti-communist, but in the trying times of war he embraced the Soviets as an unlikely ally. He once told an assistant, "I'd put Stalin on the OSS payroll if I thought it would help us defeat Hitler." British prime minister Winston Churchill made a similar declaration. When asked whether it was hypocritical of him, an anti-communist, to make favorable noises about the Soviet Union, he said, "Not at all. I have only one purpose, the destruction of Hitler, and my life is much simplified thereby. If Hitler invaded Hell I would at least make a favorable reference to the Devil in the House of Commons."

President Franklin Roosevelt felt the same way. He once told Donovan to "treat the Russians as we would treat the British." And since the British were made privy to the developments of the R&D Branch, it made sense to extend a similar invitation to the Soviets. Donovan informed the OSS staff, "A delegation of Russians is coming soon to inspect Professor Moriarty's bag of tricks."

Lovell wasn't as eager to help them as Donovan was, and he wasn't as welcoming, either. As an introductory gift, he gave the delegation of Russians a quart of pure ethyl alcohol mixed with water, which he told them was vodka. They didn't seem to notice. Throughout their visit, Lovell only demonstrated his simplest devices, such as the booby traps. He didn't want to reveal too much because he didn't think that the alliance between the two countries would last long. When it came time to demonstrate the silenced, flashless .22 automatic pistol, he showed them an altered version that was both deafening and blinding. "They mumbled some Russian equivalent of a most derogatory nature," Lovell recalled. Besides the quart of synthetic vodka, they took nothing of value home.

One area where the R&D Branch benefited the most from its close collaboration with the SOE was in developing a variety of specialty pills for agents to use on their missions. A-pills alleviated travel sickness, B-pills provided a spurt of extra energy in the form of amphetamine, E-pills contained a quick-acting anesthetic, H-pills held an incendiary device that could be mixed with gasoline to form a Molotov cocktail, and K-pills knocked a person out with a dose of morphine.

Donald Summers, a special assistant in the R&D Branch, wrote a report describing another pill that would "produce extreme illness in man but is definitely not fatal." The effects lasted for six to eight hours, during which time the recipient "will be totally incapacitated and will be afraid he will die or," Summers said with a touch of morbid humor, "perhaps he will be afraid that he will not die."

Of all the pills that were developed, the L-pills, or lethal pills, were the most notorious. The box that they came in carried the eerie instructions, "If you're ever in a position that looks hopeless, and you've lost the will to fight, take as directed." Most often, agents took their L-pill if they were caught and wanted to commit suicide before an interrogation.

When bitten through its waxy outer coating, the L-pill oozed a goo of potassium cyanide, which an R&D Branch report says smelled like "butter of almonds . . . before and after death." The pill caused death within minutes—ideally. It didn't always work as advertised. One time, a helpless agent who had bitten his L-pill convulsed on the ground for an excruciating hour and a half before succumbing.

The OSS often exaggerated the L-pill's potency to make the decision to bite it more palatable. Nevertheless, if an agent refused to bite their L-pill in a moment of crisis, but they also didn't want to be caught with it, they could hide it inside a hollowed-out Gillette razor handle. Alternatively, they could swallow it whole, let it pass through their digestive system undisturbed, and recover it for later use, ideally after a thorough washing.

Donovan enjoyed playing a trick on his aides with the L-pill. Complaining of a headache, he would take two pills out of his pocket and offhandedly murmur to himself, "I don't know which is the L tablet and which is the aspirin." His aides would look on with terror as he alternately held up his hands in a twisted game of Russian roulette, trying to determine which pill to pop into his mouth.

The L-pill wasn't a laughing matter to Donovan for long. On June 7, 1944, the second day of the Normandy invasion, he and Colonel David Bruce, the OSS director of European operations, journeyed together across the English Channel to northern France. They were headed straight for the front. Despite the danger, or perhaps because of it, Donovan longed for a taste of the action. He wanted to relive the thrill of combat that he had experienced some twenty-six years earlier in World War I.

On the crossing, their ship, the USS *Quincy*, picked up three floating corpses and ten downed crew members whose planes had been shot out of the sky. The sight of the bloated bodies invigorated Donovan, who told Bruce, "What better end for us than to die in Normandy with enemy bullets in our bellies?" Bruce, a genteel man who was married to Ailsa Mellon, the richest woman in the United States, was less enthusiastic. He had earlier advised Lovell to be bold when dealing with Donovan, but now he wondered whether a little caution might do them some good.

For their final approach to Utah Beach, Donovan and Bruce transferred to the USS *Tuscaloosa* via swinging ladder. "Bilious yellow clouds of smoke shoot forth above the mouths of our guns," Bruce wrote in his diary. "The air is acrid with powder, and a fine spray of disintegrated wadding comes down everywhere on us like lava ash. Everywhere there is noise. When we fire, the deck trembles under our feet, and the joints of the ship seem to creak and stretch."

Once near the shore, they descended to an amphibious DUKW, or "Duck" craft, which brought them into the shallows amid a strong wind. Donovan, accustomed to the fog of war, nimbly hopped off the Duck's hood and onto the beach. Bruce took his time getting down, but his patience betrayed him. He fell on top of Donovan, knocking him to the ground. In the process, Bruce's helmet gashed Donovan's throat close to the jugular vein. Blood poured from his neck. While climbing back to his feet, without even acknowledging the mishap, he told Bruce that he wanted to be buried in Arlington National Cemetery, the nation's military cemetery in Virginia. "David, you've got to get a plot near mine."

They continued up the beach. Around them they heard the

crashing of waves, the drone of airplane engines, and the zip of machine-gun bullets, which clanged against the metal hood of the Duck craft that they had just jumped off. Donovan turned to Bruce with a slight grin, "Now it will be like this all the time." As soon as he turned back around, two German planes were shot out of the sky directly overhead. Bruce shook in fear, but Donovan reveled in the mayhem. "Excitement made him snort like a racehorse," Bruce later said.

They ran past the beach to the front lines, and then beyond. Donovan wanted to interrogate French civilians in the unoccupied zone between the battling forces. They stopped running when they spotted a group of German soldiers ahead. The Germans similarly spotted the Americans and began spraying at them with their machine guns. Donovan and Bruce jumped behind a small hedgerow for cover, flattening themselves on the ground. Donovan had said that he wouldn't mind going out with bullets in his belly, but he would try to avoid that fate if possible.

Laying prostrate in the dirt, Donovan whispered, "David, we mustn't be captured, we know too much."

Bruce instinctively agreed.

"Have you got your pill?" Donovan asked.

Bruce confessed that he didn't have the "instantaneous death pellet" that Lovell had given him.

"Never mind," Donovan said, "I have two of them." He reached into one pocket after another, disgorging their contents—a passport, photographs, hotel keys, travel orders, newspaper clippings, a variety of currencies—but found no pills. "Never mind," he said again, "we can do without them, but if we get out of here you must send a message to Gibbs, the Hall Porter at Claridge's in London, telling him on no account to allow the servants to touch some dangerous medicines in my bathroom." The humor briefly distracted them from the dire situation.

Still laying beneath the hedgerow, Donovan began another quiet conversation, "I must shoot first."

Bruce mistakenly thought that Donovan was suggesting that he would shoot first at the approaching Germans, providing cover for an escape. "Yes, sir," Bruce said, "but can we do much against machine guns with our pistols?"

Donovan corrected him, "Oh, you don't understand. I mean if we are about to be captured I'll shoot you first. After all, I am your commanding officer."

Bruce realized that Donovan wasn't joking this time. Fortunately, neither the pills nor the bullets were necessary. When the Germans left, Donovan and Bruce retreated back to the beach unharmed, except for the gash in Donovan's throat.

The R&D Branch project "Natural Causes," also called "Pneumonia," involved pills of another sort. Unlike the L-pill, which was meant for suicide, Natural Causes was meant for assassination. The minutes of a meeting reveal that Lovell and his colleagues considered killing someone by "the feeding of sodium metal in capsules," which "would be particularly devastating on anyone having stomach ulcers." The metal would react in the stomach to produce salt, which meant that even "the most careful autopsy would fail." The minutes emphasize that the project "is to be considered super-secret." The meeting's participants also discussed other ways to cause a death yielding a "logical autopsy" that left no trace of foul play. Their top ideas included inserting a lethal suppository, inducing a high body temperature for a prolonged period, and injecting an air embolism into a vein.

Nothing else is known about Natural Causes, but Lovell and the R&D Branch developed several other ways to covertly kill. On one occasion, Admiral Milton Miles and Captain Cecil Coggins, both from the Office of Naval Intelligence, asked Lovell to supply them with a poison or toxin that Chinese prostitutes in Shanghai could surreptitiously slip into the drinks of occupying Japanese officers. Lovell chose botulinum toxin because it occurs naturally in certain undercooked foods and therefore would draw less suspicion. The R&D Branch encased the botulinum toxin in tiny gelatin capsules that the prostitutes could hide behind their ears until it was time to spike the drinks of the Japanese officers. Given the nature of the prostitutes' work, hiding the capsules in their clothing, as Lovell would have otherwise suggested, wasn't an option.

Vannevar Bush once approached Lovell with a similar request. He was worried that the Axis powers might start fighting with poisoned bullets. Germany probably wouldn't, he wrote in a letter to Secretary of War Harvey Bundy, but then again, "One can never tell what the Nazis themselves would do as a matter of desperation." More worrisome was Japan. "As the noose draws tighter," Bush said, "we may expect almost anything from the Oriental mind." Bush told Bundy that he had asked the R&D Branch to create poisoned bullets of its own using unnamed "powerful poisons" that the NDRC's Chemistry Branch had recently discovered. Bush never identified the specific poisons, but an R&D Branch summary report on "Toxic Materials" lists 244 substances that were investigated, including anthrax, arsenic, cadaverine, cannabis, curare, heroin, mussel poison, mustard gas, phosgene, ricin, and venom from bees, cobras, copperheads, coral snakes, and rattlesnakes.

Interestingly, Bush seems to have sung a different tune in an October 18, 1943, meeting with Harvard president James Conant and James Rogers, the OSS planning chief. Rogers wrote in his diary that Bush and Conant "protested Lovell's interest in poisons" and said that "all toxins are taboo as attack measures."

Rogers agreed and wrote, "We had best avoid this ugly business." Elsewhere he wrote in his diary, "We have monkeyed [with poisons] to my disapproval as I know it is against Army policy." But poisons and toxins intrigued those within the R&D Branch, even if their peers disapproved.

For instance, Donald Summers suggested that the R&D Branch or a similar "future organization" lace cigarettes, chewing gum, and "foodstuffs like sugar, cereal, or grains" with poison to harm select individuals. In fact, Lovell himself devised a similar plan during the war. And his target, naturally, was Adolf Hitler.

In 1943, the OSS hired Harvard psychologist Henry Murray to conduct an analysis of Hitler's personality. Murray concluded that there was "a large feminine component to his constitution," which made him "emotional," "outwardly submissive," "annoyingly subservient," and "a full-fledged masochist" when it came to sex. After reading Murray's report, Lovell decided to inject female sex hormones into Hitler's food. In theory, the hormones would make his mustache fall out, his voice turn soprano, and his chest grow breasts, thereby exacerbating his fragile masculinity.

Lovell assumed that when Hitler visited the Eagle's Nest building in southern Germany, a mountaintop compound where the Nazis held meetings, the vegetables he ate came from a nearby garden. Lovell therefore paid a local gardener to inject female sex hormones into the beets and carrots destined for Hitler's plate. But the operation didn't go as planned. Lovell later speculated that the gardener took the money and ran. "Either that," he said, "or Hitler had a big turnover in his 'tasters.'"

Not every weapon, gadget, or scheme was so esoteric. On the more practical side, the R&D Branch helped produce the first official daggers of the OSS, the first official "cloak and dagger" organization of the United States. These daggers included the broad, leaf-shaped smatchet and the slender, foot-long stiletto. Lovell hired the kitchen cutlery company Landers, Frary & Clark to manufacture the stiletto, which explains why the belt hanger on its sheath resembles a pancake spatula—it was cast from the same die.

OSS recruits studied knife fighting and general hand-to-hand combat from the man who designed these daggers himself. His nicknames included "Fearless Dan" and "The Shanghai Buster." His real name was William Fairbairn.

Combat came naturally to Fairbairn, one of fourteen children born into his Scottish working-class family. In 1900, at the age of fifteen, he had enlisted in the British Royal Marines (the recruiter falsified his age) and served as a guard at the British Legation in Seoul. Beginning in 1907, he spent two decades with the Shanghai Municipal Police monitoring the city's red-light districts and battling some of the dirtiest felons of the criminal underworld.

One evening toward the beginning of his stint in Shanghai, a gang cornered Fairbairn in an enclosed alleyway and beat him unconscious. He woke up the next day in a hospital with no recollection of how he had gotten there. When his eyes adjusted to the bright, sterile light, he saw a sign advertising jujitsu training. He enrolled in the course as soon as his injuries healed.

Fairbairn remembered the jujitsu as "a very Hard School of Learning, and the Professor knew no English, and I, no Japanese." In the beginning, he was "hung on every nail around the room" by a group of Japanese naval officers, but later, "when I was better able to give it out, instead of being on the receiving end, it was very noticeable that the Jap officers were not so regular in their attendance."

Although a slender, bespectacled man, otherwise normal if not unintimidating at only 160 pounds, Fairbairn's face, legs, arms, palms, and torso were riddled with knife scars that he had acquired in the hundreds of street fights that he engaged in over his career. One long scar went from his ear to his chin and gave him the appearance of a Hollywood villain. His asymmetrical nose bore the evidence of having been broken multiple times. In light of his unique combat experience, Fairbairn developed a no-nonsense combat style called "Gutter Fighting" to train the Shanghai police and, later, OSS recruits.

Fairbairn trained the OSS recruits at the Congressional Country Club. To begin, he would ask the most physically impressive recruit to punch him. If the recruit refused, Fairbairn kicked him in the crotch. This, in essence, is Gutter Fighting. There are no rules. OSS agent and Fairbairn trainee William Dreux explained that there was "gouging, biting, knee or foot to the groin; the short, vicious karate chops to the neck; smash your boot down on the Jerry's face when he's down. Give no quarter. Cripple him, kill him."

An OSS instructional video elaborates on the psychology of Gutter Fighting: "It's a simple matter of kill or be killed. Capture or be captured. In this phase of the instruction period, the student is taught the gentle art of murder." The video continues with OSS personnel, wearing robber-style masks over their eyes, acting out the narrator's words. "The most valuable offensive blow at close quarters is the chin jab. The hand is held open at shoulder height and the blow is delivered to the opponent's chin with all the weight of the body in the follow-through." Fairbairn considered this and the "Tiger's Claw," a clenched hand thrust at an adversary's eyes, particularly effective moves.

As for knife fighting, Dreux explained how Fairbairn awed the recruits with his mastery of technique:

It was like watching a fighter shadow boxing and punching the big bag. He advanced on the dummy like a fencer, except partly crouched and half facing the dummy, left arm up as a shield. One threatening step followed the other in a deadly, purposeful pattern, the knife held out point forward and waving back and forth in short circular motions. There were feints, and then the sudden hard stab into the dummy, accompanied by a primitive snarl as the stiletto ripped into the fabric.

General Donovan once introduced former Supreme Court justice James Byrnes and his wife to Fairbairn at the Congressional Country Club. Byrnes watched the recruits shoot target practice at a papier-mâché Hitler and run across an obstacle course of narrow wooden planks to simulate a rooftop mission. At the end of the obstacle course was a house of horrors. "It was like a huge carnival shooting arcade," said one recruit, "except you were in the games. Targets would fly up, each to receive two rounds. Sacks filled with sawdust would lurch at you. Trap doors, loose floorboards, closed doors, and blind corners would bedevil you. At one point, as you kicked open a closed door, a man would face you, his gun at the ready. But—better not fire. It was your own reflection in a full-length mirror."

Donovan and Byrnes knew that President Roosevelt loved a good show, and they figured that Fairbairn's "circus stuff," as Byrnes called it, would interest him. They decided to bring the Shanghai Buster to Shangri-La, Roosevelt's private retreat in Maryland's Catoctin Mountains (now known as Camp David). Roosevelt wasn't disappointed. According to Byrnes, he was "vastly entertained" by Fairbairn's "repertoire of stunts and stories, and by his assortment of trick weapons."

Fairbairn also occasionally gave combat demonstrations to

the OSS hierarchy. During one such demonstration, he called his young pupil Rex Applegate to the stage and said, "Lieutenant Applegate, I want to you to attack me."

Applegate hesitated. "You can't possibly mean that, sir." At 230 pounds, Applegate dwarfed Fairbairn.

"I want you to attack me *for real*," Fairbairn said. "That's an order."

Applegate recalled thinking to himself, "This dumb old bastard, I'll take care of him."

In the aftermath, Applegate couldn't remember what move Fairbairn had put on him. All he remembered was flying through the air and landing atop the front row of the audience. Fairbairn stood at the front of the stage, unscathed, the star of the show.

Fairbairn also trained British SOE recruits in Scotland. One of them was journalist George Langelaan, who remembered "the Buster" as having a one-track mind set on combat. "Off duty his conversation was limited to two words: yes and no. . . . All his interest, all his knowledge, all his intelligence—and he was intelligent—concentrated on one subject and one subject only: fighting." Fairbairn had a surprising knowledge of human anatomy, but he never learned the specific names of bones and muscles. Instead, Langelaan said, he would refer to "this" or "that" and point to whatever bodily structure that he wanted broken, torn, or twisted.

Fairbairn taught Langelaan and the other recruits his most creative Gutter Fighting techniques. If an assailant corners you against a wall and you have an umbrella, he instructed, hold it tightly in both hands, one at each end, and drag the point of the umbrella across the assailant's stomach as if you're striking a large match. This won't do much harm, but it surprises the assailant. It causes him to pull his stomach in and lean slightly

forward. While he's in this position, thrust the point of the umbrella upward directly into his chin. "Now indeed," Langelaan
repeated Fairbairn, "it is all over bar the shouting, so scream as
much as you like and call the police, but if you are the kind-
hearted person you seem to be, you will also call an ambulance
for your victim."

Langelaan learned another technique for when an assailant
grabs you by the throat with both hands. "That is easier still," he
relayed. Simply push the assailant away with both of your hands
firmly on his chest. No matter his strength, he won't be able to
hold on. "Unbelievable? You can prove it easily enough. Just ask
your husband to grip you round the throat and to do his best to
hold on—he may be delighted to oblige for once. Now push."

Fairbairn later wrote a book on Gutter Fighting that choreo-
graphs a number of moves designed to incapacitate an assailant.
For example, if someone grabs ahold of both of your wrists, "Jerk
your hands toward your body, at the same time hitting him in
the face with the top of your head." When being strangled, "Bring
your forearms up inside his arms and strike outwards. If necessary,
knee him in the testicles." Targeting the testicles is a recurring
theme in the book (the assailants are always male). But whenever
a knee to the testicles isn't enough, the book suggests a simultaneous chin jab.

Fairbairn was known to put his own testicles on the line. He
once told OSS recruit and future director of Central Intelligence
Richard Helms to "grab my privates." Helms complied, but pru-
dently. "Not good enough," Fairbairn yelled, "*Go* for me." Helms
grabbed harder and in a moment found himself flat on his back.

Fairbairn gave the recruits a number of other tips for close
combat situations. When delivering a blow with a club, he recommended aiming for the shin bone instead of the head, which
is easily guarded. Plus, the forehead is hard, the shin less so.

When delivering a blow with a bare hand, he recommended hitting with the outer edge of the hand instead of a clenched fist. The edge of the hand delivers the force of the blow over a smaller surface area, resulting in greater pain. He also taught the recruits effective holds, throws, lifts, trips, dives, and falls.

But the most important tool that Fairbairn gave the recruits was a mindset. His training made them feel invulnerable. It made them confident enough to take on any mission, no matter how dangerous. And in the world of secret warfare where the success of an operation often rests upon the shoulders of a single individual, confidence is key. One recruit said that Fairbairn "gave us more and more self-confidence which gradually grew into a sense of physical power and superiority that few men ever acquire. By the time we finished our training, I would have willingly tackled any man, whatever his strength, size or ability." Perhaps besides Fairbairn himself.

6
Psychological Warfare

While William Fairbairn was busy boosting the self-esteem of OSS recruits through combat training, others were busy finding ways to demoralize the enemy through psychological warfare. These psychological strategists hoped that as they spread propaganda and disinformation abroad, enemy soldiers would despair and lose the will to fight. If done effectively, the enemy soldiers might surrender before actual combat even became necessary.

In one of the more peculiar psychological schemes of World War II, John Carter, a journalist with connections to the White House, informed President Roosevelt about a plan to drop bombs into the craters of Japan's semi-active volcanoes. Carter said that a group of unnamed seismologists and volcanologists "were of the opinion that a hearty explosion of a semi-active volcano will start the lava flowing and might burst out of the sides." Carter then revealed the kicker: "We could convince the mass of Japanese that their gods were angry with them, by dropping bombs down the craters and starting some nice local eruptions." Neither Roosevelt nor General Henry "Hap" Arnold, chief of the Army Air Forces, dismissed the idea out of hand, but neither did they push for its implementation.

In contrast, the OSS actively pursued a number of psychological schemes. In Operation Cornflakes, the OSS produced a batch of fake German postage stamps that replaced Adolf Hitler's portrait with a skull. The image was supposed to insinuate the inevitable death of the German war effort. Beneath the image, the words DEUTSCHES REICH (German Empire) were replaced with FUTSCHES REICH (Ruined Empire). The existence of these stamps only became known after the war with the sale of President Roosevelt's private stamp collection.

In another scheme, the OSS Morale Operations Branch spread a rumor throughout Germany that there existed a League of Lonely War Women who were willing to have sex with heroic German soldiers. All that a soldier had to do to receive his carnal reward was wear a heart-shaped pin on his lapel and visit a common bar or restaurant. A member of the League would duly approach him and offer companionship for the night. On its surface, this rumor would seem to have invigorated the German soldiers, but in reality, it subtly demoralized them by making them believe that, out of a sense of patriotic duty, women were joining the League in droves. Perhaps the women who joined included the soldiers' lonely girlfriends and wives back home.

Sometimes these psychological schemes targeted specific individuals. A group of psychoanalysts once thought that they could demoralize Hitler by dropping a payload of pornography over his headquarters. In theory, Hitler would step outside, pick up the smut, glance at the naked bodies, and descend into an uncontrollable state of derangement. Exactly how this would work, or how it would help the Allies, was never quite explained.

When the psychoanalysts approached an Army Air Forces colonel for help, he became convinced that *they* were the deranged ones and threw them out of his office.

In late 1943, Stanley Lovell was struck with inspiration to concoct a psychological scheme of his own. He planned to develop a substance that smelled so foul that it would "produce unmistakable evidence of extreme personal uncleanliness," he wrote in a letter to Harris Chadwell. The idea was to distribute tubes of this fetid fragrance to little boys in China and have them spray it on the backsides of occupying Japanese officers to make it seem as if they had soiled themselves. The officers would, ideally, become embarrassed and demoralized.

Lovell hired chemical engineer Ernest Crocker, the so-called Million-Dollar Nose, to develop this special "perfume." Crocker had gotten his start in the smell industry nearly thirty years earlier when he and his roommate, chemist Lloyd Henderson, had helped the U.S. Army develop harmless chemical red herrings that smelled like poison gas and thus would scare enemy troops on the battlefield. (At the end of a workday, the two men often came home smelling so foul that they slept outside in a nearby park.) Crocker's penchant for creating deceit through odors was exactly what Lovell needed.

At the Maryland Research Laboratory, Crocker and his team from the Arthur D. Little Company (the same team that developed the Dog Drag) synthesized the smell of vomit, urine, foot odor, and rancid butter before eventually settling on a substance that bore the unmistakable stench of feces, which they dubbed "Who Me?" But a Navy doctor who had recently returned from Saipan told Crocker that the Japanese routinely spread their own sewage as fertilizer and therefore weren't fazed by the scent. Crocker subsequently changed the formula of Who Me? to produce a more "skunky" smell.

Regardless of whether Who Me? actually lowered the spirits of the Japanese officers, it certainly raised the spirits of the R&D Branch personnel. Lovell called the effort in stench warfare "comic relief" from the "grim, bloody and sordid" reality of his other weapons.

Someone soon took the joke too far and began stealing samples of Who Me? from Lovell's personal cabinet to play practical jokes around the office. Lovell retaliated by booby-trapping the cabinet to spray the compound the next time that it was opened. That very evening, the thief picked the lock on the cabinet, "which was not at all surprising," Lovell said, "since we instructed all of our saboteurs in the art of picking open all makes of locks and door latches." The spray tagged the thief red-handed. Lovell never identified who it was, but he hinted that it was someone "too highly placed to be scolded." Apparently, even the leaders of the OSS needed occasional comic relief from the war.

Ed Salinger was responsible for developing the most unusual psychological schemes of the OSS. He was a "pleasant man," according to Elizabeth MacDonald, the strategist for the Morale Operations Branch who delivered a piece of Black Joe to a saboteur in China. He had an "elongated, foxlike face, curiously pointed at the chin," she said. "He wore the very expensive clothes of a dollar-a-year man, affected an ivory cigarette holder and bow tie." But beneath his posh exterior was a devious mind.

Between 1903 and 1914, Salinger had lived in Tokyo running an import/export business that traded in everything from fine silks to surgical instruments. Through his business dealings, he became familiar with Japanese culture. He knew the language, collected the art, and studied the superstitions, which is why the OSS eventually hired him. It needed someone who understood the Japanese psyche well enough to exploit its vulnerabilities.

In one psychological scheme, Salinger suggested that the Army paint white animals on tanks that were destined for an invasion of Japan. White animals were "sacred" to the Japanese, he said, and therefore the Japanese might hesitate to attack anything, even an American tank, with a white animal on it. As the war progressed, his suggestions became even more bizarre, most notably in the case of Operation Fantasia.

As Salinger pitched it, Operation Fantasia would destroy Japanese morale by exposing Japanese soldiers and civilians to the sight of *kitsune*, glowing fox-shaped spirits with magical abilities. In the Shinto religion, these spirits often represent portents of doom. Salinger thought that if he could release glowing foxes—or at least something that looked like glowing foxes—in Japan, then the Japanese might believe that it signified the upcoming defeat of their military. "The foundation for the proposal," Salinger wrote in a memo outlining his idea, "rests upon the fact that the modern Japanese is subject to superstitions, beliefs in evil spirits and unnatural manifestations which can be provoked and stimulated." (In reality, the Japanese folklore of *yōkai*, which includes mystical entities such as *kitsune*, resembles the folklore of any other culture.)

When it came to the question of how to actually make the glowing foxes, Salinger enlisted the help of the R&D Branch. First, R&D personnel fashioned fox-shaped balloons to fly over Japanese villages. They also hired a whistle company to create a whistle that simulated the fox sounds on a phonographic record. "These whistles," Salinger wrote, "can be used in combat and a sufficient number of these should create an eerie sound of the kind calculated to meet the Japanese superstition." Additionally, the R&D Branch once again hired "Million-Dollar Nose" Crocker to create artificial fox odors. Salinger thought that the Japanese would somehow recognize these odors—just as he thought that they would somehow recognize a rare fox sound—and cower in fear. But despite his best efforts, the balloons, whistles, and odors were ultimately abandoned as impractical. Instead, the R&D Branch opted to pursue Salinger's alternative plan: catch live foxes in China and Australia, spray-paint them with glowing paint, and release them throughout Japanese villages—somehow the more practical option.

This new plan presented a number of logistical hurdles. First, what kind of paint should be used to make the foxes glow? The United States Radium Corporation provided an answer in the form of its specialized glow-in-the-dark paint containing radium, a dangerous radioactive element with a half-life three million times shorter than uranium. The health risks associated with the paint weren't unknown. As early as 1917, women detailing watch dials with it began suffering from anemia, bone fractures, and necrosis of the jaw because they had used their pursed lips to shape the contaminated brush tips into a fine point.

The next roadblock was determining whether the paint would adhere to animal fur. Salinger turned to Harry Nimphius, a veterinarian at the Central Park Zoo in New York, for help. In his tenure at the zoo, Nimphius had dealt with issues ranging from a paralyzed elephant to a canary with a broken leg, but never anything as odd as slathering an animal with glowing paint. Nimphius recruited the help of a raccoon that was more than willing to have his fur painted in exchange for his daily allotment of food. The raccoon was kept under lock and key and hidden from public view so as not to cause alarm. After several days of ordinary raccoon shenanigans, the paint stayed on.

Salinger next decided to release thirty glowing foxes in Washington, D.C.'s Rock Creek Park to make sure that they would indeed frighten people. If the foxes could spook average Americans, he reasoned, then they would certainly terrify the Japanese.

On a summer night in 1945, the glowing foxes scampered through the park with promising results. The sight of the ghostly apparitions terrified the locals. One person was so concerned that he notified the National Park Police, which reported on the incident: "Horrified citizens, shocked by the sudden sight of the leaping ghost-like animals, fled from the dark recesses of the park with the 'screaming jeemies.'" Needless to say, the test was a success.

There were still other questions to answer before Operation Fantasia could proceed. For one, how would the foxes get to the Japanese islands? Salinger had initially planned to drop them in the ocean and let them swim ashore, but it wasn't clear whether they would survive such an excursion. Could foxes swim long distances? Nimphius gave his word that they could, but Salinger wanted confirmation.

Under the cloak of an early morning fog, unidentified R&D personnel packed a group of painted foxes onto a boat destined for the middle of the Chesapeake Bay. The foxes paced inside their small cages for the duration of the journey. When the engine cut off, they became frantic. One by one, the reluctant foxes were pulled from their cages and thrown into the brackish seawater.

To the delight of the personnel, the foxes doggy-paddled to shore without a problem. The dry (or wet) run for the Japanese invasion had been a success. But only partly. By the time that the foxes reached the shore, most of the paint had washed off, and within minutes of stepping onto the beach, they licked their wet fur until the rest of the remaining paint was gone.

If Operation Fantasia was to proceed, the foxes would have to be dropped onshore. But what would stop them from running off in the wrong direction? Salinger's solution was simple: strength in numbers. "If enough foxes are released, some will get through," he wrote. And on the off chance that the foxes failed, he suggested painting readily available minks, muskrats, raccoons, or coyotes in their stead.

Salinger's bizarre scheme gets even stranger. In one newly discovered memo, he wrote that he had learned of "a peculiarly potent manifestation of the Fox legend," a version of the Shinto superstition that supposedly terrified the Japanese even more, which "appears in the form of a fox bearing death's head on his crown." His plan to capitalize on this information bears repeating in his own words: "We have made a stuffed fox with a human skull affixed to his head, equipped with a simple mechanical device for raising and lowering the jaw so as to simulate the opening and closing of the mouth of the skull. This stuffed figure will be painted to give the same luminous effect as in the case of the live foxes." Salinger suggested draping this taxidermied ventriloquist human-fox hybrid in a black cloth painted with glowing bones, then lifting it in the air with balloons to make it appear to be levitating. From the ground, the Japanese would look up and see a floating fox body, covered in glowing bones, with a human skull sitting atop its head, its jaw opening and closing as if it were talking.

And just in case none of his previous plans worked, Salinger included an addendum to his memo titled "Fox-Possessed Human Beings." According to this plan, Japanese citizens sympathetic to the Allied cause would "simulate persons possessed of the Fox spirit, who utter strange chants purportedly emanating from the Fox spirit." Essentially, they would run around in a semi-deranged state yelling about foxes. Salinger cautioned the

OSS Planning Staff that the creation of a fox-possessed human army was in the planning stages only. "There are many difficulties which would have to be overcome before the plan could be put into actual operation."

None of the aforementioned harebrained schemes ever went beyond the planning and experimental stages. As early as September 24, 1943, Stanley Lovell recommended that the OSS abandon Operation Fantasia. He couldn't understand why nobody else had questioned its logic or feasibility. At best, he thought that it would be as ineffective as exposing American G.I.s to black cats. "I trust that this will serve as a critique to us in the field of pure reason," he told his colleagues in a meeting. Lovell had established his reputation by pursuing eccentric ideas—he was Professor Moriarty, after all—but Operation Fantasia went beyond even his tolerance for absurdity.

The minutes of another meeting reveal noticeable relief in the attendees, including Lovell and Harris Chadwell, when the OSS canceled the project near the end of the war. "This problem of Fantasia has been mercifully completed," they concluded. When Bill Donovan had told Lovell that the American people would "applaud someone who can outfox the Nazis and the Japs," he didn't mean it quite so literally.

7
Detachment 101

Not everyone approved of what the R&D Branch was doing. In a diary entry from January 1943, OSS planning chief James Rogers wrote about a lunch meeting that he had with Stanley Lovell in which he called Lovell's devices "amusing murder nonsense we will never employ." Amusing murder nonsense aside, the OSS did employ many of the devices, and Carl Eifler probably got more use out of them than anyone else.

Lovell described the 250-pound Eifler as the "deadliest hombre in the whole O.S.S. menagerie." He was "an enormous mass of a man with a temper as big as his hulk." Others nicknamed him "Mastodon Incarnate" and "Colonel Thundercloud." He was known to shoot cigarettes out of his friends' mouths, dig a bullet out of his leg with a spoon handle, and grab a ten-foot king cobra by the tail and behead it with his knife.

Eifler's past was as intriguing as his personality was brazen. In 1921, at the age of fifteen, he had lied about his age to join the

Army (his size wasn't indicative of his youth). He was discharged eighteen months later when the truth came out. After brief stints with the Los Angeles fire and police patrols, he worked as an agent for U.S. Customs and the Border Patrol, detaining bootleggers and drug smugglers along the Mexican border and occasionally engaging in gunfights. He rose within the ranks to eventually become the chief customs inspector in Honolulu, Hawaii.

That's where he found himself on the fateful morning of December 7, 1941. At 7:55 A.M., Eifler answered his ringing telephone. Sergeant Vincent Curl panted for breath between rushed words, "You'd better get up here. All hell has broken loose."

"Sergeant," Eifler responded, "have you been drinking?" Eifler was a hard drinker himself and knew firsthand the audacity of a drunken soldier.

"Yes, sir, but a bunch of red planes are bombing Wheeler Field," an airbase near Pearl Harbor.

Eifler now heard the rumble of gunfire. He ran from his house. When he got to within sight of the harbor, he saw flames and a thick column of smoke billowing up from the USS *Arizona*. Its crew was firing every available weapon at a squadron of Japanese planes overhead.

Eifler noticed a young soldier standing near him, watching the carnage unfold. He asked the soldier if he had ever been in battle before. The question was rhetorical; Eifler already knew the answer just by looking at his boyish face. When the soldier said no, Eifler braced him for what was to come: "Well, hang on soldier. You're going into one."

Two months after the Japanese attack on Pearl Harbor, Eifler received a vague wire from Washington, D.C., asking him if he was available for a volunteer assignment in the Far East. He wired back declining the assignment. Soon afterward, however, he received another wire. "Glad you are joining," it said. "Will have orders issued assigning you immediately to Coordinator of Information. Leave as quickly as possible for Washington." Apparently this mysterious "volunteer" assignment was more mandatory than Eifler had thought.

Not one to disobey orders, Eifler sailed to California and caught a flight to Washington. Colonel Preston Goodfellow greeted him at COI headquarters and explained the situation: "We are sending a group of saboteurs to China. We want you to command them. Will you accept?"

The COI (soon to become the OSS) wanted these saboteurs to disrupt the Japanese occupation in the Far East, especially by destroying the Myitkyina airfield, from which the Japanese were launching surprise attacks on Allied aircraft running supply missions from India to China. Destroying the airfield, and therefore preventing the Japanese attacks, would give the United States a strategic advantage in the region. But it would also help in a more Machiavellian way. If done right, the Japanese might blame the destruction of the airfield on the many native tribes in the region and retaliate against them. Out of resentment, those tribes might then support Japan's enemy, the United States. In the cold calculus of war, this was seen as a win-win scenario. The airfield would be destroyed and the United States would gain an ally. Two Far East experts dismissed the plan as infeasible, but President Roosevelt said, "It has merit. Send it to Bill Donovan." They did, which is how it eventually fell into the hands of Carl Eifler.

Eifler took the night to think over Colonel Goodfellow's offer. The next morning, he returned to COI headquarters with his decision. "Yes, sir. I'll do it."

Eifler's first task was to recruit soldiers to join him on the assignment. One by one, he explained to them the dangers that they would encounter, the probability of never returning, and, as an inducement to join, the excitement that they were sure to experience. Jack Pamplin never forgot his first interaction with Eifler. "From behind the desk rose this mountain of a man," he said. "He walked around the desk and shook my hand, giving me the impression he intended breaking every bone. Then, with a smile that was alarming, he put his hands behind his back and said 'Hit me in the stomach as hard as you can.'"

Another recruit, William "Ray" Peers, recalled how during their first meeting, "as if it were entirely habitual," Eifler picked up a stiletto dagger and drove it several inches into the top of his desk. "He looked pleased." Eifler then entertained Peers with tall tales of what to expect if he joined the assignment. There would be adventures with pirates riding down the Yangtze River, treks with warlords on Mongolian ponies across the Gobi Desert, "parachutes, hit-and-run fire fights, resistance movements, sabotage," and other operations "crisscrossed with danger." Peers joined without any further encouragement.

Once Eifler had recruited enough men, he and seven others attended a secret training school in Canada called Camp X where they learned how to detonate explosives, resist interrogations, write hidden messages, and search for downed aircrews. Eifler's group initially called themselves Detachment 1, but out of a concern that the enemy might conclude that only one such outfit existed, they re-christened themselves Detachment 101.

General Joseph Stilwell, nicknamed "Vinegar Joe" for his biting remarks, commanded American forces in the China-Burma-India theater where Detachment 101 would be operating. His mission statement to Eifler was simple: "You have ninety days for me to hear booms from the jungle."

On May 19, 1942, Eifler flew ahead to scout out his new domain. He decided to establish Detachment 101 headquarters in Nazira, a humid subtropical town on the eastern edge of India, near the border with Burma, nestled in the foothills of the Himalayas. The climate and geography of the region were as troublesome as any enemy. Temperatures often exceeded one hundred degrees Fahrenheit. During the summer monsoon season, Eifler noted that a cleaned pistol "will develop rust pits in 24 hours, a pair of shoes not cleaned daily will rot in a week." The hilly jungle topography made things especially difficult, as detailed in a report sent back to OSS headquarters: "[Jim] Tilly got lost in the high grass . . . slashed his arms and trouser legs. He then got to the top of a hill and climbed a tree. He got nearly to the crotch and got his hand caught in a bee hive. . . . Started off through the pit grass. He went right over the cliff 30 feet and hit into a bamboo clump."

To make matters worse, the region was plagued with diseases—malaria, typhus, encephalitis—and crawling with venomous vipers, five-inch elephant leeches, and other repulsive critters. Millions of crickets and cicadas emanated a never-ending chorus of background buzzing. Among the trees, tigers silently stalked wild boars and other prey, including, on occasion, a wandering human. For fun, and for protection, Detachment 101 adopted a bear cub until it grew too big to handle. The men in camp often had a hard time determining who was doing the snarling, the bear or Eifler.

Some of the members of Detachment 101 fell victim to these jungle creatures. One night while Captain Red Maddox was sleeping, a leech attached itself to his urethra. When he woke up, his penis was so swollen that he couldn't urinate. He tried pulling at the leech, but it wouldn't budge. He was about to gouge it out with his knife when Lieutenant Pat Quinn fashioned a makeshift forceps tool out of bamboo. This created a wide enough opening to grab the leech and wrench it out.

Tales of these jungle creatures spread with abandon. In one popular rendition of a story, a man's parachute got caught in the dense canopy, leaving him dangling over the ground like a marionette. By the time that he was found, a legion of ants had eaten away his flesh, leaving only a skeleton behind.

Fortunately, Detachment 101 soon won the trust of the Kachins, a minority hill tribe native to the region. In exchange for salt, chocolate, and weapons, thousands of Kachins eventually joined Detachment 101 and taught the Americans how to survive, navigate, and fight in the jungle.

In February 1943, Detachment 101 launched its first mission. The plan was for twelve saboteurs, known as Group A, to parachute behind enemy lines and destroy the railroad bridges that supplied the Myitkyina airfield. Once Group A landed, it split into three teams, each of which targeted a different bridge. The first team accidentally detonated their charges too early, drawing unwanted attention to the area. The second team abandoned the mission because of the heightened danger. The third team, composed of Pat Quinn and Aram "Bunny" Aganoor, continued on. As they set their charges, a squadron of Japanese police spotted them. With nowhere to hide, Quinn and Aganoor sprayed the police with their automatic weapons, killing four of them, then fled into the jungle.

Yelling, gunshots, barking dogs, the beating of gongs—the

jungle erupted in noise as the police chased the saboteurs. Quinn escaped unharmed, but Aganoor was caught and killed, Detachment 101's first casualty.

The next mission was even more disastrous. The six men of Group B were dropped in the middle of Burma for another sabotage mission. Ray Peers was aboard the C-87 aircraft watching his friends land on the ground. He remembered, "We could see a discomforting sight: villagers streaming out in every direction, heading towards the drop zone. I had an aching feeling that the lines looked hostile. I couldn't get it out of my head that they were out to kill." Peers was right. The villagers captured the saboteurs and turned them over to the Japanese. After several days of torture, three of them were executed. The rest were released into the jungle during a rainstorm and were never seen or heard from again.

Over time and with additional support—including from the R&D Branch—Detachment 101 gained its composure, though its leader, Carl Eifler, lost some of his. During the next mission, Eifler planned to insert six saboteurs behind Japanese lines to cut off another supply route. A thick mangrove swamp prevented their insertion by land, so Eifler and a maritime support crew dropped them off by boat near the Burma coastline. The saboteurs were supposed to paddle ashore and bury their rafts, thereby concealing their arrival, but the landing took longer than expected and they were forced to leave the rafts sitting on the beach.

Eifler knew that the Japanese would spot the rafts and launch a manhunt. He couldn't abandon his men to die without first doing everything in his power to ensure their survival. He hatched a plan to swim ashore, tie the rafts to his waist, and tow them back to his boat.

He made it to the shore with ease, but the return trip with

the rafts was a nightmare. He was struggling to stay afloat when a towering wave flung him headfirst against a rocky outcropping. Bleeding, exhausted, and borderline unconscious, he somehow managed to reach the boat within minutes of when the crew had planned to abort the mission and abandon him for dead. The rafts had been retrieved, but it came at the cost of an injury that caused Eifler lifelong headaches, blackouts, blurred vision, and, to treat his pain, an addiction to bourbon and pain pills.

Meanwhile, General Joseph "Vinegar Joe" Stilwell was dealing with a headache of his own in the form of Chinese leader Chiang Kai-shek, whom Stilwell condescendingly called "Peanut." In Stilwell's eyes, Chiang and the Chinese Nationalist regime were irredeemably cruel, corrupt, and uncooperative in the fight against the Japanese. He equated them to the Nazis in Germany: "Same type of government, same outlook, same gangsterism."

In the fall of 1943, Stilwell summoned Eifler to New Delhi to ask him for a favor. Could he assassinate Chiang Kai-shek? Stilwell knew that Eifler possessed both the courage and experience to carry out the mission. Without hesitation, Eifler assured him that he would find a way.

In September 1943, Detachment 101 hosted a Navy lieutenant en route to China who carried with him an R&D Branch medical kit. Nobody in Detachment 101, not even Eifler, knew about all of the devices that the R&D Branch had produced. Information was hard to come by in the middle of a jungle halfway around the world. Detachment 101 member William Wilkinson wrote to OSS headquarters, "There were many situations which showed a definite need for OSS special items."

To placate Detachment 101's demand for these "special items," the R&D Branch sent over Anerometers, Black Joe, Caccolube, City Slickers, fighting knives, limpets, pocket incendiaries, silenced guns, time pencils, tire spikes, and copies of a manual on arson that Louis Fieser, the inventor of napalm, had written for the OSS. Stanley Lovell personally invented a booby trap designed for the kind of jungle warfare that Detachment 101 engaged in. The "Bushmaster" essentially consisted of a modified submachine gun that clamped to a tree. After a predetermined amount of time, a time pencil set off the trigger, causing the gun to fire until its magazine ran out of bullets.

The R&D Branch also developed a similar weapon for inserting into the ground. When stepped on, it shot a .30-caliber bullet straight up, ideally into the leg or abdomen of an enemy soldier. Ray Peers said that this device "caused untold apprehension among the Japanese. Even when we dropped the use of the device because the enemy was too alert for it, the threat of finding the mine slowed down the enemy's advance," similar to how the threat of the Rat Bomb had slowed down the Germans.

Now that Eifler had learned what the R&D Branch was capable of producing, he began sending Lovell requests for imaginative new weapons. One request was for a folding chainsaw. Another was for a self-propelled limpet that was capable of traveling one hundred yards underwater and attaching itself to a ship. There was also a request for "my old favorite Bazooka mounted in a multiple unit of 6." And finally, Eifler requested—and received—an explosive white tallow candle that detonated after the wick burned a predetermined amount.

Lovell, in turn, learned from Eifler that lighting was primitive in much of the Far East. Japanese camps often only had a single light bulb around which everyone gathered in the evenings. This gave Lovell the idea to create a device called "Blackout," a light bulb that detonated whenever it was connected to an electric current. George Kistiakowsky, the chemist who had developed the recipe for Aunt Jemima, dismissed the idea, writing in a scathing report that it would be "absolutely impossible to put enough explosive into the base of a transparent light bulb to make the result more harmful than the popping of a cracker." The Blackout never made it to the field, but something far more valuable soon arrived in Nazira.

In addition to sending over its devices to Detachment 101, the R&D Branch also sent over demolitions expert Sam Lucy to personally create dirty tricks on an as-needed basis. When Lucy arrived in Nazira, he established a field laboratory known as the R&D Section. This small section undertook a number of projects guaranteed to "keep the engineers scratching their heads," Lucy said. These included developing self-destructing messages, modifying bazookas to distribute propaganda leaflets, engineering a way to launch grenades from an M3 submachine gun, and inserting time pencils into Chinese writing brushes. Lucy's R&D Section also created "War Paint" kits that saboteurs could use to darken their skin and blend in among the locals. There were initial discussions about sending these kits to China, but Newton Jones, a member of the R&D Section, wrote in a letter, "Colonel Peers, Major Lucy, and myself all feel that War Paint and the job it is doing saving *whites* is infinitely more important."

In Nazira, the members of the R&D Section spent lots of their time camouflaging explosives to look like everyday objects, such as logs, fish, rocks, pottery, vegetables, mule turds, water jugs, animal skulls, and Buddha idols. An OSS report on these so-called false idols praises the quality of the casts but cautions, "There is a definite question as to the operational value of using religious images among people who are extremely emo-tional on religious matters." Regarding the mule turds, one OSS agent wrote to Lucy, "Dear Sam, have received your 28 March letter and the poop."

Because Detachment 101 occasionally made supply drops that fell into Japanese hands, the R&D Section naturally devised ways to sabotage these drops. On one occasion, Lucy rigged a handful of parachutes to explode upon release. The plan was to "accidentally" drop the unopened parachutes to Japanese sol-diers on the ground. In theory, the Japanese soldiers would use the parachutes on their upcoming missions. The R&D Section provided only one comment: "Won't they be surprised!"

Another time, at a forward base where a group of Kachin guerillas was expecting a supply drop, a reconnaissance plane no-ticed that the "Kachins" on the ground were actually Japanese soldiers in disguise. The R&D Section decided to employ some deception of its own and fill the supply containers with shrapnel and plastic explosives.

First Lieutenant Dennis Cavanaugh watched as members of the R&D Section loaded the containers into the B-25, handling them "like eggshells," he said. Before taking off, one of the pilots casually asked someone from R&D Section if the opening shock of the parachute would set off the charges. Nobody had consid-ered this possibility before, but it was too late to do anything about it.

Cavanaugh accompanied the containers on the flight. When they were released, he watched them fall—briefly. "BOOM-BOOM!" he later said. "Both booby-trapped containers exploded when the chutes opened, fortunately behind our plane." Nobody was hurt, but the back of the plane was riddled with holes.

On the ground, the Japanese soldiers watched the contain-ers explode in the sky. They quickly realized that Detachment

101 had seen through their disguises. As they ran for cover, the B-25 swung around and unloaded its eight forward guns into their ranks. Cavanaugh said, "We almost stopped midair" from the recoil.

The Kachins taught the members of Detachment 101 a number of dirty tricks of their own, the deadliest of which involved placing sharp, fire-hardened bamboo spikes called *punji* sticks on either side of a trail. Eifler wrote to Lovell that during an ambush, the Japanese soldiers' "natural instinct as well as their training prompted them to hit the ground beside the trail." Upon doing so, they were "immediately unmercifully spiked." Some of the Kachin guerillas even suggested dipping the tips of the *punji* sticks in poison or feces to infect the wounds of the survivors, but Ray Peers argued against it. Even though Detachment 101 engaged in all sorts of nefarious activities, he didn't want to give anyone the opportunity to claim that it also engaged in biological warfare. Lovell agreed with him—for now.

8
Target Heavy Water

In the midst of World War II, there were many reasons to think that the Germans were building an atomic bomb. For one, nuclear fission, the underlying principle of atomic bombs whereby the nucleus of an atom splits and releases energy, was discovered in Germany in 1938. Furthermore, Germany controlled Europe's only mines for uranium, one of only two elements (the other being plutonium) capable of achieving a runaway nuclear chain reaction—a bomb—through fission.

Still other tidbits of information suggested that the Germans were building an atomic bomb. For instance, German economist Erwin Respondek told Samuel Woods, the American commercial attaché in Berlin, that Germany had set aside thirty-five million reichsmarks to study technical issues related to an atomic bomb. Also, Lise Meitner, one of the co-discoverers of nuclear fission, sent a curious cable to a friend in England that raised eyebrows. Meitner wrote that she had recently visited physicist Niels Bohr in Denmark: "Met Niels and Margrethe recently both well but unhappy about events please inform Cockcroft and Maud Ray Kent." J. D. Cockroft was one of Bohr's friends, but nobody knew of a Maud Ray Kent. Cockroft concluded that the name was an imperfect anagram of "uranium taken." Perhaps, he thought, Meitner was secretly warning him that the Germans had seized all of the uranium in Denmark to build an atomic bomb. ("Maud Ray Kent" turned out to be the name of Bohr's housekeeper, Maud Ray, who was from Kent.)

In early 1943, Stanley Lovell found yet another reason to suspect that the Germans were building an atomic bomb. He was sitting at his desk in front of a stack of OSS radio reports from the previous day when his secretary, Mrs. Cooley, informed him that his morning appointments had been canceled. With time on his hands, he began looking through the reports. Near the bottom of the pile was a report from Agent 110 in Bern, Switzerland, now known to be Allen Dulles, the future director of Central Intelligence. It said, "One of my men got dry clothes and a breakfast for a French *ouvrier* who swam the Rhine to Rehen last night. Told following improbable story. Said he was forced labor guard for casks of water from Rjukan in Norway to island of Peenemünde in Baltic Sea." Lovell tossed the report aside with the others, not thinking anything of it. But his initial indifference soon turned to revelation. Why would casks of water, so abundant and cheap, need guarding? He could understand the guarding of food, fuel, prisoners, and ammunition. But water? He quickly realized that only a specific kind of water warranted such security measures: heavy water.

Given Lovell's proximity to Vannevar Bush, he had been made aware of the Manhattan Project. Heavy water, he had been told, could potentially help in building an atomic bomb. The hydrogen nuclei in ordinary water contain one proton, whereas the hydrogen nuclei in heavy water, known as deuterium, contain both a proton and a neutron. This additional neutron gives heavy water distinct chemical properties that make it an excellent candidate to serve as a moderator in a nuclear reactor. In such a reactor, lumps of uranium-238, the most common isotope of uranium, are placed in a lattice structure surrounded by a moderator, in this case heavy water. The moderator slows down the speed of the neutrons emitted from the uranium. These slow neutrons are then absorbed by other uranium atoms and convert that uranium into plutonium. This new plutonium can then be chemically separated from the remaining uranium and used to make an atomic bomb.

The OSS considered information about heavy water so valuable that if an incoming intelligence report contained the words "heavy water," it was automatically forwarded to General Donovan and President Roosevelt. Allen Dulles's report didn't mention heavy water specifically, but Lovell put two and two together.

In Dulles's report, the "French *ouvrier*" who guarded the casks of water said that they had come from Rjukan, Norway. Lovell grabbed his encyclopedia. Rjukan, he learned, was home to the Vemork hydroelectric plant, the largest power plant in the world upon its construction in 1911. Along with generating power from the Rjukan waterfall, the plant was the world's main source of heavy water. In 1940, Germany had seized the Vemork plant when it invaded Norway. Lovell's suspicions were confirmed.

Lovell wasn't the first person to link the German seizure of the Vemork plant to a potential atomic bomb. Soon after Germany invaded Norway, French intelligence officer Jacques Alliers and two of his colleagues met with the general manager of the plant and bought the entire stock of heavy water available, 185 liters, before the Germans could take it. They then shipped it from

Norway to Paris, where it was kept in a bomb-proof vault. When Germany invaded France, they smuggled it to England.

The British also had their suspicions. In November 1942, they sent two gliders full of saboteurs to blow up the Vemork plant and deny Germany its heavy water, but the operation encountered fatal problems from the beginning. On the way to the plant, the gliders experienced massive turbulence, ice accumulated on the fuselages, and the compasses failed, forcing the saboteurs to navigate by crude maps and eyesight alone, a near impossible task given that all of the observable landmarks on the ground were covered in snow.

Both gliders crashed into a mountain. Seven of the saboteurs died on impact. Of the twenty-three survivors, three were captured by the Gestapo and taken to a hospital where a German medical officer injected an air embolism into their veins. Their dead bodies were weighed down with stones and thrown into the ocean. The rest of the survivors were subsequently captured and shot in the back of the head.

Lastly, in Operation Gunnerside, a group of Norwegian saboteurs attempted to destroy the heavy water production capabilities of the Vemork plant and therefore deny Germany a means to an atomic bomb. To infiltrate the plant, the saboteurs scaled a 450-foot cliff, dodged a minefield, and lowered themselves into an intake grate. Once inside, they placed two time-delayed charges on the heavy water cells. They then made a mad dash outside, put on their skis, and fled into a frozen forest. The small explosions temporarily delayed German production of heavy water, but the Vemork plant was restored to full capacity within two months.

Stanley Lovell knew something that had escaped the French, British, and Norwegians. The French *ouvrier* in Dulles's report had indicated that the Germans were shipping the heavy water from the Vemork plant to Peenemünde, a village bordering the Baltic Sea in northern Germany. The OSS already knew that strange structures that looked like ski slopes dotted the landscape in Peenemünde. Lovell inferred that these structures "must be launching sites" for atomic bombs.

He ran out of his office, down the hall, and flung open Donovan's door. Donovan was talking to a guest, but Lovell interrupted them. "Bill," he said while panting for breath, "this may be vitally important." Donovan could tell that he was serious. He dismissed his guest and gave Lovell his full attention. Lovell laid out the evidence: "This little French workman has told us where the German heavy water comes from, but vastly more important, where the German physicists are working to make a bomb employing nuclear fission. It all adds up perfectly."

"Adds up to what?" Donovan asked.

"To a catastrophic Nazi victory. This explains the 'ski' sites."

Donovan was skeptical, but he acknowledged that Lovell was the scientist in the room, not him. "If you say this is 'hot' I'll believe it, although it sounds like Jules Verne to me."

Lovell tried to reassure him. "General, remember Hitler said, 'We will have a weapon to which there is no answer'—remember? The whole thing falls into place. . . . If we bomb the very hell out of Peenemünde, we stop it cold before it has a chance to start."

Donovan ran Lovell's hypothesis by Vannevar Bush and James Conant for good measure. Both of them agreed that Lovell was onto something. Donovan, in turn, was convinced that Peenemünde was a target of critical importance.

The information eventually made its way to Colonel David Bruce in London. On the night of August 17, 1943, the British Royal Air Force led a bombing raid on Peenemünde. Nearly six hundred heavy bombers dropped two thousand tons of payload on the village. The raid killed one thousand people—many of them Polish and Russian prisoners of war—and destroyed the mysterious structures that Lovell thought were launch sites for atomic bombs.

Lovell was partly wrong about the structures. They weren't launch sites for atomic bombs, but rather launch sites for the Nazi V-1 and V-2 rockets. The bombing raid seriously delayed Germany's ability to deploy its rockets, but the threat of the German atomic bomb remained. The Allies still needed to destroy the German heavy water.

The order to destroy the German heavy water went to Knut Haukelid, a steely-eyed Norwegian Resistance soldier who had earlier participated in Operation Gunnerside. His best chance at success would be to sink the *Hydro*, a ferry ten miles east of the Vemork plant that was scheduled to transport the barrels of German heavy water across Lake Tinn. If Haukelid could sink the *Hydro* over the deepest part of the lake, he could all but guarantee that the barrels would be lost.

On a freezing February 20, 1944, Haukelid and two companions, Rolf Sorlie and Knut Lier-Hansen, snuck onboard the *Hydro* carrying a sack of plastic explosives. They quickly located the hatchway leading to the keel where they needed to place the explosives for maximum damage. Soon afterward, they heard the footsteps of the ferry's watchman getting closer. Haukelid and Sorlie ran below deck, while Lier-Hansen ducked under the closest table. The watchman easily spotted Lier-Hansen on the ground and demanded to know what he was doing. In a moment of panic, Lier-Hansen invented a story about how he didn't mean any harm, he was just looking for a place to sleep.

He and the sympathetic watchman fell into a long conversation, inadvertently providing the perfect distraction for the other two saboteurs.

Haukelid and Sorlie spent the next two hours placing the plastic explosives on the keel. "It was an anxious job," Haukelid recalled, "and it took time. The charge and the wire had to be connected; then the detonators had to be connected to the wire and the ignition mechanism. Everything had to be put together and properly laid. It was cramped and uncomfortable down there under the deck, and about a foot of water was standing in the bilge." They ultimately placed enough explosives to blow eleven square feet out of the bottom of the ferry.

Halvard Asskildt and his fiancée, Solveig, boarded the *Hydro* for what they thought would be another typical crossing. They had been celebrating Halvard's birthday with his parents that morning and barely made it to the ferry on time. Once onboard, they sat down to catch their breath. They could now relax and enjoy the mountain scenery, the peaceful ride, and each other's company.

Halfway across the lake, the explosives detonated. The *Hydro* rapidly filled with smoke and water. "Solveig wanted me to jump," Halvard later said. "She knew she couldn't swim, but I told her she would have to jump. She said, 'Okay, you first, and I'll follow.' I jumped, but she just stayed there and went down with the boat. It's hard for me to talk about this."

Miraculously, Solveig survived the ordeal. "I was probably dragged under by the undertow from the boat," she said, "and I somehow ended up getting caught in the propeller. I was badly cut and bruised. And the second time I emerged, I managed to grab hold of the lifebuoy crate. I couldn't see a lot, but I did see a barrel next to me, although I have no idea what was in it. A man was trying to get up onto it, but he didn't manage, and he drowned."

Four Germans and fourteen Norwegians died in the explosion. Twenty-nine people survived, including Halvard and Solveig, thanks to a group of local farmers who heard the blast and raced to the wreckage. Haukelid's sabotage mission succeeded in destroying the barrels of heavy water, crippling Germany's chances of acquiring an atomic bomb before the war's end.

9
Pursuit of the Mastodon

General Donovan, true to his "Wild Bill" nickname, craved another taste of combat. While riding in a jeep through Italy in July 1943, he "got behind my light machine gun and had a field day," said Captain Paul Gale. "He shot up the Italians single-handed. He was happy as a clam when we got back." On that same trip, OSS officer Irving Goff spent time with Donovan and noted his "foolish guts." When a German plane strafed their position, Donovan didn't budge. "He wouldn't get down, and bombs droppin' all around."

Five months later, Donovan once again entered the field. On December 7, 1943, he landed on an airstrip in the heart of the jungle for a surprise visit to Detachment 101. Officially, he was there to evaluate OSS operations in the Far East, but unofficially he was there to evaluate Carl Eifler. Rumors were circulating that Eifler had become erratic on account of his head injury and subsequent addiction to bourbon and pain pills. Donovan respected Eifler, but he wouldn't hesitate to remove him from command if it served the greater good.

The two larger-than-life figures shared a number of traits, including their brawny build and brazen personality. Stanley Lovell said that Donovan found in Eifler "a fellow spirit who dared to throw heavy hazards into the teeth of Fate and who, like himself, was completely devoid of fear." But they weren't the same in all respects. Whereas Donovan was "the calm, relatively unemotional type to whom danger was only delectable when blended with duty," Eifler was "an uninhibited extrovert." There was "nothing of the braggart or show-off in William J. Donovan," Lovell said. "Somewhat less than that has to be said for Carl Eifler."

Despite his head injury, Eifler was sharp enough to sense that Donovan had come to relieve him of his command. If Eifler was going to have any chance of keeping his job, he would need to prove to Donovan that he was a competent leader. And to do that, he needed a challenge. Fortunately for Eifler, challenges in Nazira practically grew on the jungle trees.

"Would the General like to go behind the lines?" Eifler hoped that by taking Donovan on such an excursion he could demonstrate that he was capable of leading Detachment 101.

Donovan wasn't oblivious to what was happening. He knew that Eifler was trying to win him over. And yet he couldn't bring himself to forgo a wartime thrill.

"When do we leave?" Donovan asked.

"First thing in the morning, sir."

That night, OSS agent Nicol Smith roomed with Donovan. "General," he said when they were alone, "aren't you risking your life?"

"Everything is a risk," Donovan replied. "My boys are risking their lives every day."

In the morning, Donovan handed his wallet and identification papers to Smith. "If anything goes wrong, it'll be just as well if I'm incognito." He and Eifler then climbed into a small, antiquated British biplane. An observant mechanic muttered to himself, "That damned plane will have a double hernia if it gets off the ground." *If* indeed. Eifler had already crashed a plane once before while taking off from the same short runway (he walked away with minor injuries). But the prospect of crashing and dying fazed neither Eifler nor Donovan. What worried them most was the prospect of crashing, surviving, and falling into Japanese hands. Just in case they were captured, Donovan carried an L-pill in his pocket.

The plane somehow managed to take off. Several hours later, Eifler and Donovan landed at a forward base called Knothead, more than one hundred miles behind Japanese lines. When Donovan climbed out of the plane, a group of Americans rushed to his side, stunned that the head of the OSS was there in the flesh. Donovan shook their hands and listened to their stories of sabotage missions. He also met with a group of friendly Kachin soldiers, some of whom were scarcely taller than the rifles that they carried. Donovan and Eifler couldn't stay long. Headstrong as they both were, even they realized that this had been a reckless idea.

The makeshift runway at Knothead was even shorter than the one in Nazira. To help them generate speed, Eifler revved the engine while a group of Kachins held back the plane. On his signal, they let go and the plane sped down the grassy runway. With only 10 percent of the runway left, Eifler pulled at the controls, but nothing happened. In the distance, a wall of trees grew closer. Eifler pulled again. This time the plane lifted, but not high enough to clear the trees. He banked to the right, turning the plane on its side. In this perpendicular position, he somehow managed to thread through a narrow gap in the tree line.

Although the plane was now airborne, it still needed speed.

Eifler dove down a steep hill toward a river for acceleration, leveling out just five feet above the water. All the while, Donovan sat silently in the back seat relishing the adrenaline.

Once they were safely back in Nazira, Donovan finally told Eifler the reason for his visit. "Carl, I think it is time for you to return to America. I am issuing orders for you to return immediately."

Eifler insisted on staying. "Sir, I have a job to do here. I have just got things rolling. I need to stay and build my organization."

But Donovan held firm. He told Eifler that he needed him back home for "morale purposes," a cock-and-bull excuse meant to boost Eifler's own morale more than anything. Eifler wasn't convinced, but he also wasn't one to disobey orders. In December 1943, he returned to the United States.

Eifler hadn't forgotten about General Joseph Stilwell's proposition to kill Chiang Kai-shek, and it wasn't long before someone else was asking him for a similar favor. In February 1944, Robert Furman, the Manhattan Project chief of foreign intelligence, met with Eifler in a quiet room of the bustling OSS headquarters. Furman knew that Eifler was itching to go back in the field. Maybe they could help each other out. The German effort to build an atomic bomb had been wounded, perhaps fatally, when Knut Haukelid sank the *Hydro*, but Furman wanted a guarantee that it was dead.

During their meeting, Furman told Eifler about a renowned German physicist named Werner Heisenberg, a pioneer of quantum mechanics who had coined the famous Uncertainty Principle. Heisenberg had recently stopped publishing articles in physics journals and stopped teaching his usual courses at the University of Leipzig. Furman considered this an indication that

Heisenberg was now working on a secret project that demanded silence. Perhaps that project was an atomic bomb. After all, if anyone was going to lead a German effort to build an atomic bomb, it was Heisenberg.

Eifler listened attentively. He had never heard of Heisenberg or atomic bombs. He didn't understand either of them, but it didn't take a physicist to understand what Furman was getting at.

Eifler cut to the chase. "Do you want me to bump him off?"

Not exactly, Furman said. "This man's brain has a great deal to it. [He's] much too important, he's a great scientist, but we do want it denied to the enemy." A simple kidnapping would suffice. "Colonel Eifler, do you think you can kidnap this man and bring him out to us?"

Eifler assured Furman that he could.

"My God," Furman exclaimed, "we finally got somebody to say yes."

The details of the kidnapping were left to Eifler. In a meeting with three of the highest-ranking members of the OSS—Donovan, Ned Buxton, and Joseph Scribner—he proposed traveling to Switzerland, sneaking into Germany, kidnapping Heisenberg, and then smuggling him back to Switzerland. From there, they would rendezvous with a getaway plane and fly to Great Britain.

Buxton, the assistant director of the OSS, interjected to say that under no circumstances would Heisenberg set foot on British soil. This was to remain a strictly American operation.

Eifler thought for a second, then pitched an alternate idea. He would instead fly the getaway plane over the Mediterranean Sea, not to Great Britain. He and Heisenberg would parachute into the water, where an American submarine would pick them

up and bring them to the United States. It was a risky operation, but it could work.

With the plan in place, Eifler asked for advice on what he should do in case something went wrong. "All right," he said, "I have kidnapped this man and smuggled him safely back into Switzerland. Now suddenly I am surrounded by Swiss police and cannot get him to the airfield. What are my orders?"

"You are to deny Germany the use of his brain," Buxton said.

"Okay, so I bump him and am arrested for murder. Now what?"

"Then, we will deny you."

Eifler expected as much.

Eifler needed a cover story to explain why he was being sent to Switzerland. Otherwise, if he showed up without an overt reason, he might arouse suspicion and jeopardize the operation. In a letter to Donovan, Stanley Lovell suggested that Eifler lead a "Strategic Trial Unit" that would travel to U.S. military installations in Europe and South Asia and demonstrate the R&D Branch's "toys and devices." This cover story was sensitive enough to appear legitimate and, Lovell thought, important enough on its own that even if Eifler had to abandon the kidnapping, the effort would still be worthwhile. Additionally, Eifler's background in customs gave his cover story an added layer of authenticity. He would be on "orders" to write a report about how customs were handled at the Swiss border.

Before leaving the United States, Eifler visited Lovell in his office to finalize the list of devices that he planned to demonstrate abroad. Among them were limpets, time pencils, and the silenced submachine gun. The meeting also gave Eifler an opportunity to raise an additional question that few but a

Professor Moriarty could answer: How could he covertly kill Chiang Kai-shek?

It turns out, Lovell had already been thinking about assassinations for quite some time.

As part of the Natural Causes project, Lovell had contemplated how to kill someone in a way that yielded a "logical autopsy." He had also provided botulinum toxin to Chinese prostitutes with access to Japanese officers. Throughout the war, he conceived of and consulted on a number of other assassination plots that were far more elaborate.

The strangest plot involved hypnotism. Broadly interested in the phenomenon, Lovell invited Lawrence Kubie and brothers Karl and William Menninger, all three of them psychiatrists, to OSS headquarters for a discussion. He asked them whether it would be possible to take a German prisoner of war whose family had been victimized by the Gestapo and hypnotize him to "stimulate and activate that sore spot." Could hypnotism provoke this disgruntled prisoner to assassinate a member of the German hierarchy? The psychiatrists had their doubts. According to the Menningers, "A man to whom murder is repugnant and immoral cannot be made to override that personal tabu." Kubie agreed and elaborated, "If your German prisoner of war has adequate and logical reasons to kill Hitler, Heydrich, or anyone else you don't need hypnotism to entice or motivate him. If he hasn't, I am skeptical that it will accomplish anything."

Now also sufficiently skeptical of hypnotism, Lovell was surprised when Ned Buxton asked him to come to his office to meet with a hypnotist from South Carolina who specialized in posthypnotic suggestion. Buxton wanted Lovell's opinion on whether the man was legitimate or a fraud. When Lovell

walked into the office, the hypnotist said, "I have two soldiers at a nearby camp whom I have hypnotized frequently and know are fine subjects. Let me bring them to your office, Colonel Buxton, and I'll prove I can produce posthypnotic action." Lovell's ears perked up. Perhaps the psychiatrists had been wrong after all.

The next day, the hypnotist brought the two soldiers to the office. Lovell, Buxton, and General Jon Magruder watched as he placed them in a hypnotic sleep. Once they went under, he told them that whenever they next entered the office, they would experience a terrible itch on the soles of their feet. He then woke them up, dismissed them for an hour, and waited.

An hour later, the two soldiers ambled back into the office and sat down with a smirk. Without saying a word, they unlaced their boots and began furiously scratching at the bottoms of their feet. "Gotta scratch 'em," one of them said, "itch like hell."

Lovell wasn't amused. He dismissed the entire performance, later saying, "What private in the whole U.S. Army wouldn't enjoy taking off his shoes and socks before a general when he knew in advance he couldn't be disciplined for doing so? It's a wonder they kept their pants on." The psychiatrists had been right from the beginning. Hypnotism wasn't a viable method for assassination.

Lovell devised another assassination plot during an OSS staff meeting where it was announced that Adolf Hitler and Benito Mussolini were scheduled to attend an upcoming conference at Brenner Pass. When the announcement was made, a member of the Special Operations Branch blurted out, "Let us parachute a cadre of our toughest men into the area and shoot up the bastards! Sure, it'll be a suicide operation, but that's what we're organized to carry out."

General Donovan wouldn't commit to a specific plot before hearing from everyone. "How would Professor Moriarty capitalize on this situation?" All eyes turned to Lovell.

"I propose an attack which they cannot anticipate," Lovell said. "They'll meet in the conference room of an inn or a hotel. If we can have one operator for five minutes or less in that room, just before they gather there, that is really all we need."

Donovan could hear murmurs of skepticism among the rest of the OSS staff. "Gentleman," he said, "hear Professor Moriarty out, if you please. Now what do you propose to have your one man do in this conference room?"

"I suggest that he bring a vase filled with cut flowers in water, and that he place it on the conference table or nearby."

"So what?" came a cry from a West Point general.

Inside the water, Lovell explained, an agent posing as a janitor would crush a capsule containing colorless, odorless nitrogen mustard gas. "If they are in that room for twenty minutes, the invisible gas will have the peculiar property of affecting their bodies through their naked eyeballs. Everyone in that room will be permanently blinded. The optic nerve will be atrophied and never function again."

Donovan smiled. "You see, Gentlemen, why we have so depraved an idea man as Professor Moriarty on the staff! If he had been born a German I wouldn't give ten cents for Franklin Roosevelt's life."

"But General," Lovell said, "I was born a Cape Cod Republican," insinuating that Roosevelt still had something to fear.

Donovan laughed. "A villain, a scientific thug with a sense of humor. He knows that I'm a Republican, too, so it's a double-edged pleasantry."

Lovell's plan was never executed, nor the Führer. Hitler and

Mussolini surreptitiously changed the date and location of their conference before the OSS could strike.

Carl Eifler didn't require such an elaborate plot to kill Chiang Kai-shek. Instead, Lovell gave him the same botulinum toxin that he had given to the Chinese prostitutes. The next time that Eifler saw General Joseph Stilwell, he would tell him that a solution to his "Peanut" problem was at hand.

Eifler flew to Europe and demonstrated the R&D weapons to universal acclaim. Everywhere he went, military officials would ask him, "When can we secure this equipment?" He then traveled to India and told Stilwell about the botulinum toxin. But Stilwell had since developed second thoughts about assassinating Chiang. In the time since he and Eifler had last spoken, President Roosevelt had written a strongly worded telegram to Chiang demanding action. Stilwell summarized the effect of the telegram on Chiang in a jubilant letter to his wife:

> Mark this day in red on the calendar of life. At long, at very long last, F.D.R. has finally spoken plain words, and plenty of them, with a firecracker in every sentence. "Get busy or else." A hot firecracker. I handed this bundle of paprika to the Peanut and then sank back with a sigh. The harpoon hit the little bugger right in the solar plexus, and went right through him. It was a clean hit, but beyond turning green and losing the power of speech, he did not bat an eye. He just said to me, "I understand," and sat in silence, jiggling one foot. We are now a long way from the "tribal chieftain" bawling out. Two long years lost, but at least F.D.R.'s eyes have been opened and he has thrown a good hefty punch.

Chiang was now cooperating with the Allies, meaning Stilwell didn't need Eifler to kill him anymore. Nor did Eifler get a chance to kidnap physicist Werner Heisenberg. On June 23, 1944, while on a break from demonstrating the R&D Branch weapons abroad, Eifler met with Donovan at OSS headquarters to discuss the secret operation. Donovan suggested that they step out onto the balcony for privacy. Alone outside, with the traffic noise shielding their conversation from eavesdroppers, Donovan informed Eifler that the kidnapping had been scrubbed. "We've cracked the atom," Donovan said, insinuating that the United States had built an atomic bomb and would end the war soon. Eifler took the news hard, especially after having already lost command of Detachment 101. This operation was supposed to have been his redemption, not another disappointment. A few days later, he choked back tears while telling a friend that his mission was over.

In reality, the United States was still a year away from building its first atomic bomb. The real reason why Donovan pulled Eifler from the operation was because capturing Heisenberg would be a delicate affair requiring both daring and discretion. Eifler had plenty of the former but none of the latter. Discretion certainly wasn't the defining quality of a man nicknamed "Mastodon Incarnate" and who was said to have a "voice that would dwarf a circus barker into insignificance."

Even though Donovan pulled Eifler from the operation, the OSS hadn't abandoned its pursuit of Heisenberg. Instead, it hired someone else to do the job. And this time, the plan wasn't merely to kidnap Heisenberg. It was to kill him.

10
The Heisenberg Uncertainty

When World War II broke out in Europe in 1939, Moe Berg began to reconsider his career as a professional baseball player. He explained his change of heart to Arthur Daley, a reporter for *The New York Times*. "Europe is in flames, withering in a fire set by Hitler," Berg said. "All over that continent men and women and children are dying. Soon we, too, will be involved. And I'm doing what? Sitting in the bullpen telling stories to relief pitchers."

Berg, whose thick unibrow commanded his flat, suntanned face, felt an unshakable urge to join the war effort. In particular, he wanted a job in the intelligence community. A loner without a wife or children, he was accustomed to, and even preferred, the itinerant lifestyle of a secret agent. He was also a polyglot who could speak Greek, French, Latin, Spanish, German, Hebrew, Yiddish, Sanskrit, and Italian. While his facility for languages didn't necessarily translate into success on the baseball field—"I don't care how many of them college degrees you got," fellow catcher Buck Crouse once told him, "They ain't learned you to hit that curveball no better than me"—it could certainly help him conduct undercover work abroad.

Back in 1934, Berg had joined Babe Ruth and Lou Gehrig on a seventeen-game baseball exhibition tour of Japan. During the trip, along with playing games, visiting geisha houses, and making speeches in rudimentary Japanese, Berg climbed onto the roof of a Tokyo hospital and filmed the city with his movie camera. Seven years later, following the Japanese attack on Pearl Harbor, he showed the rare footage to U.S. military officials, aiding them in their strategic planning. With his baseball glory days behind him, and having proven his ability to gather valuable information abroad, Berg applied for a job at the OSS.

In September 1943, Italy surrendered to the Allied forces. Two months later, the OSS assigned Berg to Project Larson, ostensibly a mission to interrogate Italian scientists about their efforts to produce radar, rockets, and other military technologies. However, in a private meeting, Stanley Lovell told Berg that Project Larson was actually a smokescreen for another project called AZUSA. The purpose of AZUSA was to uncover what the Italian scientists knew about Werner Heisenberg and the German effort to build an atomic bomb. Berg's job would be to contact well-known scientists in Rome and make it seem as if he was interested in radar and rockets, but in reality he would slyly probe them for information about atomic bomb research.

On the eve of Berg's departure to Italy, Robert Furman, the Manhattan Project chief of foreign intelligence who had earlier recruited Carl Eifler to kidnap Heisenberg, told him that the words "atomic" and "radioactive" were taboo because they would blow his cover. Furman emphasized that Berg should instead seek information on "secret weapons" and factories with "extreme security measures" and "unusual health precautions," good proxies for the taboo words. Lastly, Furman wanted "to know: German & Italian scientists, whether alive," Berg wrote in his notes.

In Italy, Berg set his sights on two prominent Italian physicists, Edoardo Amaldi and Gian Carlo Wick, both of whom had previously worked under Enrico Fermi, a Nobel Prize–winning nuclear physicist and member of the Manhattan Project. On June 5, 1944, Amaldi agreed to an interview at his home. Berg brought along a gift of sweets that Fermi had given him for Amaldi's children. During the interview, Berg delicately steered the conversation toward the state of German physics. Amaldi said that the last German physicist whom he had seen was Otto Hahn, a co-discoverer of nuclear fission, but that was back in 1941, and they hadn't discussed fission in any depth. Since the beginning of the war, the Germans hadn't made any attempt to collaborate with Italian physicists. But Amaldi speculated that the Germans "must be working on" nuclear fission and therefore possibly an atomic bomb. Still, he was skeptical of whether they had the talent to actually create one, saying that Heisenberg was "a first-class theoretical physicist but not an experimental physicist."

Berg next interviewed Wick, who had "a great love for, and a sentimental interest in, Heisenberg," Berg wrote in his notes. Wick revealed that Heisenberg "was probably working on nuclear physics." He also shared his belief that Heisenberg was an anti-Nazi, though one with "too deep a sense of patriotism not to work for his country."

Berg wrote a report summarizing his interviews of the two physicists—translating the Italian dialogue into English when necessary—and sent it to OSS administrator Howard Dix, who forwarded it to Stanley Lovell, who in turn forwarded it to Vannevar Bush. Both Lovell and Donovan sent Berg a letter of appreciation.

On December 18, 1944, Werner Heisenberg was scheduled to give a public lecture in Zurich, Switzerland. When news of the lecture reached the United States, Generals Donovan and Leslie Groves, the director of the Manhattan Project, forwarded a new assignment to Moe Berg. Groves later hinted at what the assignment entailed:

> At one time during the war . . . it was suggested to me by someone in the Manhattan organization, I think a scientist, that if I was fearful of German progress in the atomic field I could upset it by arranging to have some of their leading scientists killed. I mentioned this to General [Wilhelm] Styer one day and said to him, "Next time you see General [George] Marshall ask him what he thinks of such an idea." Some time later Styer told me that he had carried out my wishes and that General Marshall's reply had been, "Tell Groves to take care of his own dirty work."

Berg later revealed to his friend Earl Brodie that Donovan and Groves had asked him to carry out this "dirty work." He was to attend the lecture in Zurich and, if he judged it wise, assassinate Heisenberg "right there in the auditorium," Brodie said. "It probably would have cost Berg his life—there would have been no way to escape."

Disguised as Swiss physics students, Berg and Leo Martinuzzi, an OSS companion, checked their winter coats at the door and entered the lecture hall in Zurich. Berg sat in the second row, a pistol tucked beneath his clothes and an L-pill sitting in his pocket. At the front of the room, Heisenberg paced back and forth, occasionally scribbling an equation on the blackboard.

Berg jotted down notes while Heisenberg talked. "As I listen," he wrote, "I am uncertain—see: Heisenberg's uncertainty principle—what to do to H. Discussing math while Rome burns—if they knew what I'm thinking." He took the time to describe Heisenberg's appearance: "thinnish," "heavy eyebrows," "sinister eyes." Heisenberg was apparently flattered by his would-be assassin's dutiful note-taking. "H. likes my interest in his lecture."

The subject of the lecture, S-matrix theory, was well beyond Berg's comprehension of physics, but he was at least sharp enough to sense that it had nothing to do with an atomic bomb. By the end of the lecture, he decided that Heisenberg was innocuous. The pistol, and the L-pill, remained at his side.

That same week, Swiss physicist Paul Scherrer invited Berg, Heisenberg, and several other students and colleagues to a dinner party at his home. At one point in the evening, German physicist Gregor Wentzel said to Heisenberg, "Now you have to admit that the war is lost."

"Yes," Heisenberg conceded, "but it would have been so good if we had won."

Berg interpreted this statement as an admission that the Germans were nowhere close to building an atomic bomb. Heisenberg wouldn't have displayed such a defeatist attitude if Germany possessed a weapon that could still turn the tide of the war.

When Heisenberg left the dinner party to walk back to his hotel, Berg excused himself so that he could accompany him. On the walk, Berg, speaking in Swiss-accented German to maintain his cover story, peppered Heisenberg with leading questions about nuclear physics. Heisenberg was visibly uninterested in the conversation, his curt answers as cold as the winter weather. Once again, Berg determined that Heisenberg was innocuous. He wrote to Donovan, "[German] separation of U235 isotope absolutely hopeless."

After the war, Berg was awarded the Medal of Freedom (though he declined to accept it) for his undercover work with the OSS. For the remaining three decades of his life, he told war stories, attended baseball games, and compulsively read newspapers. He relished the intrigue that others saw in him, to the point where he tried to cultivate the impression that he was still a secret agent. He became a nomad and vagabond, disappearing for weeks at a time. Sam Goudsmit, a physicist and wartime acquaintance, grew so concerned for Berg that he once placed a cryptogram in the *New York Herald Tribune* that read, when deciphered, "Moe Berg how are you?" In another message, Goudsmit wrote, "Where are you hiding? . . . Please, please, please, respond—react—write—phone—cable or, 'say it with flowers.'"

The government assigned Berg little more of the undercover work that he so desperately sought.

Heisenberg's other pursuer, Carl Eifler, felt the opposite compulsion and tried to distance himself from the demons of his past. Once the fog of war lifted, he sobered up from the addictions that had cost him the command of Detachment 101, but another haze descended upon him. For several years after the war, he experienced increasingly flagrant psychotic episodes, a result of his head injury and, presumably, undiagnosed post-traumatic stress disorder. One night, a friend living nearby in California visited Eifler at his home to check on him. As the two talked in the living room, a glaze came over Eifler's eyes. Without notice, he reared back and punched his friend square in the jaw, knocking him to the ground.

"Carl, what's the matter?" his friend stammered while struggling to his feet.

Eifler roared, "Get away from me, you Jap bastard!" He then ran to a neighborhood grocery store, broke through the windows, and wrecked the shelves of cans.

After several such outbursts, Eifler grew increasingly concerned for others' safety in his presence. But over time, the outbursts became less frequent and less severe. He eventually went back to school for divinity and psychology, earning a Ph.D. in the latter from the Illinois Institute of Technology.

When Stanley Lovell learned that Eifler had gotten a degree in divinity, he said, "I hereby warn his future congregations to heed the admonitions from his pulpit, or I would expect a dum dum," a type of bullet, "to zing down among the communicants." Lovell's warning may have applied to the old Eifler of World War II, but the new Eifler was a calm, caring, and compassionate man. His days of death and destruction were behind him.

Detachment 101 has since been credited with obtaining the highest kill-to-loss ratio of any infantry-type unit in U.S. military history. In total, its members wrecked 9 trains, demolished 51 bridges, rescued 232 downed American airmen, destroyed 277 enemy military vehicles, and killed a confirmed 5,447 enemy soldiers (10,000 estimated), all while suffering only 22 American and 184 native deaths.

In 1967, Detachment 101 held a reunion party at an officer's club in California. Mrs. Winifred Stilwell, wife of the late

General Joseph Stilwell, was the guest of honor. The next day, two dozen members of the unit and their families gathered at Eifler's house for a barbecue. They reminisced about their years of waging jungle warfare halfway around the world. The atmosphere was light and fun, until the guests noticed Eifler standing alone near the fireplace. The room got quiet. Eifler looked at his glass in somber reflection. "You know," he said, "if we had our just deserts, we'd all be hung as war criminals."

11

The Documents Division

Stanley Lovell wanted the R&D Branch to pursue tasks beyond making weapons and devices. Limpets, Black Joe, Aunt Jemima, L-pills, fighting knives, and all the rest were cunning, but they wouldn't make or break a secret agent's mission on their own.

During an OSS staff meeting, Lovell was dismayed to learn that the Germans had executed an agent whose cover was blown because he didn't have the necessary documents to corroborate his cover story. Lovell realized that an agent's success depended as much on their ability to reach a target as it did on what they did when they got there. Agents needed proper documents—letters, tickets, passports—as much as they needed weapons. Lovell therefore decided to create a secret unit within the R&D Branch, the Documents Division, to forge them.

Long before Germany invaded Poland, the nations that would eventually engage in World War II had anticipated forgery. In the 1930s, European governments embedded their official documents with watermarks, special fibers, secret chemicals, and sometimes invisible inks. The goal of the Documents Division was to out-smart these experienced and sophisticated governments at their own game.

Lovell proceeded with caution despite his resolve to help. Making weapons was one thing; this was war, after all. But forgery? And not only the forgery of enemy documents, but of Allied documents if necessary? He worried that the Treasury Department and Secret Service—originally created to suppress counterfeit currency—would arrest him as soon as the operation got underway. So did General Donovan, who initially resisted the idea. Forgery wasn't part of the bag of dirty tricks that he had in mind when he had recruited his Professor Moriarty.

Before creating the Documents Division, Lovell decided to ease his conscience and obtain official approval for the project. In a meeting with Secretary of the Treasury Henry Morgenthau Jr., he explained how the creation of a Documents Division within the R&D Branch would save the lives of OSS agents abroad. Morgenthau agreed to ask President Roosevelt for approval of the Documents Division on Lovell's behalf.

Morgenthau already knew that Roosevelt was interested in forgery. Back in 1940, author John Steinbeck and his friend Melvin Knisely, an anatomy professor at the University of Chicago, had met with Roosevelt to propose their own idea for an American forgery operation. "It was very easy to get in to see him," Steinbeck wrote in a postwar article for *Collier's*:

> I remember he sat at his desk in the Executive Offices, with French windows behind him. His face was in shadow, but as we talked, he leaned back in his chair and the sun shone on his hair and on his forehead as far down as his closed eyes. His cigarette in the long holder stuck straight

up in the air, with curls of blue smoke drifting in the sunstreaks. We had rehearsed our speech so we wouldn't take too much of his time. Finally we finished and waited. The room was very quiet. Suddenly the President opened his eyes and banged his chair forward. He was laughing. "This is strictly illegal," he said, his eyes shining. Then he added in a low voice, "And we can do it!"

Roosevelt picked up the phone and called Morgenthau. "Henry," he said, "I am sending two men to you with an idea. Listen to them and tell me what you think." Steinbeck and Knisely pitched their idea to Morgenthau, but he was less receptive. "It's against the law," he told them, "and I will have nothing to do with it."

To Lovell's delight, Morgenthau had since changed his mind about forgery. At the end of their meeting, Morgenthau told Lovell that when they next met, if he said, "the President has a cold and I was unable to see him on your problem," it meant that Roosevelt had given his full permission for the Documents Division. On the other hand, if Morgenthau said, "I took the matter up with the President and he refuses authorization," it meant exactly that.

The next day, Lovell entered a stuffy conference room filled with a dozen men, including Morgenthau. "Excuse me, Gentlemen," Morgenthau said as Lovell stepped inside, "this is Dr. Lovell of the O.S.S." Morgenthau turned to face Lovell directly. "Now, on that matter you asked me about, I was unable to see the President for approval because he has a cold. Do you understand that, Dr. Lovell?"

"Yes, I do, Mr. Secretary, and thank you."

Lovell had been given a green light from the most authoritative source in the country. Legality aside, nobody would arrest his forgers now.

But the operation was still risky. Morgenthau had cleverly verbalized the authorization in such a way that it gave Roosevelt plausible deniability. There were a dozen men in that conference room who could vouch that Morgenthau hadn't given Lovell any authorization at all, he had only said that the president had a cold. If the Documents Division faltered in any way—if it got out of hand, if the media caught wind of it, if it failed to produce results—there would be but one sacrificial goat: Stanley Lovell.

Lovell recruited expert printers, papermakers, and even criminal forgers to help him get the Documents Division up and running at OSS headquarters. One of the more intriguing characters that he recruited was a forger referred to only as "Jim the Penman." By Lovell's account, Jim was "the pleasantest, nicest man in the whole group," even though he could forge the signatures of some of the nastiest men in the world: Benito Mussolini, Heinrich Himmler, Joseph Goebbels, Adolf Hitler. Lovell had recruited Jim from a federal penitentiary where he was serving time for forging U.S. government bonds.

At the Documents Division, Jim often demonstrated his skills by having a colleague sign their name on a piece of lined paper. After studying their writing style, he would choose a suitable pen or quill and recreate their signature up and down the page, betting them a dollar that they couldn't pick out the original. He won more often than not.

Lovell once used Jim's skills to move a shipment of limpets from Nebraska to Norway. Two volunteers had agreed to transport the limpets, but Lovell feared that they would be arrested for carrying explosives. He arranged for Jim to forge a letter on White House stationery saying, "Any interference with their vital mission, any search, questioning or delay of any sort will be followed by my severest disciplinary action." Beneath the text, Jim added President Roosevelt's signature.

There's a good chance that the OSS sent Jim the Penman to Scotland to help train members of the British SOE. George Langelaan, the SOE recruit who received combat training from William Fairbairn, remembered learning forgery techniques from a man with a remarkably similar backstory.

At a training camp on the Scottish coast, Langelaan was walking through a garden on the way to the beach when he heard the sound of a violin. Intrigued, he followed the music to its source, a dingy wooden shed. Peering through the open door he saw a man in a pearl-gray waistcoat sitting in a chair, facing away, a violin tucked beneath his chin.

Langelaan stepped closer. The music stopped.

"Good morning," said the man without turning around.

Langelaan was startled. "Good morning, sir. Please excuse me. I don't know—"

"That is quite alright," interrupted the man, "but don't call me sir. They poke enough fun at me as it is." He turned around to face the intruder. "I am only one of your instructors."

Langelaan was confused. "Don't tell me we have to learn violin playing!"

"Oh no," said the man, "that's only my hobby. I make violins."

"A very interesting hobby it must be. But may I ask you what you teach us?"

At this the man flashed a smile. "The art of imitating other people's handwriting, altering and faking documents, making beautiful official rubber stamps—in other words, a real trade."

Langelaan and the rest of the SOE recruits came to know this man as "The Forger." They assumed that he was an ex-con who had been sprung from prison to aid the war effort. Nobody knew for sure, though, because nobody dared to ask him. Most likely, The Forger and Jim the Penman were one and the same. The OSS and SOE often exchanged instructors, as they had done with Fairbairn.

In Scotland, The Forger would stroll into his workshop with a briefcase full of inks and pockets overflowing with fountain pens. In less than a week, he taught himself how to imitate the handwriting of every recruit. "Whenever possible," he told them, "try to see your victim write. Note carefully how he or she holds the pen, the position of each finger, the wrist, the arm on the table and that of the body; also the slant of the paper. . . . Don't forget that simple signatures are the most difficult to imitate; fancy flourishes are generally quite easy—do those with your wrist, never the fingers."

The Forger had other tricks up his sleeve. He taught the recruits how to alter words on a document; how to make invisible inks (urine and lemon juice worked particularly well); how to lift and re-adhere wax seals, proving to Langelaan "how utterly useless" the seals actually were; and how to remove a letter from an unopened envelope and then, "far more difficult," reinsert it. For fun, he also taught them how to cheat at cards.

Langelaan's brief description of The Forger is the only known account of his work in Scotland. Otherwise, he's absent from the historical record, just like Jim the Penman—perhaps not coincidentally. As an ex-con, Jim likely skipped town once his government contract expired. Lovell was away when he left, but Jim left him a short note of appreciation on his desk, saying, "Thanks to an understanding boss." Lovell cherished the note, partly for the sentiment, but also, he swore, because it was in his own handwriting.

The OSS may have sent Jim the Penman to Scotland to help train members of the SOE, but he wasn't the only person associated with the Documents Division to travel to Europe. In April 1944, seven members of the R&D Branch established a European offshoot of the Documents Division in the former home of English architect Christopher Wren, an ornate three-story building behind the main OSS office in London. In June, they began producing printed documents and faux rubber stamps. Eight more workers soon arrived and turned the manor into an improvised workshop. They put a tailor's shop in the attic, built an engraving plant in the kitchen, installed heavy presses on the concrete floor of the garage (one lithographic press was rented from a friendly British Rotary Club for $1 a year), and made a studio to take photographs for passports and other official papers.

Among the most commonly forged documents were passports, discharge forms, ration tickets, railway passes, driver's licenses, and travel papers. Each document had to look completely authentic, down to every minute detail, from the hue of an ink to the texture of the paper. Even the photographs had to match the specific style of their supposed country of origin. For example, the German Army had a rule that photographs on identity documents couldn't show a person's right ear.

The forged documents even needed to match the physical appearance of the particular agent that they belonged to. René Povel, the librarian of the Documents Division, artificially aged documents with what one report refers to as "a chemical of his own invention." Another method involved rubbing the documents in ashes or coffee grounds and rounding the corners with sandpaper. Still another method involved scattering them on the floor of the office for everyone to walk over. If the documents were still too stiff, the women at the office would stuff them in their bras, or the men in their armpits, for days at a time to soften them up.

Passports were among the most difficult documents to forge.

For the best results, the workers in the Documents Division took an authentic passport—usually obtained from a prisoner of war or scavenged from a dead body—chemically removed the writing, and filled in the blanks with fake information.

Obtaining fake American passports was sometimes just as challenging. During World War II, Ruth Shipley, the passport chief at the State Department, wielded unprecedented authority to issue—or deny—passports as she saw fit. A stickler for the rules, she put up a stern defense against issuing fake passports to the freewheeling OSS. She eventually caved when General Donovan argued that either she could issue the fake passports or the OSS would forge its own.

Donovan once visited the OSS offices in London and toured the Documents Division. The workers had just finished reproducing a Gestapo identification card and decided to impress him with a demonstration of their handiwork. They found an old photograph of Donovan in uniform, retouched it to make it look as if he were wearing civilian clothing, reduced the size of the image, and attached it to the Gestapo card. A skilled forger then signed it in Donovan's handwriting, "Wilhelm von Donovan."

Donovan became visibly upset when presented with the card. He insisted that he had never posed for such a photograph. Carl Strahle, a printer in the Documents Division, tried to calm him down. "Sir, you know what we do here—"

"But this signature," Donovan said, "Where did you get my signature?"

"General, we probably have some of the best forgers in the world in this shop."

Donovan's mood suddenly changed. "This could be great. I can take this to Congress and show it to them when they want to know where all the money goes."

A German Army Corps once inadvertently praised the Documents Division, saying, "The enemy forges identity papers so perfectly that only trained experts of the Security Police can recognise the falsification." But after the war, the official *War Report of the OSS* did admit one mistake. Most of the documents that were otherwise perfect in form, color, and texture "differed greatly when examined under ultra-violet light." The workers in the Documents Division never corrected the defect because they correctly assumed that the enemy would never discover it.

A flawless—or near flawless—forgery could save an agent's life, but the wrong document in the wrong hands could spell disaster. If an agent was caught with an incriminating document on them, they could be killed on the spot. The R&D Branch therefore developed multiple ways to quickly dispose of documents. One method involved printing messages on edible Japanese Yoshino paper. When agents complained about the bland taste of the paper, it was laced with saccharin for sweetness. The R&D Branch also created an ingenious sheet metal briefcase for document disposal. An agent could place documents inside, close the briefcase, and detonate a charge that shredded them into illegible scraps.

Beyond forging documents, the Documents Division also counterfeited foreign currencies. Stanley Lovell handpicked Willis Reddick, a dapper printer from Illinois with a strong jaw and pencil-line mustache, to lead the operation. Reddick, in turn, hired commercial artists from *Collier's* and *The Saturday Evening Post*, poached workers from the Bureau of Engraving and Printing, and recruited other artists and printers from Army basic training camps. "These sad sacks," he later said, speaking of the Army recruits, "figured it had to be better than carrying a rifle or following a tank." Unlike Lovell, Reddick put little faith in convicts sprung from prison. "How good could they be? They got caught."

As a first order of business, Lovell asked Reddick to explore the possibility of counterfeiting enough reichsmarks to flood the market and ruin the German economy.

> He was the boss so I went down to the Bureau of Engraving. I said we were exploring the idea of flooding Germany with counterfeit [reichsmarks] and what did they think. They thought I was crazy. But they did some figuring, how many millions of notes we'd have to do to make any kind of impression in a country the size of Germany. It was hopeless. When you got right down to it, even if they could turn out the notes on the Bureau's presses—of course they'd have to stop making U.S. notes—the delivery problem was impossible. We'd have to be sending bombers day and night all over Germany for weeks and weeks letting them hurl out bales of money. And then all the Germans would have to do is issue a new series of notes and our stuff would be dead. It wouldn't be cheap, either. Just making the notes would run $10 million.

Reddick thereafter focused on smaller operations, starting with one to help Carl Eifler and Detachment 101. In September 1943, Eifler sent samples of Japanese occupation currency from Burma to Washington, D.C., with a request that the Documents Division duplicate them. Reddick approached Alvin Hall, the head of the Bureau of Engraving and Printing, for help, but Hall refused to get involved. He told Reddick, "Major, don't you know that counterfeiting is an international crime and that we're the signatory to various anti-counterfeiting conventions? Count us out on this."

Reddick then asked the president of the American Bank Note Company for help. "The guy was horrified," Reddick said in a postwar interview. "He said his firm wouldn't lend itself to such a terrible scheme. Bank note people all over the world knew and trusted each other—like a secret fraternity, the way he made it sound—and war or no war they wouldn't do this to one another." When Reddick next approached the head of another large bank note manufacturer, the man explained, "We're not in the printing business; we're in the *trust* business. Governments entrust to us their most precious child—their currency." If that trust evaporated, then so would his business. He also refused to help.

The Documents Division was on its own—mostly. The Bureau of Engraving and Printing secretly gave Reddick special machinery for printing bank notes. To account for the missing machines in its inventory, the Bureau listed them as having been sunk on a ship in the Atlantic.

In late 1943, Reddick forwarded the newly minted Japanese bills to Eifler. Carl Strahle was so impressed with the finished product that he told Reddick in worried tones, "Suppose these guys decide to start knocking out the British five-pound note? They could do it, you know."

Eifler had also sent samples of the Japanese occupation currency to Calcutta for counterfeiting, but the results were far inferior to those of the Documents Division. Eifler refused to give the Calcutta counterfeits to his men. Instead, he used them in a different way. Whenever Detachment 101 discovered a local tribesman who was secretly conspiring with the Japanese, Eifler made sure that a few of the Calcutta counterfeits fell into his hands.

Over time, the Japanese would inevitably trace these botched bills back to the tribesman, who would then be killed. In one fell swoop, Eifler would eliminate an enemy and simultaneously sow doubt between the Japanese and their informants.

One of the more difficult currencies to counterfeit was the Maria Theresa thaler, a silver Austrian coin depicting a plump Empress Maria Theresa on one side and an elaborate double-headed eagle with a coat of arms on the other. The coins had gone out of production in 1870 but were still popular throughout Indonesia.

Lovell acquired some sample thalers from a collector in New York for reference. The workers in the Documents Division were apprehensive about the job. If they failed to replicate every single ridge and groove, anyone found carrying the coins could be executed.

Lovell spared no expense. When pouring the molds for the coins, he insisted that the workers use real silver instead of a cheaper alloy. That way, even if someone bit down on the coins or listened to the pitch at which they rang, there would be no difference between them and the real thing. "It was the most honest job we ever did," Lovell recalled with pride. He never learned whether the coins made a difference in Indonesia, but he hoped that they were worth their weight in silver.

Japanese occupation currency in the Philippines was even more difficult to counterfeit. Not only did the intricate banana tree design pose a challenge to the artists, but the paper fibers in the bills came from the kudzu and mitsumata trees found only in Japan.

Luckily, the OSS located a stock of Japanese paper in the United States. Lovell wanted to buy it himself, but he quickly realized that he couldn't because if he did, someone might question why the OSS needed Japanese paper and conclude that there was a counterfeiting operation underway. Lovell needed a cutout to buy it for him.

He turned to James Byrnes, the former Supreme Court justice who had introduced William Fairbairn to President Roosevelt at the Shangri-La retreat. Byrnes surreptitiously bought the Japanese paper and transferred it to a warehouse in New Jersey for Lovell to grab. "How he did it, I'll never know," Lovell said.

The Philippine bills were a rush order, so there wasn't enough time to artificially age them before sending them out. This posed a problem. The locals would become suspicious if American soldiers started paying for goods and services with crisp new bills. The only solution was to take the aging process on the go.

The bills were stuffed inside five-gallon metal containers full of sand and water. To deter greedy soldiers from snagging fistfuls of cash on the trip, the containers were labeled "Finance Forms," a boring albeit accurate bureaucratic term.

General Douglas MacArthur received the literal payload in the Pacific theater and used it to support intelligence agents and guerilla resistance movements. The soldiers who received the bills dried them by spreading them out on the ground. If a batch arrived during the rainy season, "which seemed to be all the time," Lieutenant Bob Stahl said, "we sat beside fires waving wads of currency over the heat to drive out the moisture."

MacArthur wrote a grateful letter to Donovan, who in turn thanked Lovell, "Well done, Professor Moriarty."

12
The Camouflage Division

An undercover agent's appearance was scrutinized just as much as their documents, and the discovery of any inconsistencies carried equally severe consequences. If the Documents Division could make forged documents look legitimate, perhaps another division could do the same for the undercover agents themselves.

In 1944, the R&D Branch opened a Camouflage Division two blocks away from the Documents Division in London. It occupied four small rooms of a large house, two of which held a tailor and a leather workshop. Outside, a squash court served as storage space for inventory.

The Camouflage Division supplied all of the clothing, equipment, and accessories that undercover agents needed for their disguises abroad. Its workers had to know everything from the differences in what a Bavarian peasant wore during the winter versus the summer to the differences in the everyday items carried by the residents of Hamburg versus those of Breslau. They had to be able to transform any agent into a passable French miner, German soldier, Danish fisherman, or Dutch longshoreman at a moment's notice.

The workers often scoured the manifests of refugee ships headed for the United States, contacted the passengers, and asked them if they would cooperate with the OSS. If so, a member of the OSS would visit them, ostensibly to gather information about the social, economic, and military conditions in Europe, but also to purchase their authentic European clothing. The refugees always needed the money and rarely cared about why the OSS needed their clothes. If for some reason the refugees refused to cooperate, authentic European clothing could often be found in secondhand shops in Manhattan's Lower East Side.

On the off chance that a disguise couldn't be found, the OSS instructed its undercover agents to remember that "people as a whole fortunately are unobservant." Never despair. Instead, find a crowd to hide in. "Look and act like others and you will not be noticed."

Evangeline Bell was one of the many workers who created these disguises for the Camouflage Division in London. A diplomat's daughter with a husky voice, she had studied Chinese history and French literature at Radcliffe College, the "Harvard Annex" for women, and spoke French, German, Chinese, Italian, and Japanese.

On a tour of the OSS offices in London, General Donovan once suggested that Bell transfer to New Delhi where her knowledge of the Far East would better serve her, but Colonel David Bruce, Donovan's accomplice at Normandy and the OSS director of European operations, petitioned for her to stay.

He had fallen in love with her despite being married to Ailsa Mellon, the richest woman in the United States. Bell and Bruce eventually got married in 1945, a mere three days after Bruce's divorce was finalized.

On her time with the Camouflage Division, Bell said that she would sometimes "burst into tears because of the combined tension of the bombings and work. I remember the German planes flying up the Thames like angry hornets. When I heard a V-1 coming, I would put my hands over my eyes, thumbs in my ears because of the intense noise. I had the feeling that I had to make the most of my days while I was living." She experienced tremendous stress, both because of the explosions and because of the high stakes of her job. "One mistake," she said, "and our people could be executed. Their lives depended upon what they wore or carried."

During its first six months of operation, the Camouflage Division outfitted 314 agents for undercover missions into Axis-controlled territory. A complete outfit consisted of a suit, shirt, tie, socks, shoes, gloves, hat, underwear, overcoat, wallet, knife, notebook, handkerchief, cigarettes, matches, suitcase, soap, towel, razor, razor blades, toothbrush, and toothpaste. One lucky agent received a thousand-dollar golden cigarette case that an unnamed woman in Paris gifted the OSS. The case provided him with escape money in case he got in trouble and "needed to get cracking," said OSS officer Robert Springsteen. It was fairly common for agents to carry gold rings, watches, and lighters, or even diamonds, to avoid carrying large sums of cash. And if the presence of gold conflicted with an agent's humble cover story, the items were plated in nickel to conceal their true value.

Agents occasionally requested unusual items that the workers in the Camouflage Division had difficulty supplying. These included a Volkswagen, two complete French chef's costumes, and a specific shade of Elizabeth Arden lipstick. But no matter how unusual the request, the workers did their best to supply the items. An agent who felt properly equipped was more confident, and a more confident agent had a better chance of success. According to William Turnbull, a London R&D hand, "If an individual is thoroughly confident of what he has with him and is therefore self-assured, it is my experience that he can get away with murder, but if he is worried about any little item he has with him, he lacks self-assurance and is well on the way to being blown." William Fairbairn had given OSS recruits the confidence to kill, and while wallets, toothbrushes, and chef's costumes were trivial compared to practical combat skills, they had the potential to inspire just as much confidence.

When necessary, the workers built false bottoms into briefcases, drilled "message chambers" into shoe soles, and sewed secret pockets into pants. (All sewing had to match that of the clothing's supposed country of origin; the Germans used parallel threading instead of crisscross.) The Germans, however, soon discovered these simple tricks. In an OSS training film on enemy search methods, the narrator explains:

> When it comes to clothes and personal effects, investigators take nothing for granted. They begin on the premise that every item contains a message and carry on from there. . . . Sweat bands, hat bands, linings are studied and ripped out if necessary. A coat gets a going over that would make its tailor squirm. The lining, shoulder padding, seams, and pockets are checked and double checked. Labels come off. Buttons are examined. Shirts and underwear get the ultraviolet ray treatment

for invisible laundry marks. Sewing is checked against the possibility of writing coded messages on thread. Shoes are potential gold mines of evidence, gold mines soon assayed. The space between the sole, the hollows of the heels, the canvas lining under the tongue, and the shoelace tips are all searched. . . . When the naked eye fails, magnifying glasses and microscopes take over, searching for pin pricks and marking containing coded messages. No area is too small or too insignificant for the investigator's attention.

This undercover arms race led to the creation of ingenious concealment methods, such as screw-top buttons that contained a tiny cavity inside. The screw threads on these buttons were reversed so that twisting them open in the ordinary fashion would tighten them instead. "Right up to Germany's surrender," Stanley Lovell boasted, "we never learned of one instance of this simplest of deceptions being discovered by enemy inspectors or police."

One of the cleverest deceptions involved hiding secret messages in lipstick. Workers would melt the lipstick into a molten wax, pour it around the message, and recast it to fit the original tube. Similarly, they sometimes molded messages into suppositories for insertion into the body's natural cavities.

Aided by Hollywood makeup artists, the workers in the Camouflage Division taught OSS agents a number of tricks to help them alter their appearance. For instance, agents rubbed iodine on their teeth to stain them yellow. They stuffed wads of cotton in their cheeks to fill out their face. They inserted rubber nipples into their nostrils to widen their nose. They put newspaper in

William Donovan, head of the OSS.
OSS/National Archives

Stanley Lovell in college
at Cornell.
The Cornellian Yearbook

"Professor Moriarty" upon
joining the OSS.
OSS/National Archives

STANLEY P LOVELL

Vannevar Bush, Lovell's idol,
mentor, and correspondent.
Office of Emergency Management/
Library of Congress

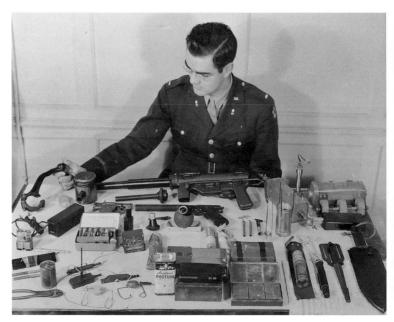

Chemical engineer Ernest Crocker with a display of R&D Branch weapons and devices.
OSS/National Archives

Catching bats for the Bat Bomb.
U.S. Air Force/Briscoe Center

A lump of Aunt Jemima ready for detonation.
OSS/National Archives

An R&D Branch weapons demonstration.

Test of a Javaman "missile."
OSS/National Archives

Carl Eifler, head of Detachment 101, holding a *punji* stick.
OSS/U.S. Army

Carl Eifler and William Donovan in Nazira.
OSS/U.S. Army

Printer Willis Reddick sits between two workers inside the Documents Division office in London.
OSS/National Archives

Members of the Documents and Camouflage Divisions, including
Evangeline Bell (sixth from left), Willis Reddick (seventh from left),
William Turnbull (tenth from left), and Carl Strahle (twelfth from left).

OSS/National Archives

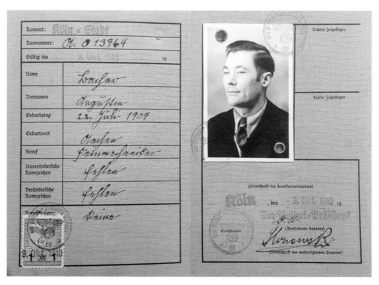

A forged German passport from the Documents Division
(note the hidden right ear).

OSS/National Archives

Inside the storeroom of the Camouflage Division office in London.

OSS/National Archives

Three disguises from the Camouflage Division.

OSS/National Archives

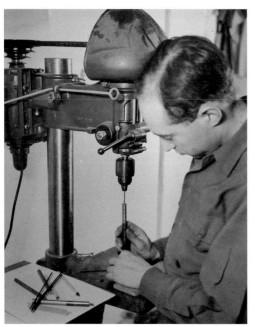

A worker drilling a message chamber
into a pencil.
OSS/National Archives

A worker making suppositories for carrying
secret messages.
OSS/National Archives

Workers creating camouflaged message drops for spies and saboteurs.
OSS/National Archives

their shoes to appear taller (this had the added benefit of changing their gait and posture). They pinned back their ears with liquid adhesive to alter their profile. They rubbed their hands on rusty iron, and then on their skin, to darken their complexion. They whitened the hair on their temples and drew charcoal pencil in their wrinkles to appear older. Female agents changed their hairstyle, wore different makeup, and padded their bras to further disguise themselves.

Lovell once described the simple tricks that he used to alter the appearance of a prominent Dutchman "so well-known and so outstanding in his appearance that discovery would have resulted in certain death":

> At a conference in London one of the group suggested that his great crop of black hair be shaved off and he be given a special chemical which would maintain baldness. His striking blue-black eyes had to be changed somehow, so I suggested contact lenses into which were made a pale, washed-out, gray iris. Knowing something about shoemaking, I ventured the thought that if one of his shoes was built up internally, he would have to walk with a slight limp. At least his gait and posture would be altered beyond recognition. I heard that, so camouflaged and provided with counterfeit papers, ration coupons, identification cards and all other necessary documentation, he was smuggled into Holland.

In a 1943 letter to Whitney Shepardson, the head of the OSS Secret Intelligence Branch, Lovell revealed that he had just learned of a new disguise technique from the SOE. The British had apparently used X-ray radiation to make an agent's hair fall out. "Complete baldness with a persistence of four to five months is effected," Lovell wrote.

OSS agent Virginia Hall underwent many of these alterations for her own mission into occupied France. In fact, her disguise was more elaborate than most others on account of her left leg. It was missing.

In 1933, at the age of twenty-seven, Hall had lost her leg on a snipe hunting expedition in Turkey. While she and her friends were walking across the wetlands looking for the small birds, they encountered a wire fence. Hall scaled the fence with ease, but as she neared the top, she lost her balance and her shotgun slipped off her shoulder. She reflexively reached out to grab it, but in doing so her hand accidentally struck the trigger and fired a round into the top of her left foot. Her friends raced her to a hospital, saving her life, but the doctors couldn't save her leg. Gangrene set in the open wound. Her leg turned black and radiated a searing pain. Her pus-soaked bandages smelled of death. The infection spread to the point where she was forced to undergo an amputation.

At the beginning of World War II, Hall worked with the SOE in France. She trained resistance forces, drove ambulances around the country, and relayed information on German troop movements back to British intelligence. She was never caught, but the Gestapo issued an order for her arrest: "The woman who limps is one of the most dangerous Allied agents in France. We must find and destroy her."

The Germans almost did find and destroy her, but before they could, Hall escaped to Spain on a bone-chilling winter hike over the Pyrenees mountains. (Army Air Forces pilot Chuck Yeager made a similar journey over the Pyrenees and called the "endless" climb "a bitch of bitches.") Along the way, her artificial leg, nicknamed Cuthbert, slowed but never stopped her. At one point, the bottom of her stump began oozing blood. She transmitted a message to London, "Cuthbert is giving me trouble." An uninformed intelligence officer messaged back, "If Cuthbert is giving you trouble, have him eliminated."

Given the obvious danger that Hall faced in returning to France for the OSS, the workers in the Camouflage Division urged her to undergo facial surgery to prevent anyone from recognizing her. She declined.

Nevertheless, with the assistance of the Camouflage Division, Hall transformed herself into an old French peasant. She dyed her brown hair a dirty gray. She penciled in wrinkles around her eyes. She wore full skirts, oversized sweaters, and thick shawls to change the apparent shape of her body—and to conceal her pistol. A London dentist ground down her teeth to match the deplorable oral hygiene of a poor French countrywoman. She carried a forged identity card in her pocket bearing the false name Marcelle Montagne. Lastly, she adopted a miserable backstory to help explain her limp. Given the wartime conditions in occupied France—chronic food shortages along with recurring epidemics of boils, typhoid, diphtheria, scarlet fever, and tuberculosis—any miserable backstory rang true.

To reach France, Hall traveled in a small dinghy across the English Channel (she couldn't parachute on account of her leg). In Lyon, she befriended Germaine Guérin, the flamboyant owner of the city's most successful brothel. Guérin's prostitutes often spiked their German clients' drinks with heroin and searched their pockets for information. Hall called these prostitutes her "tart friends" who knew "a hell of a lot."

Under Hall's direction, French Resistance soldiers destroyed bridges, derailed freight trains, and downed telephone lines. Her motto to them was "shoot, burn, destroy, leave." In her spare time, she tended a flock of goats in case anyone inquired into what this supposed French peasant did for a living. Plus, the shepherd's staff had the unintended benefit of steadying her gait. In 1944, when Hall's mother wrote to the OSS asking whether her daughter was alright, secretary Charlotte Norris wrote back, "You have every reason to be proud of her. Virginia is doing a spectacular, man-sized job."

After the war, General Donovan awarded Hall the Distinguished Service Cross, the country's second-highest military decoration behind the Medal of Honor. President Harry Truman had wanted to give her the medal personally in a public ceremony, but Hall declined the honor. The public ceremony would compromise her cover. She wanted to go back in the field.

In necessary cases, changes to an agent's appearance went much deeper than a surface transformation. Hall had refused facial surgery, but others didn't. The OSS relied on a handful of surgeons connected to the SOE to apply this "permanent make-up," as the British called it.

George Langelaan, the agent who had learned Gutter Fighting from William Fairbairn and had walked in on The Forger playing his violin, underwent facial surgery for his mission abroad. The Allies planned to drop him in central France to train resistance forces. Langelaan had spent most of his life in central France and knew the terrain as well as anyone. But this also meant that he knew many people living there. If anyone recognized him, his cover would be blown. His commanding officer suggested a solution: "What would you say to another face?"

Langelaan was not a handsome man. His protuberant ears—

"they had always kept a good couple of sizes ahead," he joked—stuck out from his head like jug handles. Having agreed to the surgery, he daydreamed of looking like a famous movie star. Clark Gable or Gary Cooper would do, he thought. But the surgeon had other ideas. The purpose of altering Langelaan's appearance was to make him unrecognizable. A Clark Gable walking through the streets of France would draw unnecessary attention, the last thing that an undercover agent needs.

During a consultation, the surgeon "plastered my face with putty," Langelaan said, "stuffed my gums and nostrils with cotton wool, pulled my nose up and down and in various other directions, lifted or lowered my cheeks, eyelids, eyebrows, and ears with stinking glue and fishskin, the peeling of which proved each time a tear-provoking operation." Once the surgeon was satisfied, he suggested making the changes permanent.

Two days later, Langelaan climbed onto the operating table. Afterward, he called himself "the owner of two elegant ears" and "a fine round chin" that had been smoothed out with a piece of bone borrowed from his thigh. To further disguise his face, he wore glasses, slicked down his dark hair, and grew a thick moustache. His appearance resembled the novelty disguise item Groucho Glasses, named after comedic actor Groucho Marx. Ironically, Langelaan looked like a movie star after all, albeit not a Clark Gable.

For complete authenticity, his shirts, ties, shoes, socks, and underwear were swapped with those from Parisian shops. He even traded his beloved English Dunhill pipe for a cheaper French Ropp. Once properly attired, he reported to a house in London where he received fake identity documents. He later recalled seeing a man inside who was "kept busy walking up and down on identity cards, ration cards and French military papers, French Army demobilization certificates, etc., one of the best ways of 'aging' them rapidly." Another man ironed the documents to turn them yellow. A third continuously folded and unfolded the same piece of paper to give it an authentic wear pattern. The marching man stopped when he saw Langelaan. "In which pocket do you usually carry your wallet?" he asked. Langelaan said his hip pocket, prompting the man to bend and chew the corners of the papers accordingly.

Langelaan's identity card, dated 1939, identified him as Gérard Touché and claimed that he had been born in a small town in northern France. The Allies knew that the town's archives had been destroyed in 1940, guaranteeing that nobody could investigate his past.

Langelaan committed his Touché cover story to memory: "I was single but had in the back pocket of my wallet a wisp of fair hair which belonged to a girl with whom I was supposed to have corresponded while in the Army, a girl of whom I also carried one or two very deep tender letters and a photograph." The hair actually belonged to Langelaan's wife. "I also had a photo of myself in a French uniform and standing arm and arm with a postman, my sister's husband who had been killed in a dive-bombing attack near Lille." The "postman" was actually an English colleague who couldn't speak a word of French but did a fine job of looking the part.

On the day of departure, Langelaan and the other agents scheduled to drop with him drank expensive wine and smoked cigars, after which they vacuumed their coats to remove any lingering traces of English tobacco. They then received their guns, daggers, and L-pills and left for the airfield.

The flight was freezing and uncomfortable. On the far side of the English Channel, with France in view, the plane descended in preparation for the drop. Langelaan approached the edge of the fuselage. Looking down he saw woods, fields, and a silver river spanned by a chalk-white bridge. Near his head a green light flashed on, followed by a shout of "Go!" He jumped through the "Joe Hole" and into the void. "That drop!" he remembered. "That fearful, nightmarish, endless drop! It seemed that this time it would never end, and I was going to shout when my harness tightened with a jerk."

While drifting to the ground, he looked down and saw a mysterious man running beneath him. Langelaan became tense. Was it the enemy? Had the plane been watched? With a final yank on his harness, he eased his descent, hit the ground, and instinctively grabbed his pistol in preparation for a shootout.

"Welcome to France," said the mysterious man. "Oh, you can put your gun away. There's no danger here!" The man was a friendly resistance soldier there to help the agents find their destinations. Langelaan immediately set off for the Café-Hôtel de la Boule d'Or where he would teach twenty-odd members of a resistance cell how to conduct sabotage operations and disrupt the German occupation.

On one sunny weekday afternoon, Langelaan went to a nearby café with a bottle of wine and a crossword puzzle to pass the time between meetings of the cell. A square-shouldered man approached his table and asked, "Are you Monsieur Touché?"

"Yes," Langelaan said.

The man wanted to talk outside.

"Certainly, just a second while I pay for my drink."

"That's alright," the man said. "It is paid."

Langelaan knew that he was caught. Two more square-shouldered men approached the table and escorted him outside. There was no "talk." The goons took him to a nearby prison in

Périgueux. Unbeknownst to Langelaan, a few days earlier another agent had been caught and exposed Langelaan in the process.

A prison guard searched through Langelaan's clothes for paraphernalia. He then punched Langelaan in the face—his brand-new face—and placed him in a cell. Langelaan lived in solitary confinement for weeks, devoid of any amusement to punctuate the boredom. He slept on a thin straw mattress for up to eighteen hours a day. There was nothing else to do. His body, he said, "had become numb and torpid."

The worst part was the food, or the lack thereof. During his first month in prison, Langelaan lost over forty pounds. He was given watered-down coffee for breakfast, watered-down soup with a few beans for lunch, and the same watered-down soup plus a fistful of bread for dinner. On the rare occasion when a tiny piece of bone appeared in the soup, he gnawed on it gingerly so that it lasted all day. His only solace from the boredom and hunger was whatever inner contemplation his mind could conjure.

Until, that is, he heard a faint tapping noise echoing in his cell. He listened closely and noticed a distinct pattern in the cadence of the taps. It was Morse code. Another prisoner was sending a message through the pipes. Langelaan translated the code: "Who can hear me?" The two prisoners became quick friends. When they learned that they shared a passion for chess, they each made a chess set from lint and tapped their moves back and forth across the pipes.

One day—the days all blended together—a guard approached Langelaan's cell and demanded to know how he communicated with the other prisoners.

"I know things which the other prisoners and even the jailers don't know," Langelaan said. "I can give you the exact time. It is twelve minutes past three, *mon Colonel*."

The guard said that he was wrong. It was a quarter past.

Langelaan begged to differ. "Well, that is something else you can check when you get outside, *mon Colonel*. You will see that I am right and that your watch is three minutes fast." Langelaan had made a rudimentary sundial from the window bars and a series of marks on the floor. He calibrated the readings according to the local church bells and the city's noontime siren tests.

The perturbed guard looked down and saw the lint chess set. "What are you doing there?"

"Playing chess, *mon Colonel*." There was no use denying it.

"You play chess alone?"

"No, I am playing with the prisoner in cell 43 on the ground floor."

Just before the guard had appeared, Langelaan had received a move over the pipes. He now grabbed a rook and placed it on the intended space.

The guard was confused. "How do you know that the prisoner in cell 43 has moved his rook?"

"He transmitted his move a second or two ago, while we were talking, *mon Colonel*." Langelaan was insinuating that they swapped moves telepathically.

"I don't believe you," said the guard.

"Why not go down to his cell?" Langelaan knew that the guard wouldn't be able to resist the challenge. "If you wish, I shall only transmit my move when you get there."

The guard took the bait, left, and began the two-minute walk to cell 43. Langelaan turned to his pipe and furiously tapped a message: "Urgent. Visit. Carry on game, but await visit before playing my move a2–a3. Tell visitor you are warned his visit. Great fun."

Sure enough, when the guard arrived at the cell, the prisoner greeted him. "Come in, please. I was expecting you." He then moved a piece of lint.

The guard could only admire their ingenuity. "I don't know how you do it, but I must say you do it extremely well."

Langelaan's situation took a more serious turn when he was sentenced to death, a sentence that a captured agent could expect sooner or later. He was transferred to a prison farther south called Mauzac, an open-air camp surrounded by barbed wire. Compared to the prison in Périgueux, Langelaan considered Mauzac a paradise. "The open air, the large barracks full of sunshine, the wash basins, everything seemed so marvelous."

Langelaan learned that several other death row inmates at Mauzac had parachuted behind enemy lines. They soon formed a fraternal group, The Companions of the Floating Silk, and agreed to escape together. For weeks on end they noted when the patrol guards made their rounds. On the night of the escape attempt, the prisoners placed makeshift dummies in their beds and covered their shoes with socks to muffle their footsteps. A turncoat guard had promised to warn them when the coast was clear by lighting his pipe. In exchange for his cooperation, the prisoners promised to take him to London with them.

The guard lit his pipe at three in the morning. The prisoners carefully opened their barracks door, which they had greased the night before to prevent squeaking. The lead prisoner, Michael Trotobas, ran to the perimeter fence and cut the lowest strands of barbed wire. One by one, the rest of the prisoners made the same mad dash across the yard and crawled through the fence to freedom. Langelaan was last. He was halfway under the fence when a guard approached. Trotobas, who had stayed back to hold the up the fence, whispered, "I'll take care of him." He was about to attack when the guard asked, "Is it the English?"

"Yes," Trotobas said, the escapees were from the English barracks.

"I thought so. Well, don't make so much noise."

The prisoners sprinted across a field to the nearest farmhouse. They spent the next fortnight hiding in a hayloft, leaving only at night to scrounge for food, money, and clothing, waiting for the search party to lose interest in them.

When their wait was finally over, Langelaan stole a bicycle, rode it to a nearby train station, and bought a ticket to Lyon. Anyone traveling without luggage invited suspicion, but luck was with Langelaan. Upon arriving in Lyon, "Just in front of me," he later said, "a woman with two heavy bags and a baby was struggling slowly along in the crowd. She gladly accepted my offer to help, and, taking the child on one arm and one of her bags under the other, I gave her my ticket to give up with hers as we passed the barrier, thus looking for all the world like husband and wife."

From Lyon, Langelaan headed south and crossed the Pyrenees mountains on foot, just as Virginia Hall had done. On the Spanish side of the mountains, he quite literally stumbled into a military garrison. The Spanish guards placed him in a jail cell where the fleas and lice had as much of an appetite as he did. After having spent over a year in various French and Spanish prisons, he was eventually bused to an airstrip and put on a flight back to England.

Langelaan credited his success, and his survival, to the ingenious disguise, weapons, and knowledge that he had been given in preparation for his mission. By contrast, German agents were wholly unprepared for their equivalent missions. "They never seemed to bother much about the countless little details which can so easily give a man away," Langelaan said. "Several

[German] suspects were easily confounded by their underwear which still bore the tabs or imprint of the German manufacturer. One German agent was captured within twelve hours of his landing in England simply because a railwayman happened to pick up a chocolate wrapper which he had thrown away and which was printed in German!"

The Allies saved an untold number of lives because they paid due diligence to the smallest details of an agent's documents, clothing, appearance, and accessories. Hall and Langelaan were just two agents to go behind enemy lines equipped—and reconfigured—in such a way, but there were many others.

13
Undercover Missions

The workers in the Documents and Camouflage Divisions of the R&D Branch spent countless hours manipulating documents, clothing, appearances, and accessories to cohere with the cover stories fabricated for each individual agent, but the cover stories themselves were the foundation upon which everything else was built. In order to survive an undercover mission, agents needed to commit every detail of their cover story to memory, and they needed to make sure that they didn't subconsciously lapse into old habits. "*Know* the character or characters that you will have to be, inside and out," says an OSS instruction manual on disguises and cover stories. "Study the type of men of the cover you might quickly have to fade into. Study everything about them—and then practice. The necessity for really thoughtful study, constant observation and practice cannot be emphasized too strongly."

Forgetting trivial details could spell disaster for an undercover agent. The British once uncovered a spy in Egypt because he forgot to urinate in the ordinary fashion of the natives, knees slightly bent. Charles Fraser-Smith, Stanley Lovell's British counterpart, recalled two instances when German agents were caught because of elementary errors: "One walked into a pub at nine A.M. and asked for a beer, with no apparent knowledge of British licensing hours. Another tried to take a train. When asked for the fare of 'ten and six,' he handed the booking clerk ten pounds and six shillings! Off he went to prison camp."

American agents in Europe learned to identify these minute cultural distinctions, such as whether to pour tea or milk first, smoking cigarettes down to the stub as the French did, walking with hands dangling instead of in pockets, and "eating continental," keeping a knife and fork in their respective hands instead of shifting them after each mouthful of food.

Turhan Celik, a Turkish student and OSS recruit in Istanbul, was almost found out for something much more intimate. His assignment was to set a honey trap on a female Nazi spy responsible for the deaths of several American pilots. He pretended to be a member of the American embassy staff in Istanbul, thereby luring her into wanting to sleep with him for information. But in reality, he was the one getting information from her.

Everything was going well until one night after sex the woman wondered aloud if Celik had lied about his American identity. He stayed calm and asked her why she would suspect such a thing. "Darling," she whispered to him in bed, "it's just that you don't make love like an American. They don't know how, and they are not sexually powerful like European men."

Her suspicions apparently didn't last long. She soon asked Celik if he could get her a passport from the American embassy. The OSS used the opportunity to double-cross her. Since the OSS couldn't arrest her in neutral Turkey, it persuaded the American embassy to grant her passage to Canada via Syria.

When she arrived in Syria for her layover, she was quickly arrested, tried, and executed as a Nazi spy.

At the OSS office in London, workers Lazare Teper and Henry Sutton created the cover stories for OSS agents. Nicknamed the Bach Section after Teper's favorite composer, the two men provided agents with fake names and backgrounds, as well as information about the military unit that they supposedly belonged to, the geography of the places where they were supposed to have been, the color of the school buses in their supposed hometown, and the burial place of their supposedly deceased parents (a favorite question of the Gestapo). Teper and Sutton gathered all of these miscellaneous facts by talking with prisoners of war and reading small-town newspapers from hundreds of European cities.

The meticulously detailed cover story of "Antonin Vesely" serves as an example of their handiwork:

> I was born on 20 February 1907, at Mährish-Ostrau Protectorate, the son of Jan Vesely, a railroad worker, and of Maria (maiden name) Jirka, housewife. I am a Roman Catholic and single. My father was born on 15 March 1877 and died of angina pectoris on 22 April 1938. He was buried at the city cemetery in Mährisch-Ostrau. My mother, Maria Vesely, maiden name Jirka, was born on 7 August 1883 in Mährisch-Ostrau as the only daughter of the cobbler Franto Jirka, Mährisch-Ostrau; she died on 10 January 1944 of heart failure and is buried with my father there in the family grave.
>
> I went to elementary school (*Volksschule*) in Mährisch-Ostrau from 1913 to 1921 and graduated there. From

October 1921 to October 1924 I was apprenticed at the machine and repair shop Jaroslav Janiszeck in Mährisch-Ostrau, where I learned welding and lathe-band operating. I continued to work with this firm with minor interruptions until summer 1940, when by recommendation of my uncle who was a foreman at the Ringhoffer-tatrawerke A.G. (Zavody Ringhoffer Tatra A.S.—Czech name for firm) in Praha-Smechov, Martouzska 200, I quit my job in Mährisch-Ostrau to work with this firm in the welding department. There were about 4000 to 5000 workers employed in 1940 on the production of cars and trucks. In Prague I lived at: Praha-Sarchov, Zborouska 27.

Kennkarte was issued by the Polizeidirektion in Prague on 4 February 1941.

In May 1944 I was transferred by the Labor Office in Prague to the Junkerswerke, Striegauerstr. (near Gaudon airport) to work again as a welder in the welding department on repair of fuselages, steering mechanisms and wings. There were about 1800 workers of which 75% were foreigners. The plant consisted of 6 large buildings. I lived in Breslau at Tauentzienstrasse 175.

The plant was nearly completely destroyed by Russian air attacks and most of the machinery was damaged or destroyed. I was told to report to the Labor Office in Breslau where I was given an order to evacuate to Berlin and report there at the Arbeitsamt.

Teper and Sutton occasionally used their best cover stories on multiple agents, which led to at least one embarrassing situation. Kermit Roosevelt Jr., an OSS officer (and the grandson of former president Theodore Roosevelt), wrote in an official history of the OSS that agent "Aramis" was picked up in a raid in Paris and discovered "that the man who was questioned before him told the same story he himself planned to use when his turn came." Sometimes improvisation was an agent's only hope for survival.

By May 1945, the Documents Division, Camouflage Division, and Bach Section had assisted hundreds of agents on their undercover missions. Some of the agents were Americans, but many of them were foreigners who spoke the local language of their destination. Some were even German soldiers. To recruit them, a German-speaking OSS officer would initiate conversations with German prisoners of war. If any of them expressed a distaste for Hitler, the officer would engage.

Agent "Louis" parachuted into Germany with forged identification documents, a Nazi party card, and a *stammbuch* (genealogy) proving his Aryan ancestry. He pretended to be a German prisoner of war who had escaped from his American captors. When he later returned to the Allies, he said that his documents were never suspected of being forgeries and that the Germans even offered him dinners and presents in honor of his bravery. Another agent, "Mark," was ironically congratulated by a German military officer for having the only proper documents in a lineup of German (or supposedly German) soldiers.

In the greatest testament to the skills of those who worked under the umbrella of the R&D Branch, one unnamed OSS agent posing as a German soldier completed his mission and reported back to U.S. Army Headquarters, but his forged documents and disguise were so good that the Americans suspected that he was, in fact, an actual German soldier. The agent was thrown in jail as a prisoner of war—of his own country—until the OSS office in London intervened.

The Army soon developed a system of passwords that soldiers

could use to determine whether returning agents were genuine Americans. The soldiers, however, became so lax with the passwords that another system was devised. In this new system, the soldiers would simply ask the agents a series of questions that any American should know. If the agents knew the answers, they were probably American.

Colonel James Curtis and Lyman Kirkpatrick were once stopped and subjected to this questioning because Curtis's cavalryman's mustache looked suspiciously German.

"Where did you get your basic training?" a soldier asked Curtis.

"West Point."

"What's that?"

"That is the United States Military Academy."

"What was your port of embarkation?"

"Fort Hamilton."

"Who won the World Series?"

Curtis said that he didn't follow baseball, causing a renewed look of suspicion to flash across the soldier's eyes.

Kirkpatrick spoke up: "The Cards."

"We didn't ask you," the soldier snapped. He glared at Curtis. "Who's our pin-up girl?"

"Betty Grable."

With this answer the tension melted away. Curtis and Kirkpatrick were allowed to proceed.

Undercover missions weren't limited to men, either. Women made particularly effective agents abroad. For one, their cover stories didn't need to account for why they weren't with a military detachment. Secondly, women were generally seen as being less interested in political and military affairs. This alleged lack of interest made them less suspicious, which in turn made them better equipped to conduct espionage.

"Maria," a resilient twenty-year-old from a mining town south of Strasbourg, volunteered to become an OSS agent. During the German occupation of France, she had been the mistress of a Gestapo officer. She hoped that by aiding the Allies she could clear her conscience and escape the stigma that followed her for sleeping with a German.

The OSS eagerly accepted her help. She was bright, fluent in both French and German, and possessed an intimate knowledge of the region's geography. The Bach Section developed her cover story: She was a military nurse who had traveled from Strasbourg to Tübingen in search of a German officer with whom she had fallen in love. A memo notes, "We used the name of an officer actually known to have been killed in action."

Just before takeoff on the night that she was scheduled to jump, Maria informed Peter Viertel, her handler, that she was pregnant with the Gestapo officer's baby. She said that she wanted to continue with the mission, but in exchange, she wanted him to arrange for her to have an abortion when she returned. Viertel reluctantly agreed to her terms. Besides, he thought to himself, the jolt of her parachute opening might take care of the unwanted pregnancy anyway.

According to an OSS report, Maria was "controlled many times, and was enthusiastic about her cover." Nobody ever suspected that she was a spy. When she returned to Allied territory, she met with Viertel and debriefed him on her mission. She had upheld her end of the bargain; now it was time for him to uphold his. Viertel asked Peter Sichel, another OSS officer, to take her to a hospital in Strasbourg. When they arrived, Sichel explained to the physician that Maria had exhibited extraordinary heroism in Germany. She had sacrificed herself for the war effort and, unfortunately, had become pregnant in the process. The physician immediately understood what was being asked of him. He told Sichel not to worry, he would perform the procedure for free. It was the least that he could do, he said, for a woman who had fought *"pour la belle France."*

Small but consequential errors inevitably crept into agents' documents, appearances, and cover stories. "Jacques" was detained at a Nazi collection point because of an error in his documents, but he managed to escape. While on the run, he met with another agent, "Paul," who gave him a second set of phony documents in case they encountered any more trouble. Jacques then wrapped his head in bandages to avoid being recognized. Paul drove him to the edge of the woods opposite the Rhine where Jacques planned to swim across the river and flee the country. An R&D Branch report notes, "He has not been seen since."

A Nazi officer once questioned "Klaus" about the authenticity of his documents because of a clerical error. On one page, his commanding officer was listed as "Hardenberg." On another, it was listed as "Hardendorf." Klaus was immediately arrested. An OSS report says that he managed to escape custody, though it doesn't explain how.

"Herbert" parachuted into Germany with what he thought were excellent forged documents. But when he looked at them more closely, he noticed that one page identified him as a paymaster while another identified him as a surgeon. He faced certain death should anyone notice.

Disguised as a German civilian, he was deactivating a bridge mine when two German lieutenants walked behind him and asked for his identification papers. Herbert pretended to reach for the papers but instead grabbed his pistol. Before the lieutenants could react, he shot them both.

"Adrian" parachuted into Germany in March 1945. His cover story was that he was a railroad electrician who had been sent from Poznan to Augsburg for a job. On his way from the drop point to Augsburg, he drew a quick sketch of a nearby airfield. In Augsburg, a guard noticed that Adrian was missing travel orders. Plus, his name didn't appear on a master list of workers who had been sent from Poznan. Adrian was arrested and sent to a nearby prison in Halle. On the ride over, he quietly ripped up the incriminating sketch of the airfield and swallowed the pieces of paper.

At the prison, Adrian was stripped, searched, and told to drink an emetic solution to make him vomit. When he refused, an officer hit him in the jaw with a rifle, knocking out five of his teeth. He then drank the emetic solution. The police didn't find anything incriminating in his vomit, but they still weren't satisfied. They proceeded to roll Adrian's body between two rubber cylinders to make him disgorge whatever remained in his stomach. This time they found the pieces of paper.

For the next five days, for eight hours a day, Adrian was interrogated and beaten with clubs. On the sixth day, an American bombing campaign struck Halle. By chance, one of the bombs dislodged the door to Adrian's prison block, allowing him and several other prisoners to escape.

Several days later, Russian forces found Adrian barely alive in a forest. When he was reunited with American forces, the Army Counter Intelligence Corps recruited him to help identify captured Nazi officers, among whom were two of his former torturers. In a split-second decision fueled by rage, he pulled a pistol out of a colleague's holster and shot them both at point blank range. No disciplinary action was ever taken.

Other OSS agents were on the receiving end of a hasty trigger finger. "Evrard" parachuted into Germany with documents identifying him as a distinguished engineer. The documents looked flawless, but a German officer decided to phone his "employer" just in case. Of course, the employer couldn't identify him because he had never worked there. Evrard was killed on the spot.

Sometimes death offered the most charitable end. In April 1943, Gestapo officers in Toulouse, France, captured "Louis," an OSS radio operator. They placed him in the back of a car and transferred him to the local police headquarters. Along the way, as the car slowed to navigate a busy marketplace, Louis sprang for the door handle to escape, but the door wouldn't budge. As punishment for his failed escape attempt, "I got a blow to the head that almost split my skull," he said in a postwar interview, "then in the face, until I was blind. I was immediately handcuffed with my hands behind my back. No doubt the Germans would have killed me on the spot except that they wanted to reserve this pleasure for later."

When they arrived at the police headquarters, the officers dragged Louis out of the car by his throat. "Then the Krauts pretended to open the gate by knocking my head against the bars." Once inside, "They gave me the works: rawhide whips, clubs, and fists rained on me." Louis denied being a spy, even when the officers showed him the confiscated radio equipment that he had used to send messages back to the OSS.

The enraged officers took Louis upstairs for another round of torture. "I was hung by a strong rope tied around the middle of my body and run through a pulley in the roof just over the stair shaft. Then I was whipped hanging in space with nothing to hold on to." The officers swung wooden bats at his dangling body as if he were a piñata. "I must say that at this moment death would have been pleasant." In a test of his will, the officers handed him a revolver. "I put it to my head and pulled the trigger." *Click*. It was unloaded.

Louis employed a clever strategy to survive his confinement. He pretended to gradually sympathize with Nazi ideology. He renounced the "sins" of his past, despite feeling internal pangs of conscience for doing so. "I would go up to be handcuffed so docilely that they finally would put the cuffs in my pocket instead of putting them on my hands." His false conversion was a guise to win the trust of his captors. "In reality I was thinking of nothing but how to escape, how to murder my guard."

Louis's patience ultimately paid off, though it took a year and a half before he could spring his plan. Now that the Germans thought that he was a genuine Nazi sympathizer, they wanted his help. They asked him to send disinformation back to the OSS through his radio. He did, but he cleverly signed off with "SK," a German signal, instead of "VA," his usual signal, indicating that he was compromised. In a more audacious plan, the Germans asked him to meet with other OSS agents and persuade them to defect. When Louis got the chance to leave the prison to betray his fellow agents, he ran.

"Adrienne" was one of the few agents who endured even more hardships than Louis. OSS officer Robert Alcorn provided the only account of her harrowing story. He described the twenty-eight-year-old Adrienne as "tall and slender with an attractive figure. Her hair was dark and worn in a long bob, softly curling, and she had pale blue eyes, the envy, I'm sure, of every brunette who ever knew her." A Belgian native, she volunteered to work with the OSS in response to the Germans occupation of her country.

On a cold, moonlit night in late 1944, Adrienne and two assisting agents, "Pierre" and "Georges," parachuted into a field near the Belgian-German border. Their mission was to work their way into the German interior and report back on troop movements.

Adrienne quickly buried her parachute, jump slacks, and camouflage smock under a thin layer of dirt. As she rose to her feet, she heard rustling in the grass to her left. Footsteps. She was immobilized with fear—until she realized who it was.

"Pierre," she whispered, "C'est Adrienne."

Her husky teammate crept toward her voice. The two spies embraced, though their brief moment of joy was tinged with apprehension. Where was Georges? Had he been injured on landing? Did he need their help? Together they searched for him in the field.

While walking through the tall grass, Pierre grabbed Adrienne's hand. "It is better this way," he said. "If we are surprised then we are only lovers walking in a field. Right?"

Suddenly a flood of light illuminated the field, stopping them in their tracks. The words "Achtung! HALT!" cut through the silence. Adrienne and Pierre clenched each other's hands. They were caught.

Armed Nazi soldiers eerily silhouetted by the floodlights, guns at the ready, walked toward them. The soldiers pulled the "lovers" apart and searched them for illicit items. They found a gun and a knife on Pierre. Under Adrienne's skirt they found a revolver strapped to her leg. With her skirt still raised, the soldiers poked at her body and made obscene remarks. Pierre lunged at them in her defense, but one of the soldiers thrust a rifle butt in his face, knocking him unconscious.

The soldiers led Adrienne to a waiting car and forced her inside. During the unnerving drive—she didn't know where to— she felt a hand slide underneath her skirt and across her upper leg. She instinctively slapped the face of the Nazi sitting beside her. For a split second, her audacity stunned him into silence, but his shock quickly turned into blind rage. He yelled for the driver to pull over.

The soldiers pulled Adrienne out of the car. Four of them took turns raping her.

Adrienne regained consciousness on the cold floor of a barren, brightly lit cell. Its only furnishing was a bucket for her waste. Her body was beaten and bruised. Her spirit was broken. She could hardly move, and didn't want to anyway. She wanted to die. She reached to the back of her head where an L-pill had been concealed in her hair, but her hand touched a bare scalp. Her head had been shaved and the pill was gone.

Looking around the prison, Adrienne saw Pierre and Georges in cells of their own. If nothing else, at least she knew that they were alive.

All three OSS agents were interrogated at length, often under pain of torture. During one session, the guards ripped out Pierre's fingernails. During others, they placed electrodes in his ears and his nostrils, and on his testicles. In the most sadistic act of all, they forced Adrienne to watch as they attached raw meat to the male prisoners' naked, emaciated bodies. Adrienne didn't understand why until she saw a pack of hungry police dogs snarling in the corner. After the ferocious attack, as deafening cries echoed throughout the prison, Pierre writhed on the stone floor in a pool of his own blood. With his last ounce of strength, he kicked at a passing guard, who shot him dead.

The next time that a guard entered Adrienne's cell to abuse her, she kicked and clawed at him with as violent a passion as she could muster. In the chaos of their struggle, she clamped her teeth down on the fatty flesh of his cheek. She refused to let go, even as his warm blood oozed into her mouth. Eventually the guards subdued her with blows to her body, but they didn't kill her as she had hoped. They instead kept her alive to make her suffer. An hour later, as punishment for biting, they put her in restraints and ripped out her teeth.

Despite the torture, Adrienne refused to reveal any of her secrets. The Nazis eventually realized that they wouldn't break her and so transferred her to the Dachau concentration camp. That's where American forces found her in April 1945.

General Bill Donovan and Robert Alcorn visited Dachau upon its liberation. Surrounding the camp were lush trees and sunlit fields. Alcorn recalled that "even the stark barracks of Dachau, behind their high barriers of barbed wire, looked ordinary rather than sinister." But the interior of the camp was anything but ordinary. "Army personnel, mounted on huge bulldozers, were pushing high stacks of rotting bodies into enormous pits which had been scooped out of the soft earth. Most of the men were wearing gas masks against the stench and the rest had covered their faces and nostrils with handkerchiefs." Donovan was aghast. "Dear God, Bob," he said. "Can you believe this? And it's only one camp out of many."

An orderly escorted the two men to a barracks where Adrienne lay incapacitated. Alcorn later described seeing her head resting on a pillow, "No hair on it whatsoever. The pale blue eyes were staring wildly from deeply sunken sockets that seemed to be ringed with black kid." She looked as if she were about to die. "The cheeks were grey and sunken and there were no teeth in the face at all so that the once full mouth had fallen in on the gums in the grotesque manner of advanced age." In her pitiable state she managed to eke out the words, "*Mon General. Mon General Donovan.* You are here. And I am alive."

Donovan took her hand:

> Slowly, quietly and firmly, he talked to her with the wonderful mellowness of his voice. He told her that she would soon be taken back to a real hospital where she could rest and gain her strength. He told her, and I crossed my fingers for him, that she looked fine and would soon be well again. She clung to his hand as he rose from the bed and implored him with her eyes not to leave. He held her hand for a few lingering moments while he explained to her that the war was all but over, that he must leave now so that she could rest and then, in a short while, when she was well, he would see her again. And so we left.

Adrienne slowly rehabilitated. She eventually returned to Belgium, intent on starting a new life, but she never managed to escape the trauma of her past. Within a year, she was found hanging from a rope tied to a rod in her closet.

14
Biological Warfare

On October 27, 1940, Archie Crouch, an American mission-ary in Ningbo, China, watched a lone Japanese airplane fly over-head. Later that day, he wrote in his diary that a "plume of what appeared to be dense smoke billowed out behind the fuselage. I thought it must be on fire, but then the cloud dispersed down-ward quickly, like rain from a thunderhead on a summer day, and the plane flew away." The plane had dropped wheat onto the city center. Impoverished Chinese villagers rushed to collect the manna from the sky. Within a week, Crouch wrote, "The first bubonic plague symptoms appeared among people who lived in the center of the city."

Unbeknownst to the Chinese villagers, the Japanese had con-taminated the wheat with plague-infested fleas. Dozens of the villagers soon began dying of the disease. Schools were closed down. The sick were quarantined. A guild of masons built a fourteen-foot brick wall around the heart of the city, but it wasn't enough to confine the Black Death.

The city elders turned to fire. "Trails of sulfur were laid out like a rat maze through the condemned area," Crouch wrote. "Ignited in strategic places, fires from the burning Sulphur raced through the maze like sparkling snakes. . . . The heart of the city was quickly reduced to a pile of glowing embers, and the assumption was that no rat and no flea could possibly escape."

One year later, in response to Japan's actions in China, the United States formed a Committee on Biological Warfare to determine how best to fight a war with biological weapons. Based out of the National Academy of Sciences and composed of nine leading biologists, the committee developed several tactics for consideration: "Typhoid could be introduced by sabotage into water and milk supplies. . . . Botulinus toxin might be conveyed in lethal amounts through water supplies. . . . Plague could be introduced into any of the large cities or ports by releasing infected rats or fleas. . . . Diptheria can be spread by dissemination of cultures in shelters, subways, street cars, motion picture theaters, factories, stores, etc." In its final report, the committee concluded, "The best defense is offense and the threat of offense."

In light of the committee's recommendations, Secretary of War Henry Stimson told President Franklin Roosevelt that while biological warfare was undoubtedly "dirty business," he agreed with the committee that "we must be prepared." Roosevelt had his own reservations about biological warfare—he especially didn't want to launch a first strike—but he acknowledged that the United States needed to develop biological weapons, just in case.

The British had already come to the same conclusion. In July 1942, British scientists began conducting biological weapons tests on Gruinard Island, a desolate mile-long island off the

Scottish coast. For their first test, the scientists—donning gas masks and orange biohazard suits—prepared a bomb filled with a highly virulent strain of anthrax. Downwind were dozens of sheep confined in small wooden cages resembling pillories. When the bomb detonated, a sturdy island wind carried the brownish cloud of anthrax spores toward the target sheep. Just a few days later, all but two of the sheep were dead.

The scientists flung the infected sheep carcasses over a nearby cliff for disposal. They then exploded a shelf of rock that was supposed to bury the carcasses in ten feet of earth, but the force of the rock crashing against the ground propelled one of the carcasses out to sea. It eventually drifted to the mainland where a curious dog happened upon it, contracted anthrax, and spread the disease to at least twenty-five other animals in the area. The scientists subsequently built a small furnace on the island to cremate the infected sheep carcasses and prevent any similar mishaps in the future.

The Americans weren't far behind their British allies. In early 1943, the U.S. Army established Camp Detrick in Frederick, Maryland, as the country's main biological warfare installation. The abandoned flying strip that Camp Detrick was built upon had originally belonged to the OSS, but Stanley Lovell lobbied the organization to transfer it to the Army. Brigadier General Alden Waitt wrote in a letter of thanks to Lovell, "I feel that you were responsible in a large measure for our being able to take it over. I know that OSS released the field at considerable sacrifice."

Inside the laboratories and industrial facilities that sprung up at Camp Detrick, scientists mass-produced botulinum toxin, anthrax spores, and other "pandemic organisms," as Lovell called them. And as the American stockpile of deadly biological agents grew, so did the number of animals that they were tested on. In its first two and a half years alone, Camp Detrick went through

598,604 white mice, 32,339 guinea pigs, 16,178 rats, 5,222 rabbits, 4,578 hamsters, 399 cotton rats, 225 frogs, 166 monkeys, 98 brown mice, 75 Wistar rats, 48 canaries, 34 dogs, 30 sheep, 25 ferrets, 11 cats, 5 pigs, and 2 roosters.

Not everyone approved of these developments. Lovell said that General Donovan "despised" the idea of biological warfare "as most heroes who had withstood shot and shell were prone to do." Vannevar Bush "became profane when it was mentioned." Roosevelt himself disliked the idea, but for matters of defense, he let the research continue.

Although the Army ran Camp Detrick, Lovell's R&D Branch conducted its own related research. As early as July 20, 1942, OSS planning chief James Rogers wrote in his diary, "I am studying biological warfare." He called it "the densest secret of war" and "curious, dangerous stuff." But even that was revealing too much. "I dare not write even here. . . . This war is just murder."

A year later, Rogers met with Vannevar Bush and James Conant, the country's leading coordinators of wartime scientific research, to discuss the future of the R&D Branch. He wrote in his diary that both Bush and Conant considered the OSS "aimless, political, and socialite," but that they saw promise in "Lovell's section." Bush and Conant agreed to continue supporting the R&D Branch under four conditions: if Rogers agreed that it was worthwhile, if a list of objectives was made, if it interested the NDRC scientists, and if the R&D Branch "would hereafter avoid biological warfare" and let the Army pursue the matter exclusively. Lovell had, in their opinion, adopted some troubling views that they wanted to rein in.

Lovell developed into a pragmatist over the course of the war. He had been reluctant to create deadly weapons when Donovan had first recruited him to lead the R&D Branch, but now, when faced with the devastating realities of war, he simply wanted it to end—by whatever means necessary. In fact, after having seen and heard of the gruesome fates that many soldiers had faced, some of whom he had known personally, Lovell came to view biological warfare as the *ethical* alternative to conventional warfare. Exposing a soldier to a lethal or incapacitating disease was, he said, "infinitely less barbarous than to stab him in the viscera, twist the bayonet to contaminate the wound thoroughly and leave him to die from the horrors of general septicemia." If a soldier was going to die from an infection either way, then why not at least spare him the gruesome wound? Was that not the more humane option? Wouldn't biological weapons end the war quicker and ultimately spare unnecessary suffering?

Bush and Conant wanted the United States to stockpile biological weapons as a deterrent to foreign aggression, but they disagreed with Lovell about the ethics of instigating biological warfare. In their minds, Lovell had failed to consider the broader consequences of such an action. What kind of precedent would it set for future wars? What if the diseases spread to civilian populations? How would it affect American credibility? Was there any reason to think that biological warfare was even effective? But Lovell dismissed their arguments. He had already made up his mind.

On December 31, 1943, the National Academy of Sciences hosted a secret meeting of ten scientists, military officers, and business leaders to discuss recent advances in biological warfare. Among the distinguished group were George Merck, president of the Merck pharmaceutical company; Ira Baldwin, a leading bacteriologist and the scientific director of the Biological Warfare Laboratories at Camp Detrick; John Marquand, a war correspondent and novelist who had recently won the Pulitzer Prize for his book *The Late George Apley*; and Stanley Lovell. When it was Lovell's turn to speak, he said that "a new front could not be opened in Europe without taking b.w. [biological warfare] into consideration." He then inquired about whether a certain sugar refinery in Germany "could be used to produce 'X,'" the code name for anthrax. Baldwin assured him that this was "entirely possible."

Among the diseases that most interested the group were anthrax, botulism, brucellosis, cholera, dysentery, mussel poisoning, plague, psittacosis, tularemia, typhus, and valley fever. Additionally, James Hamilton, an R&D Branch scientist, said that Lovell was investigating a substance code-named "peach fuzz" that had "tremendous possibilities, and might prove to be a most lethal BW weapon."

Given the morbid nature of their work, everyone at the meeting at some point had to confront the same moral dilemma that Lovell had faced. In a postwar interview, Baldwin, a part-time preacher with pacifist Quaker grandparents, explained his rationale for creating biological weapons. "There is no question that the idea of using biological agents to kill people represented a complete shift in thinking," he said. "But it only took me about twenty-four hours to think my way through it. After all, the immorality of war is war itself. You start out with the idea in war of killing people, and that to me is the immoral part of it." Baldwin had come to the same pragmatic conclusion as Lovell. War is hell, he reasoned. The quicker it's over, the better, even if that means resorting to biological weapons.

The meeting at the National Academy of Sciences strengthened Lovell's belief in biological weapons. Following the meeting, he and the other scientists in the R&D Branch developed several methods to disperse biological agents in case the need ever arose. One method involved using a time pencil to detonate an aerosol bomb that contained an airborne disease. Another method involved scattering contaminated powders throughout irrigation ditches to ruin enemy crops. One compound, "LN 8," could reportedly wither crop leaves in a single day. Within a week, a summary report says, "the stalks fall over and the plant dies or fails to bear fruit." The idea, common throughout history, was to deprive enemy soldiers of food and therefore weaken their will to fight. As the saying goes, an army marches on its stomach.

Admiral William Leahy, President Roosevelt's chief of staff and the highest-ranking active-duty member in the entire U.S. military, was firmly opposed to the plan to poison crops. He later recalled that in July 1944, while sailing with Roosevelt to Honolulu, "There was a spirited discussion of bacteriological warfare in the President's cabin. By that time the scientists thought, for example, that they could destroy completely the rice crop of Japan. Some of those present advocated the adoption of such measures." Leahy was horrified. "Mr. President," he pleaded, "this would violate every Christian ethic I have ever heard of, and all of the known laws of war. It would be an attack on the noncombatant population of the enemy."

The Joint Chiefs of Staff, however, saw great promise in the plan. According to a declassified R&D Branch report from August 3, 1945, it was understood that "the Joint Chiefs of Staff have given their approval to the use of plant BW provided the theatre commander wishes to use it." But the theater commanders sided with Leahy and refused to issue the order.

Instead, three days later, the United States dropped an atomic bomb on Hiroshima, instantly incinerating the Japanese city and tens of thousands of its inhabitants. Another three days later, a second atomic bomb was dropped on Nagasaki. Over the following months, the death toll from the bombs climbed as thousands of people succumbed to their burns, wounds, and to radiation sickness. A fifth-grade boy in Hiroshima compiled a list of the horrors that he saw in the aftermath of the explosion:

> The flames which blaze up here and there from the collapsed houses as though to illuminate the darkness. The child making a suffering, groaning sound, his burned face swollen up balloon-like and jerking as he wanders among the fires. The old man, the skin of his face and body peeling off like a potato skin, mumbling prayers while he flees with faltering steps. Another man pressing with both hands the wound from which blood is steadily dripping, rushing around as though he has gone mad and calling the names of his wife and child—ah—my hair seems to stand on ends just to remember. This is the way war really looks.

Vannevar Bush and James Conant had tried to suppress Lovell's work on biological weapons, but they both supported the decision to drop the atomic bombs. As did Lovell. Decades after the war, he debated the issue with his grandson, Jonathan, who disagreed. "What about nuclear waste?" Jonathan said. "What about opening Pandora's Box and not being able to close it?"

Lovell dismissed the arguments with a wave of his hand. "We're an inventive people, we'll figure it out." Scientists would somehow tame the monster that they had created.

Admiral Leahy, on the other hand, remained steadfast in his disapproval. In his view, the atomic bomb wasn't really a "bomb" or an "explosive." It was more akin to a plague. "It is a poisonous thing," he said, and it deserved to be seen in as harsh a light as any biological weapon. "Wars cannot be won by destroying women and children."

Meanwhile, the American intelligence community was receiving reports that the Soviets, Germans, and Japanese were conducting dangerous biological warfare experiments of their own.

In mid-1945, members of the Alsos Mission, a secret group of American scientists and military personnel collecting wartime scientific intelligence in Europe, uncovered German reports of horrific Russian biological warfare experiments. According to a German zoologist referred to as "Dr. Arper" in an Alsos report, but whose name was most likely "von Apen," he had visited Russia and witnessed biological warfare trials "carried out by B.W. aircraft sprays on nomad tribes, as a result of which the whole tribe was infected with 100% positive success. After the trial the survivors were all annihilated by air action. 50–60 of such trials had been carried out."

Arper (or von Apen) also alleged that the Soviets had developed a plan to drop flea-infested rats bred for strength and aggression onto enemy territory to serve as vectors for disease. Neither Alsos nor the Germans found much evidence to corroborate these claims. Alsos did, however, find evidence showing that the Germans had conducted similar experiments of their own.

At the end of the war, Alsos captured Kurt Blome, a German biological weapons expert with a gaunt face and a sinister dueling scar across his upper lip. During his interrogation, Blome said that Heinrich Himmler, the chief architect of the Holocaust, had ordered him to study how to disseminate plague pathogens. He further said that he and his colleagues had planned to release plague-infected rats from U-boats near enemy shores, but they realized that the plan was impractical when thirty test rats failed to find the shore and drowned.

Following his rat experiments, Blome turned his attention to humans, though he vigorously denied doing so to an Alsos interrogator who called him "a liar and a medical charlatan." During the postwar Nuremberg trials, a series of military tribunals held to try Nazi leaders for war crimes, Blome's colleague Walter Schreiber testified that "experiments were carried out at the institute in Posen," Blome's research facility. "I do not know any details about them. I only know that aircraft were used for spraying tests with bacteria emulsion, and that insects harmful to plants, such as beetles, were experimented with." When the Soviet Red Army advanced toward Posen, Blome "was very worried at the fact that the installations for experiments on human beings at this institute, the purpose of which was obvious, might be easily recognized by the Russians for what they were." He tried to destroy the institute with a Stuka bomb, "but that, too, was not possible," Schreiber said. "Therefore, he asked me to see to it that he be permitted to continue work at Sachsenburg on his plague cultures, which he had saved."

Schreiber further described experiments whereby concentration camp prisoners were infected with typhus or submerged in ice water until they froze to death (roughly ninety people died this way). Other deranged experiments that he failed to mention involved subjecting prisoners to mustard gas, euthanasia, sterilization, and high-altitude pressure chambers.

Seven out of the twenty-three men on trial with Blome in Nuremberg were sentenced to death by hanging. After the sentence was carried out, their corpses were cremated in nearby concentration camp ovens, an ironic end for the perpetrators of the Holocaust. Blome himself was acquitted. The prosecution couldn't find any conclusive evidence linking him to human experiments, only the *intent* to conduct human experiments. After his trial, the U.S. military offered him a contract under Operation Paperclip, a secret intelligence program to harness German brainpower, to come to the United States and produce biological agents. The offer eventually fell through, but Blome still became a paid consultant to the United States in Europe. He was never again arrested or charged with any war crime.

In Japan, the infamous Unit 731 was responsible for conducting most of the country's biological warfare experiments, including the bubonic plague drops over China. At the beginning of the war, the unit's leader, Shirō Ishii, a microbiologist and notorious womanizer, told his scientists, "Our God-given mission as doctors is to challenge all forms of disease-causing micro-organisms, block all paths for their intrusion into the body, annihilate foreign matter resident in our bodies, and devise the best possible treatments. However," he continued, "the research work on which we are now to embark is the complete opposite of those principles."

The unit's depraved experiments on humans involved frostbite, flamethrowers, water torture, electrocution, vivisections without anesthesia, the forced transfer of venereal diseases, and infecting prisoners with plague, anthrax, smallpox, and cholera. The unit also developed poisoned chocolate and chewing gum, fountain pens that delivered dangerous toxins, and an "Imperial sake," a stimulant that was given to kamikaze pilots. Among Unit 731's thousands of victims, or "logs," were a handful of American prisoners of war. Most of the victims, however, were

Chinese citizens, soldiers, prisoners, and mental patients who had been captured in occupied Manchuria.

American scientists at Camp Detrick were eager to learn of the results of Unit 731's experiments. Here was a unique dataset that contained revelations about the human body and its reaction to various diseases. Fearing that the data might fall into the hands of the Soviets, General Douglas MacArthur secured a deal with the members of Unit 731 whereby in exchange for exclusive access to their data, the United States would grant them amnesty from prosecution for war crimes. Shirō Ishii agreed to the terms and handed over thousands of microscope slides containing tissue from his victims. The slides were then sent to the scientists at Camp Detrick, who said that the data "greatly supplemented and amplified" their own research.

One anonymous virologist attached to Unit 731 later explained his rationale for performing these heinous experiments: "At that time, the general thinking at the unit was that it was necessary to sacrifice three *maruta*," the Japanese term for logs, "in order to save one hundred Japanese soldiers." In his calculus, the ends justified the means.

An anonymous hygiene specialist for Unit 731 recalled feeling a surge of patriotism whenever a batch of bacteria that he had cultivated killed five Chinese prisoners. "We're medal earners," he told his colleagues. In early 1945, this same hygiene specialist was sent away to fight against the approaching Americans. "That was rough," he said. "Nothing in Unit 731 was even a fraction that bad."

Yuasa Ken, an Army doctor attached to Unit 731, came to the same conclusion. He was remorseful for what he had done, but, he said, "the greatest crime . . . was not vivisection but joining the army as a medical doctor, treating sick and wounded soldiers to release them to fight again. This is the most criminal act: returning killer soldiers." He, Lovell, and Baldwin had all independently concluded that the ordinary acts of war were the grisliest acts of all.

15
Chemical Warfare

Before World War II, Germany had been at the forefront of chemical weapons research, just as it had been at the forefront of so many other scientific and technological disciplines. In 1936, a group of German scientists studying insecticides at the chemical company IG Farben discovered the first nerve agents, among the most toxic substances ever created. Nerve agents work by inhibiting the body's ability to create acetylcholinesterase, an enzyme that promotes the breakdown of acetylcholine. When someone is exposed to a nerve agent, the resulting excess of acetylcholine paralyzes their muscles, leading to a loss of control of bodily functions—including breathing—and death. Among the nerve agents that the Germans discovered were tabun and sarin, a substance so potent that a fraction of an ounce applied to the skin is fatal in humans.

During World War II, Adolf Hitler, himself the victim of a British poison gas attack in World War I, ordered the mass production of nerve agents and other deadly chemical compounds. (The United States caught up after the war when, as part of Operation Paperclip, it hired German chemists to synthesize its own nerve agents.) Some of these compounds, such as the cyanide-based pesticide Zyklon B, were used to commit genocide in Nazi concentration camps.

Because Germany was also at the forefront of rocket technology, Stanley Lovell worried that the German military would combine its dual advantages and launch rockets containing nerve agents, poison gas, or other chemical compounds. And his fear wasn't unfounded. In 1943, he received a report from an agent in the field describing how German soldiers believed that "the Luftwaffe will prepare a dreadful attack on England using gas bombs."

Vannevar Bush shared the same fear. In a postwar interview, he said that he had been "very much afraid of what Germany might have done on gas, particularly because we knew about some of the things *we'd* done," though he didn't clarify what this meant.

On January 12, 1944, Bush briefed General Dwight Eisenhower on the potential for Germany to initiate chemical warfare with its rockets. When he finished talking, Eisenhower sat back and said, "Well, you've scared the hell out of me."

To Eisenhower's relief, the German rockets weren't ready in time to repel the Normandy invasion, which began on June 6, 1944, D-Day. But they were soon afterward. The next week, as Bush climbed into a car with Secretary of War Henry Stimson to ride to Capitol Hill, he received word that the first German V-1 rockets had hit London.

Stimson asked on the drive, "About this V-1 business, Van, how do you feel?"

"I feel damned relieved," Bush said, surprising Stimson. The rockets had carried only conventional explosives and none of the chemical compounds that he had feared.

The Germans launched several thousand V-1 and V-2 rockets during the last year of the war. "It was like 4th of July," said Army mechanic Charles Dee. "They had these sparks flying out of the back of them. We didn't pay much attention to them while we could still hear that motor running. But as soon as that motor stopped, we knew that bomb was coming down, and of course, it became quite a bit of concern from then on." A single V-2 rocket once killed 160 people and injured 108 others when it struck a Woolworth's department store in South London, causing the building to implode. But overall, the total damage inflicted by the rockets "was not great," Bush said. Or at least it wasn't as great as it could have been had they contained poison gas or nerve agents.

Like General Donovan, British prime minister Winston Churchill was a war hero who had withstood shot and shell. Unlike Donovan, however, he disregarded the taboo surrounding chemical weapons. One month after D-Day, while V-1 rockets rained down on London, Churchill considered using poison gas against Germany. In a four-page memo to his chief of staff, General Hastings Ismay, Churchill wrote with characteristic wit, "It is absurd to consider morality on this topic when everybody used it in the last war without a word of complaint from the moralists or the Church. . . . It is simply a question of fashion changing as she does between long and short skirts for women. . . . It may be several weeks or even months before I shall ask you to drench Germany with poison gas, and if we do it, let us do it one hundred per cent." Churchill never followed through, but by the end of the war, Stanley Lovell was advocating for the United States to do something very similar.

President Franklin Roosevelt established a no-first-use policy for chemical weapons, just as he had done for biological weapons. The United States nevertheless manufactured chemical weapons as a deterrent and retaliatory force. Between 1940 and 1945, scientists at Edgewood Arsenal, the country's largest chemical weapons facility, produced 146,000 tons of chemical agents, including mustard agent, cyanogen chloride, and hydrocyanic acid, most of which was packed into bombs, mortars, and artillery shells.

Lovell disagreed with Roosevelt's no-first-use policy. His philosophy of chemical weapons mirrored his philosophy of biological weapons. He encouraged their use as long as they could expedite the war's end and *spare* unnecessary agony and death. While Donovan and Louis Fieser, the inventor of napalm, were vocal in their denunciations of chemical warfare, Lovell considered it no more barbaric, and perhaps even less barbaric, than shooting a soldier in the stomach, crushing him with a tank, or setting him on fire. It had been Fieser's invention, after all, that enabled the firebombing of Tokyo, a massacre that resulted in a hundred thousand deaths and prompted the U.S. Strategic Bombing Survey to conclude that "probably more persons lost their lives by fire at Tokyo in a six-hour period than at any time in the history of man."

Lovell specifically wanted to deploy chemical weapons against the Japanese soldiers dug in on Iwo Jima, a small volcanic island in the Philippine Sea. If captured, Iwo Jima could serve as an important staging ground for aerial attacks on the

Japanese mainland. Lovell relied on two arguments to justify his position. First, only two major powers had refused to ratify the 1925 Geneva Protocol banning the use of biological and chemical weapons: Japan and the United States. Secondly, Lovell wasn't the only person who wanted to deploy chemical weapons against Iwo Jima. In fact, the idea had originated elsewhere.

In early 1944, the Joint Chiefs of Staff asked the British military for advice on the best strategies for deploying chemical weapons against Japan, just in case the need ever arose. The task of responding to the Joint Chiefs fell to John Lethbridge, a British major general who had recently completed an investigation to determine how best to defeat the Japanese military.

In his resulting report, Lethbridge made three main recommendations regarding Iwo Jima. First, as summarized by Lovell, "Jam the Iwo Jima radio transmitter." Second, "Soak the little island with gas shells." And third, "Change the yellow banding of the shells so that even the gunners would never know they had fired other than high explosive shells, a few of which were to be interspersed with the gas." Once the poison gas had dissipated and the island was safe for human habitation, "Our forces were to land and without a single casualty capture a vital stepping-stone to Tokyo."

The actual wording of the Lethbridge Report is even more disturbing than Lovell insinuated. The gas attack, it says, "must be administered with complete ruthlessness and upon a vast scale, employing a mixture of agents that will not only cause mutilation and death, but by the very diversity of effects create terror and panic in the minds of the victims."

According to Lovell, the Joint Chiefs of Staff secretly

approved the plan to shell Iwo Jima with poison gas. But before the plan could be implemented, it needed the additional approval of the theater commander, Admiral Chester Nimitz. Lovell wasn't going to let this inconvenient piece of bureaucratic red tape get in his way. He decided to personally visit Nimitz in Hawaii to get his approval.

Lovell never forgot the flight to Pearl Harbor. Before taking off, the pilot told him that their plane was "in terrible shape" and that he was going to simulate engine failure on the flight in order to scare a handful of Navy admirals into giving him a better one. Once they were airborne, the pilot sputtered over the intercom, "Number One port engine is failing, gentlemen. I'm switching it off." There was a strong vibration. "We're going to climb all we can and then do a power dive to try to get our dead engine firing. Thank you." The power dive "was never forgotten by anyone aboard," Lovell later said. The passengers' stomachs leapt into their chests. Those who could bear to look out the windows watched the blue wall of the Pacific Ocean race toward them. The pilot pulled out of the dive mere seconds before crashing. Everyone onboard breathed a sigh of relief, including Lovell. "Despite my tip-off," he confessed, "I had died a coward's thousand deaths." The pilot's gambit apparently paid off. His old plane never made another Hawaiian run.

Safely on Hawaiian ground, Lovell met with Admiral Nimitz to get his approval for the plan to shell Iwo Jima with poison gas. To help cinch the case, Lovell argued that the Japanese had built a complex tunnel system on Iwo Jima. Conventional bombs would destroy the tunnels, whereas chemical weapons wouldn't. The Americans might need to use those tunnels to defend the island in case the Japanese tried to retake it. Nimitz listened intently but didn't commit to anything. Lovell never-theless sailed back to the mainland thinking that he had won him over.

When Lovell returned to Washington, D.C., he learned that the Lethbridge Report had made it all the way to the White House, but President Roosevelt nixed the plan with the stroke of a pen. "All prior endorsements denied—Franklin D. Roos-evelt, Commander-in-Chief." Roosevelt hadn't been persuaded to abandon his no-first-use policy.

Twenty years later, Lovell still disagreed with the decision. "The fact is," he said, "the sole business of war is to kill, slaughter, maim and incapacitate human beings. Once war is declared, to reason is treason." This was an odd pronouncement coming from the chemist who had once championed rational thinking over blind belief.

But Lovell's stance wasn't completely devoid of reason. "Gas warfare need not kill your enemy," he said in justification of his position. "It may be far smarter to use a gas that bewil-ders him so that, for an hour or more, he simply can't think. . . . For the first time since Cain killed Abel this would make war-fare highly amusing." In his view, exposing enemy soldiers to nonlethal chemical agents was indisputably more humane than killing them.

In fact, Lovell had briefly experimented with nonlethal chemical agents during the war. Under his direction, the R&D Branch subjected dozens of human test subjects to dimethyl diglycolate and litharge-glycerine, code-named "TB" and "VG," which caused temporary blindness and induced vomiting. The results were indeed "highly amusing," at least for the observers. Nonetheless, Lovell never did address the counterarguments to his position, such as whether instigating chemical warfare would lead to escalation, set a bad precedent, ruin American credibility, or even be effective.

Corporal Melford Jarstad was one of sixty thousand Marines who participated in the invasion of Iwo Jima. When he reached the island aboard the USS *Storm King*, he was greeted by a scene of carnage. "They were hauling casualties back out to the ships," he said in a postwar interview. "The noise from the bombardment and the action ashore was horrific." Jarstad and nine other men dragged a 37 mm antitank gun ashore, "not knowing what to expect as we moved up. It was definitely a 'fog of war.'" As they struggled up the beach, mortar shells blasted away the volcanic sand around them. "It is not like you see in the movies," he said. "Iwo Jima was inch by inch."

On that first sleepless night, Jarstad and another terrified Marine sat in a hastily dug foxhole and downed little bottles of brandy to calm their nerves. At one point, the other Marine whispered, "I think I hear one coming." They called for a flare. Sure enough, Jarstad said, "a Japanese was on his back trying to crawl under the barbwire in front of us. My foxhole mate fired and shot right through the top of his helmet, killing him instantly." That same night, "a hand grenade went off a short way up the hill and blew the arm off one of our infantry. You can't imagine the nights. We had to stay awake."

On February 23, 1945, photographer Joe Rosenthal took one of the most famous photographs of the entire war when six Marines, three of whom would later die in battle, raised the American flag atop Iwo Jima's Mount Suribachi. After a month of fierce fighting and 26,040 American casualties, including nearly 8,000 deaths, U.S. forces captured the island.

In light of the devastation at Iwo Jima, several important

military figures came to agree with Lovell's position on chemical warfare. David Lilienthal remembered General George Marshall, the U.S. Army chief of staff, saying as much in a postwar
meeting. "After the terrible losses at Iwo Jima," Lilienthal wrote
in his diary, "he was prepared to use gas at Okinawa."

During the postwar Nuremberg trials, General Donovan asked
Lovell to submit questions for the German prisoners. Lovell
suggested one question in particular: "Why no nerve gas at Normandy?" In other words, he wanted to know why the Germans
hadn't used their stockpile of nerve agents to stop the Normandy invasion.

According to Lovell, an interrogator asked this question to
Hermann Göring just days before the shrewd Nazi leader killed
himself with a cyanide pill. Lovell paraphrased their conversation as follows.

"We know you had Gas Blau which would have stopped the
Normandy invasion. Why didn't you use it?"

"*Die pferde* (the horses)," said Göring.

"What have horses to do with it?"

"Everything. A horse lies down in the shafts or between the
thills as soon as his breathing is restricted. We never have had a
gas mask a horse would tolerate."

"What has that to do with Normandy?"

"We did not have enough gasoline to adequately supply the
German air force and the Panzer Divisions, so we used horse
transport in all operations. You must have known that the first
thing we did in Poland, France, everywhere, was to seize the
horses. All our materiel was horse-drawn. Had we used gas you
would have retaliated and you would have instantly immobilized us."

"Was it that serious, Marshal?"

"I tell you, you would have won the war years ago if you had used gas—not on our soldiers, but on our transportation system. Your intelligence men are asses!"

Perhaps this conversation actually happened, or perhaps it sprung from Lovell's fertile imagination as a justification for his advocacy of chemical warfare. Either way, Lovell had certainly come a long way from the unassuming chemist who had once thought that "a Professor Moriarty is as un-American as sin is unpopular at a revival meeting."

16
Truth Drugs

On September 7, 1916, Dr. Robert House administered scopolamine as a sedative to a woman in labor. Within thirty minutes, the woman was reduced to a half-conscious state known as "twilight sleep." After a successful delivery, House asked the woman's husband to retrieve the scales to weigh the baby, but the husband couldn't find them. The debilitated woman, "apparently sound asleep," House wrote in a summary of the incident, "spoke up and said, 'They are in the kitchen on a nail behind the picture.'"

Her answer stunned House. How had she been able to respond in her incapacitated state? House reasoned that the scopolamine must have had something to do with it. Maybe, he thought, the drug lowered her inhibitions and prevented her from holding her tongue. Upon questioning her further, "I observed that, without exception, the patient always replied with the truth." Maybe scopolamine also temporarily suppressed her imagination and prevented her from inventing lies. If so, House realized that he had just discovered a truth drug.

The idea that drugs could elicit truthful statements wasn't anything new. Pliny the Elder had written the maxim *in vino veritas* (in wine lies the truth) some two thousand years earlier. If a drug as ancient as alcohol could loosen lips, House saw no reason why newer drugs, such as scopolamine, couldn't do it even better.

In 1922, House conducted scopolamine truth tests on two alleged criminals to see if it would make them confess to the crimes. One of the test subjects was "a very intelligent white man" named Scrivener who was accused of robbing a pharmacy in Dallas. The other, House said, was "a negro of average intelligence" named Ed Smith who was accused of murder.

House started with Scrivener. He dosed him with a combination of morphine, chloroform, and scopolamine and then assailed him with questions: What's your age? What's your birthday? Where were you born? Did you rob Guy's Pharmacy? Scrivener denied the robbery. House believed him, but a Dallas County jury didn't. He was found guilty and sentenced to fifteen years in prison.

As for Ed Smith, the "negro of average intelligence," the judge dismissed the murder charge due to insufficient evidence. But scopolamine did help Smith in a roundabout way. His lawyer asked two witnesses for the state if they would agree to undergo a scopolamine test to determine whether they were telling the truth. Both declined, undermining their credibility.

Word that scopolamine was a potential truth drug quickly spread. One prisoner convicted of murdering a man in Travis County, Texas, wrote to House with a plea for a "test of twilight serum." There was "no evidence against me," he said, "only I was a poor Mexican. I would certainly be glad if I could be a subject of this serum, and if it be in your power, would you please forward this letter to the proper authorities? I ask for a test upon my innocence, sir, that I may be eliminated from charges as a result."

By 1925, House had conducted eighty-six scopolamine tests on people accused of crimes ranging from kidnapping to axe murder. The tests secured the release of twenty-six of them, but House's influence in the courts was quickly fading. In 1923, *Frye v. United States* set the precedent that scientific evidence was admissible in court only if it was obtained through methods that the relevant scientific community considered reliable. Truth drugs didn't fit the bill.

In 1926, House felt the brunt of the *Frye* standard when he administered a scopolamine test to George Hudson, a black man accused of raping a white woman. The presiding judge in the case refused to admit the transcript of the test into evidence. Hudson was subsequently convicted of the crime. His defense appealed the ruling, but two years later, a new judge, Robert Franklin, upheld his predecessor's decision. In a piercing verdict, he wrote, "We are not told from what well this serum is drawn or in what alembic its truth compelling powers are distilled. Its origin is as nebulous as its effect is uncertain." The "clap-trap" truth drug deserved no consideration from the jury.

Although scopolamine tests had been undermined in the courts, scientists emboldened by House's research began searching for other truth drugs. And soon, the intelligence agencies of the world realized that truth drugs, if they existed, would have a dramatic impact on how interrogations were conducted. No longer would an interrogator have to resort to the hard-nosed tactics of torture, which often resulted in false confessions anyway (people will say anything to make the pain stop). No longer would an interrogator have to wait days or weeks or months for a subject to break. Instead, they could slip the subject a truth drug, sit back, and record the secrets that spilled forth.

During World War II, multiple countries experimented with truth drugs. Germany was again at the forefront of the research. On July 24, 1942, the British intercepted a German Enigma coded message that relayed the following information from a Nazi officer to a medical center in Berlin: "Experiments to date of injecting parachutists with scopolamine were successful. Therefore experiments with mescaline are to be undertaken, since these injections produce an enhanced effect through intoxication." Little else is known about these experiments because the records were destroyed.

The Germans did, however, conduct additional experiments with truth drugs inside their concentration camps. At the Auschwitz concentration camp, Dr. Bruno Weber gave his prisoner test subjects a cocktail of drugs that included morphine and barbiturates. Two of the prisoners took the concoction and collapsed onto the floor. A doctor who was present later said, "Within the context of Auschwitz, what difference did two prisoners make?" Werner Rohde, a medical officer at Auschwitz, was even less bothered and burst into laughter, saying, "At least they died a pleasant death."

At the Dachau concentration camp, prisoners were given mescaline, a psychedelic drug made from the peyote cactus, mixed with coffee in an attempt to "eliminate the will of the person examined," said prison medic Walter Neff. The drug made the prisoners vomit, hallucinate, and, on occasion, divulge information. Neff noted, "The examining person succeeded in every case in drawing even the most intimate secrets from the [prisoners] when the question was cleverly put." Unsurprisingly, those secrets included the fact that the prisoners harbored "sentiments of hatred and revenge" for the Dachau staff.

The British also experimented with truth drugs, though according to one British medical officer, "Truth drugs were discontinued in the army after a very short period of time" because they failed to produce reliable results. A postwar CIA report on foreign interrogation techniques says that the British administered sodium amytal "in top echelon cases." These administrations were "strictly unauthorized and no account of it was made in writing." To disguise what they were doing, the British would line up over a dozen people for a round of shots and give their target the drug while everyone else received distilled water.

The same CIA report also says that it was "strongly rumored" that the Soviets administered truth drugs and other "very crude torture mechanisms in their interrogations," including "whipping, pinching of fingers," and "making the person stand in cold water during winter time for many hours." In 1956, CIA contractors Harold Wolff and Lawrence Hinkle concluded that the Soviets hadn't made extensive use of truth drugs but had instead employed the same interrogation techniques that had been used for centuries: hunger, beatings, isolation, stress positions, and sleep deprivation.

The United States National Research Council, the operating arm of the National Academy of Sciences, tasked the OSS with creating a truth drug program of its own. Responsibility for the program naturally fell to the one branch capable of carrying it out: Stanley Lovell's R&D Branch.

In a project meeting, Lovell admitted to his colleagues that truth drugs were "considered fantastic by the realists, unethical by the moralists, and downright ludicrous by the physicians."

Nevertheless, he said, "The need for such a national weapon was too acute to deny any and every possible attempt to find it." He listed four criteria for determining whether a substance was an effective truth drug: it could be administered unwittingly, it induced a talkative mood, it wasn't harmful or addictive, and it left no suspicion in the subject of having been drugged.

Two months later, in early 1943, General Donovan established a Truth Drug Committee under the direction of Winfred Overholser, the head of St. Elizabeth's Hospital, to perform preliminary experiments with peyote, mescaline, scopolamine, and various barbiturates. None of these drugs met all four of Lovell's criteria. Some were too toxic, while others had a detectable odor or taste. But then the Truth Drug Committee turned its attention to *Cannabis indica*, marijuana.

A decade earlier, Harry Anslinger, the commissioner of the Bureau of Narcotics, had waged a propaganda war to persuade Americans that marijuana was a danger to society. Anslinger realized that if he could make Americans fear marijuana, then they would demand that the Bureau of Narcotics take action to protect them from it. And if that happened, then Congress would give the Bureau of Narcotics more money, something that Anslinger desperately wanted amid the budget cuts of the Great Depression.

Determined to convince Congress to criminalize the drug, Anslinger spread rumors that marijuana turned people into criminals, psychopaths, and sexual deviants. He even helped popularize the term *marijuana*, as opposed to *cannabis*, because it sounded foreign and more threatening. "If the hideous monster Frankenstein came face-to-face with the hideous monster Marihuana," he once said, "he would drop dead of fright." Like the "hideous monster Frankenstein," Anslinger's crusade against marijuana had been animated through sheer cunning.

The crusade worked. In 1937, Congress passed the Marihuana Tax Act, which effectively banned marijuana for recreational use and gave the Bureau of Narcotics the justification that it needed for a bigger budget. Ironically, just a few years later, Anslinger found himself sitting on the Truth Drug Committee, advising the government to investigate the very drug that he had demonized.

The Truth Drug Committee soon conducted its first experiment with marijuana. Committee member Lawrence Kubie, the psychiatrist whom Lovell had consulted about hypnotism, gave four enlisted volunteers a mixture of alcohol and tetrahydrocannabinol (THC) acetate, the main psychoactive ingredient in marijuana. In a subsequent report, Kubie wrote that the results proved "unsatisfactory, in that the men suffered considerable physical discomfort without disclosing information which had been furnished them." He got the same disappointing results when wafting THC fumes throughout the room. He then considered injecting the substance into "mashed potatoes, butter, salad dressing, or in such things as candy," but he realized that this was impractical because in an operational setting, an unwitting target might eat too little to experience symptoms or too much and "cause him to lose consciousness in the same manner as one who is completely drunk, and no further questioning will be possible."

Regardless, the Truth Drug Committee saw a glimmer of hope in THC, at least when compared to the other drugs that it had tested. THC "appeared to relax all inhibitions and to deaden the areas of the brain which govern an individual's discretion and caution," Kubie wrote. "It also accentuates the senses and makes manifest any strong characteristics of the individual. Sexual inhibitions are lowered, and the sense of humor is accentuated to the point where any statement or situation can be extremely funny to the subject."

In the spring of 1943, the Truth Drug Committee decided to conduct another THC experiment. This time, the committee members wanted to test the drug on subjects who were hiding important secrets to determine whether it would make them crack under the influence.

Nobody had more secrets—or more important secrets—than the scientists working on the Manhattan Project, the secret effort to build an atomic bomb. "Our secret was so great," said one Manhattan Project officer, "I guess we were safer than anyone else." Put another way, the scientists working on the Manhattan Project were so accustomed to keeping secrets that they weren't likely to reveal that they were involved in a truth drug experiment. The Manhattan Project administration complied with the Truth Drug Committee's request for guinea pigs and supplied a dozen subjects.

For the experiment, each of the twelve subjects swallowed a vial of liquid THC. According to a scientist who was present, "It didn't work the way we wanted. Apparently the human system would not take it all at once orally. The subjects would lean over and vomit." One man was sent to the hospital; none revealed their secrets.

Subsequent experiments showed that the most effective way to make someone talk was to give them a cigarette that had been injected with THC. During these experiments, Army volunteers were given the tainted cigarettes and told that it was a remedy for shell-shock. A few minutes after administration, "The subject gradually becomes relaxed, and experiences a sensation of well-being," Lovell wrote in a report. "In a few minutes this state passes into one in which thoughts flow with considerable freedom, and in which a conversation becomes animated and accelerated. Inhibitions fall away, and the subjects talk with abandon and indiscretion. During this talkative and irresponsible period, which lasts from one to two hours, skillful interrogation usually elicits information which would not be revealed under other circumstances."

Lovell had found his truth drug and his preferred method of administering it. "The treatment is by no means a magic key to the secrets of the mind," he acknowledged, "but it does constitute an assistance to interrogation of inestimable value to the government of the United States." Now it was time to address a more important question: Would the THC cigarettes work on an unwitting target in a real-world scenario, not just on volunteers in an experiment?

Nobody in the R&D Branch had any experience dosing unwitting targets with drugs. Lovell therefore turned to the Bureau of Narcotics for help, an organization with connections to both drugs and criminal informants to test them on. Harry Anslinger, the commissioner who had waged a propaganda war on marijuana, assigned maverick narcotics agent George White to assist the R&D Branch with its truth drug research. White had already worked with the OSS once before as an instructor at Camp X, a British training school in Canada, where he taught OSS and SOE recruits how to perform and resist interrogations. His new assignment further ushered him into the world of dirty tricks.

George White was a short and squat, bald-headed, "fat slob," according to his ex-wife. Lovell didn't disagree. He described White as "roly-poly," with a shirt that progressed "in wide loops from neck to trousers, with tension on the buttons that seemed more than bearable." But behind his "innocent, round face" was "the most deadly and dedicated public servant I've ever met."

White was indeed deadly. Once while abroad on an assignment for the OSS, he murdered—or as he put it, "interfered terminally" with—an elderly looking Chinese man whom he suspected was a Japanese agent in disguise. White's protégé Ira "Ike" Feldman later said, "He used to keep a picture of the bloody corpse on the wall in his office."

In another notorious incident, White personally arrested renowned jazz singer Billie Holiday after raiding her hotel room and finding opium. Holiday was later acquitted of the crime, leaving White sour. "I was one of the best narcotics agents in the business," he said. "This was one of the few cases I lost." Feldman agreed that White was one of the best in the business, among other things: "White was a son of a bitch, but he was a great cop. He made that fruitcake [J. Edgar] Hoover look like Nancy Drew."

Despite White's affiliation with the Bureau of Narcotics, his new assignment with the R&D Branch didn't call for getting tough on drugs, but rather for getting on them. A glutton for adventure—and pretty much everything else—White happily experimented on himself with the truth drugs. On one occasion, he poured liquid THC onto a pile of burning charcoal and inhaled the fumes until he got high. Another time, he ingested it until he passed out.

His main assignment with the R&D Branch, however, was to surreptitiously slip the truth drug to his criminal contacts and monitor their reactions. As his first target, he chose New York gangster August del Gracio. For the previous six weeks, White had been cultivating del Gracio as an unlikely ally in an attempt to secure the Italian Mafia's help in preparing the way for an American invasion of Sicily. The two men had established enough of a rapport for White to feel confident that he could administer the truth drug without del Gracio becoming suspicious.

White wrote in an intelligence report that del Gracio was "intimately acquainted with all the major criminals" around New York and "had numerous secrets he was most anxious to conceal, the revelation of which might well result in his imprisonment." Would the truth drug make an honest man of him? White had his doubts. "The subject prides himself on the fact that he has never been an informer and that he has been instrumental in killing some persons who have been informants."

On May 27, 1943, White invited del Gracio over to his apartment for what appeared to be one of their usual talks. When del Gracio walked in the door, he told White that he couldn't stay long because a friend was waiting for him in the car. White said that he understood. He then coolly offered del Gracio some liquor and a tainted cigarette.

Minutes later, "having noticed no perceptible effect," White wrote in his report, he gave del Gracio another cigarette. With this additional dose of THC, del Gracio became obviously high and "extremely garrulous." He monopolized the conversation for the next two hours, completely forgetting about his friend in the car. "Whatever you do," he told White, "don't ever use any of the stuff I'm telling you." Subtly, White steered the conversation toward criminal activities, whereupon "with no further encouragement subject divulged the following information: [*redacted*]." On declassifying White's intelligence report, the government removed del Gracio's confession.

White was obtaining incredible information, but he eventually interrupted del Gracio and asked him to leave. White was expecting other guests soon and it would look suspicious to have a notorious gangster sitting on his couch when they arrived.

Two days later, del Gracio returned to the apartment. White took the opportunity to give him two more tainted cigarettes. Within half an hour, del Gracio named multiple public officials who were being extorted or had taken bribes. He also claimed that he could arrange to have labor leader John L. Lewis murdered for organizing a number of coal strikes that hurt the American economy and war effort.

Del Gracio leaned back in his chair and closed his eyes. The room was spinning. He felt pins and needles sticking in his hands. He didn't know what was wrong with him, and White didn't want him to start jumping to conclusions. In a bout of quick thinking, White handed him a glass of brandy. Del Gracio drank it and collapsed onto the couch. When he woke up an hour later, White told him not to worry, he was probably just feeling weak because he hadn't eaten all day—drinking liquor on an empty stomach sometimes has that effect.

Del Gracio never suspected that he had been drugged. After all, White was a Bureau of Narcotics agent, not a dope peddler. But White had indeed been doling out drugs, and he was enthusiastic about their powers. He concluded in his report, "There is no question but that the administration of the drug was responsible for loosening the subject's tongue."

Following the successful experiments on del Gracio, the Truth Drug Committee sent White and an unnamed lawyer to military bases in Memphis, Atlanta, and New Orleans to give the tainted cigarettes to soldiers suspected of harboring communist sympathies. The lawyer later described the duo's modus operandi:

Before we went in, George and I would buy cigarettes, remove them from the bottom of the pack, use a hypodermic needle to put in the fluid, and leave the cigarette in a shot glass to dry. Then, we resealed the pack. . . . We sat down with a particular soldier and tried to win his confidence. We would say something like "This is better than being overseas and getting shot at," and we would try to break them. We started asking questions from their [FBI] folder, and we would let them see that we had the folder on them. . . . We had a pitcher of ice water on the table, and we knew the drug had taken effect when they reached for a glass. The stuff actually worked. . . . Everyone but one—and he didn't smoke—gave us more information than we had before.

The lawyer once tried the cigarettes for himself and said that they gave him "a feeling of walking a couple of feet off the floor. I had a pleasant sensation of well-being." For fun, he gave them to a few of his unsuspecting colleagues. Afterward, he said, "The fellows from my office wouldn't take a cigarette from me for the rest of the war."

The scientists in the R&D Branch conducted other truth drug experiments with varying results. They once interrogated forty OSS personnel, half of whom were high, and counted the number of words that they spoke per minute. The subjects who smoked the tainted cigarettes spoke 40 percent more than those who didn't. Predictably, they also showed signs of increased hunger and relaxation. Some of them became nauseous, but that was the extent of their negative side effects.

Meanwhile, Harry Anslinger was busy calling marijuana "highly dangerous" in public, saying that it led to "mental deterioration" and "insanity," and alleging that marijuana users were "irresponsible and liable to commit violent crimes" because the drug put them in a "delirious rage."

Stanley Lovell was personally involved in at least one other truth drug experiment. Toward the end of the war, he visited a prisoner-of-war camp in Virginia where an American Army officer was interrogating a distinguished German submarine commander, possibly Werner Henke. The interrogator wanted to extract two main pieces of information: the depth to which German submarines could dive and the state of morale among German submarine crews. Lovell could see that the interrogator wasn't making any progress, so during a break, he handed him two cigarettes. One was normal, the other was laced with THC.

The interrogator walked back into the room and offered the German a cigarette. Lovell eavesdropped on their conversation through a speaker connected to a microphone in the room.

Nothing about the German's steadfast demeanor changed. He refused to say much of anything, and when he did talk, he only revealed cursory information. The interrogator, however, gradually became more voluble. At one point, he announced, "I'm going to tell you something, Heine," his nickname for the German. "My boss, Major Quinn, is making passes at my wife. I'm going to shoot him sure as hell if he doesn't stop it." The cigarettes had apparently been switched. A colonel eavesdropping with Lovell leaned over and said, "Our boy has your truth drug. This ought to be real good!"

The interrogator launched into a tirade against Major Quinn loud enough for everyone in the vicinity to hear, with or without the speaker. Lovell never repeated what was said, but he described the outburst as "virile, forthright, vulgar and no doubt so slanderous a court-martial was indicated." The eavesdropping colonel shrugged it off: "He's doped—doesn't know what he's saying."

Lovell thought the same thing—until the next morning when his assistant sheepishly admitted that he had accidentally packed the wrong supplies the previous day. The cigarettes hadn't contained the truth drug at all. But if that was true, Lovell wondered, then what would explain the interrogator's behavior?

Lovell eventually solved of the puzzle. The interrogator had purposefully smoked what he thought was the tainted cigarette because he wanted an excuse to threaten his superior for eyeing his wife. Lovell was more impressed than mad. "There's more than one way to tell off your boss," he said, "but only a clever opportunist can do it in uniform and be exempt from even a reprimand."

General Donovan disbanded the Truth Drug Committee not long after he learned about George White's successful experiments on August del Gracio. His motivations for doing so are unclear, but he may have been anxious about the potential political turmoil over such a program or reluctant to undermine the rights of prisoners of war as established in the Geneva Conventions, or he may have feared retaliation against Allied prisoners if the experiments became widely known. Whatever the reason, Donovan made it clear to the Truth Drug Committee that he "did not want to know more about the subject."

In the end, the truth drug proved to be about as effective as alcohol. It did slightly increase talkativeness, but as one counterintelligence officer said, "If you have a blowtorch up someone's ass," they'll talk. Like torture, the truth drug could get someone to talk, but it couldn't guarantee that they would tell the truth. An R&D Branch summary report on truth drugs concludes with a single solemn sentence, "Indications are that uninhibited truthfulness cannot be obtained by this method."

Dr. Robert House had been wrong to think that he had found a drug that could prevent someone from inventing lies, and so was the R&D Branch. The truth drug had been a pipe dream from the very beginning.

Little else is known about American efforts to administer truth drugs in World War II. The historical record doesn't say, for instance, whether they were ever used in the field. Nevertheless, one cunning colonel fighting in the jungles of Burma came up with something even better.

Carl Eifler, the "Mastodon Incarnate" leader of Detachment 101, never received truth drugs from Lovell, but he acted as if he had. In late 1943, a U.S. fighter plane in Burma shot down a Japanese pilot, who crash-landed in a Kachin village. The Kachins, loyal to the Americans, agreed to detain the pilot until someone from Detachment 101 could come get him. But there was a problem. Detachment 101 headquarters in Nazira was dozens of miles away across impenetrable jungle terrain. How could the Americans retrieve this valuable prisoner?

Eifler devised a plan. He ordered the Kachins to sneak the Japanese pilot to the nearest airstrip. Eifler himself would fly in on a rudimentary 1920s-era British biplane, snag the pilot, and fly back to Nazira where he could administer an interrogation.

There were plenty of obstacles to overcome for the plan to work. Eifler assumed that on the return flight, the Japanese pilot would try to crash the plane in an attempt to kill them both.

Eifler therefore asked a hospital in Chabua to send him a drug that could incapacitate the pilot for the short duration of the flight. The hospital obliged and sent Eifler a syringe full of pentothal, a rapid-onset central nervous system depressant and general anesthetic.

Eifler flew to the secluded jungle airstrip. When he reached the Japanese pilot, he tied a tourniquet around his arm, plunged the needle into his vein, and injected the pentothal. The pilot fainted within minutes. Eifler then strapped his limp body into the back seat of the plane. For added security, he placed a noose around his neck and held onto the other end of the rope. If the pilot woke up in the middle of the flight and caused any trouble, Eifler would strangle him to death.

On the return flight, Eifler ran into a blinding rainstorm. He could barely see in front of him and was forced to navigate by instruments alone. To make matters worse, he was surrounded by towering mountains. One wrong turn, or even a slight change of direction, and he would crash. Regardless, he somehow managed to return to Nazira with the pilot still incapacitated.

When the pilot woke up, Eifler used an interpreter to ask him to locate his base on a map. The pilot refused to answer. Question after question, he remained silent. But Eifler did glean something from the interrogation. By watching the pilot's involuntary reactions to the questions—a slight grimace here, a twitch of the eye there—he suspected that the pilot secretly understood English. Eifler hatched a sneaky plan to prove his hunch.

On Eifler's command, a doctor walked into the room and placed a syringe, a needle, and a vial of "truth serum" onto a wooden table. Eifler paced back and forth, audibly murmuring to himself, "I just don't want to do this to this man." For dramatic effect, he walked over to a window and looked outside as if in deep contemplation. "Chang," he said to the interpreter, "see if he won't tell us anything." Again, the interpreter asked a question. Again, no answer. "You know," Eifler said, "I hate to do this and dishonor a fellow officer, don't you?" His voice was filled with regret. "I would rather have killed him than do this now. Chang, try again so we can spare him." But again, the pilot remained silent.

Eifler turned to the waiting doctor. "Well, you see I have no other choice. Go ahead." After giving the command, he walked toward the door, indicating that he couldn't bear to watch what was about to happen.

"Wait, I'll talk!" the pilot screamed in fear. Eifler stopped mid-stride, feigning surprise that the pilot had just spoken English. The performance had worked. The pilot revealed the location of his base, south of Mandalay. Within a week, a squadron of B-25 bombers destroyed it. Ironically, the mere threat of a truth drug was more effective than any of the truth drugs that the R&D Branch tested.

There exists one intriguing hint that the R&D Branch performed other truth drug experiments beyond what's acknowledged in its declassified files. Hours into a 1964 interview, Vannevar Bush said that whenever Stanley Lovell encountered a tough problem, "He'd come to me about it" for help. One of those problems was "when lysergic acid showed up and it was regarded as a very dangerous thing and put under wraps." According to Bush, the R&D Branch injected this substance into cigarettes, just as it had done with THC, but instead of giving someone the munchies or making them laugh, it "would give a man symptoms of schizophrenia for some seven or eight hours. It looked like a very dangerous affair."

In 1938, chemist Albert Hofmann had first synthesized a

hallucinogenic drug called lysergic acid diethylamide (LSD) at the Sandoz pharmaceutical company in Switzerland. It initially aroused little interest in the physicians and pharmacologists at Sandoz, leading the company to shelve it for the next five years. But during that time, Hofmann held a nagging suspicion that LSD had more to offer.

In the spring of 1943, he re-synthesized the compound for further examination. During the process, twenty micrograms of LSD, equivalent to the weight of a single eyelash, accidentally contacted his skin and gave him unusual sensations. Three days later, his interest piqued, Hofmann purposefully ingested 250 micrograms of LSD. Within half an hour, he was "affected by a remarkable restlessness, combined with a slight dizziness," he recalled. When he got home that day, "I lay down and sank into a not-unpleasant intoxicated-like condition, characterized by an extremely stimulated imagination. In a dreamlike state, with eyes closed (I found the daylight to be unpleasantly glaring), I perceived an uninterrupted stream of fantastic pictures, extraordinary shapes with intense, kaleidoscopic play of colors." He had just experienced the world's first acid trip.

It was previously assumed that the American intelligence community obtained LSD in the late 1940s or early 1950s, around the time when a handful of declassified CIA memos describe the substance. "Tasteless, odorless and capable of easily being concealed," one memo says, a heavy dose of LSD "could rest on the head of a pin." Another memo calls LSD the most potent "of all substances now known to affect the mind." In 1953, Harris Chadwell, who had since joined the CIA, wrote, "An infinitesimally small dose will produce mental derangement."

Bush's interview shows that Lovell had obtained LSD, or a similar lysergic acid derivative, years before previously thought. And what was he doing with the drug? Presumably human experimentation. After all, Bush knew that it "would give a man symptoms of schizophrenia for some seven or eight hours."

During his interview, Bush discussed the long-term influence of those experiments. "At the end of the war," he said, "this sort of thing went over to the CIA. And they've continued with it. I had some relations with CIA at various times when they asked me to look into things and so forth."

Stanley Lovell's most consequential legacy wasn't the deadly weapons, cunning schemes, forged documents, or secret disguises that the R&D Branch created. It was the inspiration that his truth drug experiments gave to a new generation of CIA scientists who would conduct one of the most infamous programs in American history.

17
Lovell's Twilight

On April 30, 1945, with Germany surrounded and the Allies advancing on Berlin, Adolf Hitler descended into the bowels of the *Führerbunker* and shot himself in the right temple. His wife of one day, Eva Braun, killed herself with a cyanide pill. Those who found their bodies noted the distinct smell of almonds present in the room.

Three weeks after the Allied victory in Europe, General Dwight Eisenhower issued a statement praising the spies and saboteurs whom the R&D Branch had supplied: "I consider that the disruption of enemy rail communications, the harassing of German road moves and the continual and increasing strain placed on the German war economy and internal security services throughout occupied Europe by the organized forces of the resistance, played a very considerable part in our complete and final victory." General George Marshall similarly noted that the resistance movement "has surpassed all our expectation, and it was they who, in delaying the arrival of German reinforcements and in preventing the regrouping of enemy divisions in the interior, assured the success of our landings." In fact, many of America's top military leaders issued statements praising the OSS for its work, including Henry "Hap" Arnold, Matthew Ridgway, Walter Bedell Smith, Carl Spaatz, and Joseph Stilwell.

But not all of the assessments of the OSS were positive. Some people still mocked the organization as vigorously as they had when it was created. Benjamin Dixon, a U.S. Army intelligence officer celebrating the Allied victory in a small town in Belgium, drunkenly acknowledged that the OSS was a "fantastic damn organization" whose personnel "seduce German spies; they parachute into Sicily one day and two days later they're dancing on the St. Regis roof. They dynamite aqueducts, urinate in Luftwaffe gas tanks, and play games with I.G. Farben and Krupp, but," he waved his arms in the air, "ninety per cent of this has not a goddamned thing to do with the war."

Colonel Richard Park, also of Army intelligence, launched the most aggressive campaign to discredit the OSS. In April 1945, President Roosevelt asked Park to make an informal assessment of the organization to determine whether it should continue in peacetime. The resulting report was full of unsubstantiated rumors and blatant distortions of the record. Its main theme was that the OSS consisted of bumbling amateurs who had leaked secrets, wasted government funds, and engaged in ill-advised and unauthorized activities. Regarding Area F, the OSS training camp at the Congressional Country Club, Park wrote, "The main purpose of this school was to subject a man to liquor tests to see how he would react to drinking," a dig at Lovell's truth drug experiments. "If the OSS is permitted to continue," he warned, "it may do serious harm to citizens, business interests and national interests of the United States."

General Donovan lobbied for the OSS to continue in peacetime, but in light of the Park Report, President Harry Truman, Roosevelt's successor, issued an executive order dissolving it. The Research and Analysis Branch was transferred to the State Department and the intelligence agents were transferred to the War Department, but everything else was liquidated, including the R&D Branch. Almost overnight, the OSS headquarters "seemed to become a mausoleum," said Elizabeth MacDonald when she returned from her assignment in China. "There was no bustle, no urgency. There were no people. I felt something like the returning Confederate soldier looking over the burned-off ground that had once been his home."

On September 28, 1945, two thousand OSS personnel gathered at the Riverside Roller Skating Rink and listened to Donovan give a farewell message:

> We have come to the end of an unusual experiment. This experiment was to determine whether a group of Americans constituting a cross section of racial origins, of abilities, temperaments, and talents could meet and risk an encounter with the long-established and well-trained enemy organizations. How well that experiment has succeeded is measured by your accomplishments and by the recognitions of your achievements. . . .
>
> When I speak of your achievements that does not mean we did not make mistakes. We were not afraid to make mistakes because we were not afraid to try things that had not been tried before. All of us would like to think that we could have done a better job, but all of you must know that, whatever the errors or failures, you have done an honest and self-respecting job. But more than

that, because there existed in this organization a sense of solidarity, you must also have the conviction that this agency, in which each of you played a part, was an effective force.

Within a few days each one of us will be going to new tasks whether in civilian life or in government work. You can go with the assurance that you have made a beginning in showing the people of America that only by decisions of national policy based upon accurate information can we have the chance of a peace that will endure.

Donovan himself would go on to join the staff of the Nuremberg trials where he interviewed Holocaust survivors and tracked down other evidence of Germany's war crimes. Afterward, he resumed his law practice, unsuccessfully ran for the Senate, and in 1953 became the ambassador to Thailand. While serving as ambassador, he began suffering from dementia, which ultimately took his life on February 8, 1959. When President Dwight Eisenhower learned of Donovan's death, he remarked, "What a man! We have lost the last hero."

Before the OSS was officially dissolved in late 1945, Stanley Lovell left the organization to care for his sick wife. His mother had unexpectedly died of illness when he was a child, and he was determined not to let the same fate befall the most important woman in his life. Soon after his departure from the OSS, Howard Dix told Moe Berg that Donovan was "very greatly disappointed" about losing Lovell. "We are all going to miss Stan but I imagine that he will drop in here every once in a while."

On the advice of German historian Oswald Spengler, Lovell had joined the war effort to defend democracy against dictatorship. At the beginning of the war, he had been reluctant to create the kinds of dirty tricks that Wild Bill Donovan expected of his Professor Moriarty, but his views changed when he rationalized that the death and destruction of conventional warfare was no different than the death and destruction of unconventional warfare. What difference did it make if a saboteur planted an explosive or a plane dropped it from the sky? Or if a soldier died from anthrax or an infected wound? Or if an enemy battalion was felled by machine guns or chemical weapons? Or if a city was destroyed by firebombing or an atomic bomb?

Lovell never developed any of the compunctions that haunted Robert Oppenheimer, the father of the atomic bomb, who came to believe that "the physicists have known sin." As far as Lovell was concerned, the only sin would have been to prolong the worst war in human history. Forget the precedent that employing weapons of mass destruction would set for the future. Millions of people were needlessly dying in the present.

No doubt influencing Lovell's opinion was the fact that on the very day that the atomic bomb razed Hiroshima, his only son, Richard, stood on a boat midway across the Pacific waiting to participate in an invasion of Japan.

Throughout the war, Lovell had been surrounded by highly credentialed colleagues. The Maryland Research Laboratory alone employed nine Ph.D. scientists. In 1946, Lovell decided to get a doctorate of his own, albeit not in the traditional sense. His friend Roger Adams, a former member of the Truth Drug

Committee, helped him obtain one through a diploma mill. Afterward, Lovell wrote Adams a comical poem of gratitude:

> By the Turkman Gate in Delhi sits an Abdul Vizatelli
> Who has doctorates in science there for sale.
> With a sponsor who is famous you can get a writ
>   mandamus
> Or a genuine Ph-D through the mail.
> Now I knew at bets and poker Roger never played a joker
> So I only did the things he told me to.
> And I say it at my peril—be the New Year fine or sterile,
> All my academic honors stem from you.

Lovell's most cherished credential came two years later when President Truman awarded him the Presidential Medal for Merit, at the time the highest civilian decoration of the United States. The doctorate had scored him an ego boost, but the Medal for Merit was a source of genuine pride for the rest of his life.

The OSS had been dissolved, but the United States wasn't without a centralized intelligence organization for long. In January 1946, President Truman established the postwar successor to the OSS, the Central Intelligence Group (soon to become the Central Intelligence Agency). A year later, Hoyt Vandenberg, the new director of Central Intelligence, offered "Dr." Lovell the opportunity to head an updated version of the R&D Branch for three more years. Lovell was initially interested in the position, but he declined after learning that Vandenberg would be stepping down a few months later.

Lovell occasionally did consulting work for the CIA. For the most part, though, he traded in his cloak and dagger for a suit and briefcase. After the war, he returned to the world of private business and formed the Lovell Chemical Company. "Better Products Through Research" its slogan proclaimed. (Vannevar Bush said that the slogan "certainly sticks out your chin and asks for it.") Over the next thirty years, Lovell obtained dozens of patents, many of which dealt with the construction of shoes. His other patents involved products as varied as splints, gas masks, petri dishes, vacuum cleaners, and packing containers.

Lovell made a small fortune when his company won an Army contract to manufacture water filters. Neither he nor his company had actually invented the filters. Instead, he had gotten their design as a sort of "intellectual reparations." In the wake of World War II, while Germany lay in ruins, government agencies and private companies, including Lovell's, pilfered the country's patents and business records. Some estimates have placed the value of the stolen intellectual property as high as $10 billion. Lovell obtained his share when he demonstrated that he could mass-produce the German filters, leading to the Army contract. He then sold the rights to the filter technology for $200,000 to his employee John Bush, Vannevar Bush's son, who formed the Millipore Filter Corporation. Among other things, Millipore would go on to produce the filters for the Apollo astronauts on their missions to space.

In 1947, Lovell wrote to Vannevar Bush—strangely enough in the third person—about his rationale for starting the Lovell Chemical Company. "A person whom I know very well," meaning himself, "decided after leaving war work, not to return to the employ of a large corporation, but to start his own business. His motives were not only a desire for profit, but a sincere belief that small enterprise was more wholesome for the country, that relations with labor would be on a more personal basis, and that all in all it would be more fun for everybody concerned." The company prospered "due to the times, a lot of good luck and some mature judgment." And the German filters.

Lovell never tired of telling war stories to anyone who would listen, and those who listened rarely tired of hearing them. His neighbor Erwin Canham, the editor of *The Christian Science Monitor,* said that he "never forgot with what fascination our group of breathless neighbors sat around in a circle" and listened to Lovell tell stories of "inventive adventure."

Lovell had been interested in the craft of storytelling ever since his days of editing the student newspaper at Cornell. He hadn't written for a popular audience since his visit to Oswald Spengler in 1934, but now that he had more stories to tell, he gave it another try. In 1963, he published a memoir of his war years, *Of Spies and Stratagems* (forming the acronym "OSS"). He prefaced the book with a warning: "To the best of my belief these accounts are truthful, but much of what I have to tell was so sensitive a nature that it is truth based more on my trust of individuals than on documents." A handful of reviewers panned the book for being full of exaggerations. Lovell defended himself against the criticism, once telling a newspaper reporter, "Not one word—so help me God—not one word in that book is not the truth!"

But the reviewers had a point. Although many of the stories in the book are corroborated by archival records and independent sources, some aren't. It's possible, and in some cases probable, that Lovell embellished the truth. For example, the book includes the fanciful story of how in mid-1943 Lovell received a mysterious order to report to the Pentagon, the nation's military headquarters. The United States had recently suffered a demoralizing defeat against Axis forces in the Battle of Kasserine Pass, resulting in ten thousand American casualties and the loss of fifty miles of terrain. In a secret meeting with a group of anonymous military officials, Lovell was asked to develop something, anything, to destroy the German forces stationed in Spanish Morocco.

As Lovell told it, he developed a secret plan called Operation Capricious (a play on words, *capri* meaning "goat" in Latin). The plan called for dropping goat dung from airplanes onto German bases in Morocco. The dung itself would be harmless, but not its added ingredients. Lovell would lace the dung with tularemia, an infectious disease that causes fever, ulcers, skin lesions, enlarged lymph nodes, and in some cases death. The dung would attract aggressive Moroccan houseflies, which would disseminate tularemia to the German soldiers. The beauty of the plan lay in the fact that the American hand was hidden. The Germans wouldn't know the origins of this specific outbreak, and therefore they wouldn't retaliate with biological weapons of their own.

According to Lovell, Operation Capricious never got off the ground because, before its implementation, Germany recalled its troops from Morocco and sent them to fight against the Soviets in the horrific battle of Stalingrad, one of the bloodiest battles in world history. At Stalingrad, bombs, tanks, rifles, grenades, snipers, bayonets, machine guns, and artillery shells turned the icy Russian city into an unrecognizable moonscape. In the aftermath of the battle, barbed wire, busted debris, and body parts littered the ground. Russian children used frozen German corpses as sleds. Few of the city's buildings were left standing, and the ones that were consisted of little more than mangled shells. Lovell was relieved that the Germans had left Morocco before the United States instigated biological warfare, but he couldn't help but feel sorry for them given the alternative.

At least that's what he wrote in his book. There are two reasons to doubt this story. First, no evidence corroborating Operation Capricious has ever been found. Secondly, and most convincingly, the chronology of the story doesn't make any sense. The Battle of Kasserine Pass happened after the Battle of Stalingrad.

Vannevar Bush took Lovell's book much more seriously than the reviewers did. In a postwar interview, he said that it "spilled the whole affair" about OSS secret methods. "I think there are too many suggestions in that bag of tricks for, oh bank robbers or something of the sort."

Shortly after the book was published, Lovell wrote a surprisingly candid letter to Richard Helms, a former OSS officer and the head of the CIA Directorate of Plans. In the letter, Lovell revealed that he had purposefully written the book "in a light vein with some (attempted) humor in order that it would be read by young men and women, and their interests directed to C.I.A. recruitment." He then suggested that Helms meet with him to discuss "several of the plans we never used, but which I held to be so potentially powerful I can never put them in writing."

Helms responded the following week. He was particularly pleased that Lovell had written the book in a way to help recruitment. Helms and Allen Dulles, the head of the CIA, had long encouraged authors to romanticize the intelligence community in an effort to boost its reputation. Dulles even fed plots to Helen MacInnes, a popular author of espionage novels.

As for Lovell's suggestion to discuss "plans we never used,"

Helms said that he had passed the word along to Sidney Gottlieb, "a senior officer now intimately concerned with the specialized problems that were once yours." Unbeknownst to Helms, Gottlieb already knew plenty about Lovell and the R&D Branch.

Besides writing his memoir, Lovell's other postwar hobbies included painting, gardening, and playing the piano. He also read the great plays of history, a hobby that morphed into an obsession. A skeptic at heart, he became convinced that William Shakespeare wasn't the true author of the works that bear his name. Lovell instead subscribed to the Oxfordian theory of Shakespearean authorship, which claims that Edward de Vere, the seventeenth Earl of Oxford, actually wrote Shakespeare's plays.

Lovell became so obsessed with the issue that he wrote a short pamphlet, "A Mystery Beyond Words," to prove the Oxfordian theory. "Come with me into the greatest detective problem ever posed," he teased his readers in the opening paragraphs. "I can promise a most interesting plot."

Lovell flat-out dismissed the idea that William Shakespeare, "an unschooled, penny-pinching peasant from Stratford," could have achieved the genius displayed in the writing attributed to him. He then denounced the claim that Francis Bacon was the author of Shakespeare's plays: "It was so absurd—every reference to 'pig' or 'ham' was held to really mean 'bacon.'" Finally, he gave his own "proofs" for why de Vere was the true author. In one proof, he noted how Elizabethan writers "delighted in concealing their names in cryptograms and double meanings." Perhaps the true author concealed his name somewhere. Lo and behold, Lovell found what he was looking for in a line from sonnet seventy-six: "That every word doth almost tell my name." He rewrote the line to reveal the hidden message: "E. Ver-y word doth almost tell my name." And what name doth the word "E. Ver-y" almost tell? De Vere. Voilà. Never mind that de Vere died before several of Shakespeare's plays were written.

Throughout his later years, Lovell maintained a cordial correspondence with Vannevar Bush. In general, the conversations between the chemist and the engineer were as amusing as their personalities. Bush once asked Lovell for the names of the books that had been loaned to him. Bush couldn't remember because he was in the hospital and "so full of coke I could hardly see out of the window."

On another occasion, Lovell wrote to Bush about the benefits of painting with tapered nylon monofilament brushes. He considered himself an amateur painter, but, he said, "I do a whole lot better job than Picasso." Bush began a letter in response, "Dear Stan, I want to have an argument with you about painting techniques."

Bush once inquired about their mutual interest in fishing. (Bush often went fishing with former president Herbert Hoover.) He asked if Lovell could "get one of your youngsters who can work a slide rule, if chemists ever use slide rules," to fabricate a transparent fish hook. Bush was sure that the hook "would inevitably sell like hot cakes." He added, "I have a few ideas on it but do not wish to spoil your fun."

Lovell immediately began devising a variety of glass and plastic hooks. The effort "has provoked as much trial and error as ever engaged a Division of NDRC," he wrote to Bush. In a follow-up letter, he penned a short poem on the matter:

> O! What a tangled web we weave
> When first we practice to deceive

The fish.
All plastic fishhooks drive us mad
To rather use an iron brad
I wish.

Two years and one week after Bush's original request for a transparent hook, Lovell claimed to have found a solution "which will completely remove all sportsmanship from angling and so stack the cards against the finny tribe that it will be like taking candy from small children." He never lost his childlike enthusiasm for invention.

In 1962, at the height of the Cold War, Lovell wrote a short magazine article for *The Saturday Evening Post* reflecting on the "devilish" devices of the R&D Branch. "Some were undramatic," he said. "Some were rather funny, at least to us. And some, of course, were weapons of death and destruction." Among his favorites were the Beano grenade, Aunt Jemima exploding flour, and the silenced .22 automatic pistol.

Two photographs of the elder Lovell accompany the article. In one, he's sitting in his office, wearing a sophisticated suit and glasses. His dark hair is slicked back. In his right hand is a Beano grenade. In his left hand is a silenced .22 pointed at the ceiling, his finger on the trigger. He appears refined and confident. James Bond couldn't have struck a better pose. This is the image that Lovell pictured when he thought of himself.

The second photograph portrays Lovell in a completely different light, both literally and figuratively. An eerie glow illuminates a blank wall behind him. He sits in shadow facing the camera, his face lit from below as if he were about to tell a ghost story. His wrinkles are deep and his jowls are heavy. Four elaborate daggers levitate in the foreground, framing his smirking face. He appears spooky and eccentric. This is the image that others pictured when they thought of Lovell. (He later said that it had taken the "Demon Photographer" four hours "to get that Fu Manchu picture. I swear he blew a black powder on my sweaty face, insulted me beyond sufferance and sure got a picture to scare the little children.")

At the end of the article, Lovell stopped reflecting on the past and turned his attention toward the present. "Doctor Moriarty"—he couldn't resist flaunting his Ph.D.—"disappeared into the somewhat anticlimactic role of an industrial scientist. The kind of dirty tricks which boiled up from his witches' cauldron have not been in demand. But looking at the world now, a man can perhaps be forgiven for wondering if they may not be needed again." Curiously enough, just such a program was already underway.

18
A Legacy of Lessons

In 1951, Stanley Lovell had an occasion to consult for the CIA. Allen Dulles wanted advice on whether he should create a branch within the CIA to develop dirty tricks, similar to what the R&D Branch had done for the OSS. Lovell was emphatic that he should. "Warfare is no longer a matter of chivalry but of subversion," he told him, "and subversion has its own special arsenal of tools and weapons. Only Research and Development is capable of creating such an arsenal." On Lovell's advice, Dulles created the Technical Services Staff (TSS), the CIA successor to the OSS R&D Branch.

What did the TSS do? In a series of legal depositions from the 1980s, attorney Thomas Maddox asked Sidney Gottlieb, a former head of the TSS, "Did it produce the gadgets and things we have associated with James Bond?" The kinds of things that Lovell had done?

"That's the right idea," Gottlieb said. "You are in the right ballpark."

When Gottlieb had joined the TSS in the summer of 1951 shortly after its creation, he had worked on the "more classical application of chemistry to the intelligence field, things like secret writing, the use of chemistry in the printing process, areas like that." The TSS resembled Lovell's R&D Branch in both spirit and function. In fact, the similarities went much deeper than that.

Sidney Gottlieb was an odd man. Born in New York City on August 3, 1918, to Orthodox Jewish immigrants from Hungary, he talked with a stutter, walked with a limp (because of a club foot), and compulsively drank goat milk. He was always a little bit different.

He was also unusually smart. In 1940, he graduated from the University of Wisconsin with a bachelor's degree in chemistry. His mentor at Wisconsin, Ira Baldwin (the same Ira Baldwin who would work with Lovell on biological weapons), wrote in a glowing letter of recommendation, "Mr. Gottlieb is a very high type of Jewish boy. . . . He has a brilliant mind, is thoroughly honest and reliable, and is modest and unassuming." In 1943, Gottlieb earned his doctorate—legitimately—in bio-organic chemistry from the California Institute of Technology.

Eight years later, Gottlieb joined the TSS. He had been there for only two years when, in 1953, he was asked to lead what would become one of the most infamous programs in American history, a secret CIA effort to study mind control. This program would eventually grow to encompass 149 subprojects, some of which involved dangerous—even deadly—experiments on prisoners, mental patients, government officials, and random, unwitting, nonconsenting citizens. It was called MKULTRA.

Gottlieb would later stress that in order to understand MKULTRA, it was necessary to understand the context in which it was created. At the beginning of the Cold War, the CIA "felt that the Soviet Union, and perhaps Red China, and other potential enemies of this country, were in possession of techniques that either were being used or could potentially be used in this country that we had no understanding of. And these techniques were particularly methods of influencing the human mind to make a person behave in some specified manner that was desired by an enemy." The CIA feared that its enemies possessed unknown methods of mind control and would use them for nefarious ends.

Such a fear wasn't as strange as it sounds, and Gottlieb knew that it sounded strange. "I might add all of this might seem far-fetched now. But I would beg you to try to live in another context, namely that of 30 years ago, when it was—" He paused. "Things were thought possible then."

There were many reasons why Gottlieb and others within the CIA believed that China, the Soviet Union, and potentially other countries possessed methods of mind control. For one, Soviet dictator Joseph Stalin had led a series of show trials in the 1930s to remove his political opponents from influential positions in the Communist Party. Strangely, many of the defendants vehemently agreed that they were guilty. Why? Perhaps, Gottlieb thought, because they had been drugged, hypnotized, or subjected to some other form of mind control.

Even more alarming was the fact that during the Korean War, dozens of American prisoners of war falsely claimed to have conducted biological warfare against the Koreans. Several downed

American pilots said that their bomber payloads had included anthrax, typhus, cholera, and bubonic plague. Why had they confessed to false crimes? Had the Koreans or Chinese subjected them to mind control? Director of Central Intelligence Allen Dulles wanted to determine whether such a thing was possible. On April 13, 1953, at the urging of Richard Helms, he established MKULTRA under the direction of Sidney Gottlieb.

MKULTRA wasn't the first CIA program dedicated to studying mind control. Two earlier programs, code-named Bluebird and Artichoke, investigated the phenomenon with tepid interest. Many of the experiments conducted under these programs involved hypnotism. Morse Allen, the head of Bluebird, routinely hypnotized his secretaries into performing unconscionable acts, such as shooting each other with a gun (which Allen would unload when they weren't looking). Overall, the results of his experiments were inconclusive. Allen wasn't sure if the hypnotism had worked or if his secretaries were simply indulging him because they didn't want to upset their boss.

Under Gottlieb's direction, MKULTRA took the mind control experiments to a new level. Many of the early MKULTRA experiments involved drugging unwitting subjects with LSD to see how it affected their behavior. Gottlieb even hired renowned magician John Mulholland to teach the TSS personnel how to slip drugs into drinks without getting caught. Thereafter, it wasn't unusual for a prankster to spike the office coffee pot.

Within the CIA, the TSS was well-known for performing these irresponsible pranks. Gottlieb often told the story of a time when he was flying back to Washington, D.C. He walked up the narrow aisle of the plane and asked the stewardess for a martini. As he returned to his seat, a man smoking a pipe stopped him

and nonchalantly asked, "Is that LSD you're drinking?" The man
was Allen Dulles.

The irresponsible pranks soon got out of hand. Throughout
the early 1950s, two groups of scientists occasionally met at a
scenic two-story stone cabin on Deep Creek Lake in Maryland
to discuss their ongoing work, exchange research results, and,
if time allowed, try their hands at some fishing. One group was
from the TSS. The other was from Camp Detrick, the country's
main biological warfare installation, which Stanley Lovell and
Ira Baldwin had helped establish. More specifically, the latter
group was from a secret division within Camp Detrick called
the Special Operations Division (SOD), which developed special weapons and gadgets. Gottlieb said that the SOD "was very
much like the earlier Division 19."

In November 1953, four scientists from the TSS, including
Gottlieb and his underling Robert Lashbrook, met with seven
scientists from the SOD at the cabin on Deep Creek Lake for
one of their periodic work retreats. As dusk fell on November
19, Gottlieb and Lashbrook decided to conduct an impromptu
experiment. They secretly slipped a small amount of LSD into a
Cointreau liquor bottle and started pouring drinks.

Twenty minutes later, most of the men who had been dosed
began laughing uncontrollably. Their conversations became unin-
telligible. The walls of the cabin began to spin. At 1:00 A.M., everyone stumbled to their rooms and went to sleep. Everyone, that is,
except for a restless Frank Olson.

Olson was a bacteriologist specializing in aerobiology within
the SOD. He had gotten a job at Camp Detrick through the
machinations of Ira Baldwin, his former thesis advisor at Wisconsin. When Olson returned home from the Deep Creek retreat,

his wife, Alice, remembered him being "a totally different person," she said in a later deposition. He was short with his words, devoid of affection, and extremely paranoid.

Four days later, the Olsons ate lunch with Vincent Ruwet and John Malinowski, both of whom had attended the Deep Creek retreat. When Malinowski went to the bathroom, Frank Olson whispered to his wife, "I can't eat this food. It's poisoned."

"It stopped me cold," Alice recalled. "This was a rational man who I suddenly realized was not rational."

Gottlieb and Lashbrook similarly noticed a change in Olson's personality. Out of concern, they arranged for him to see Dr. Harold Abramson, a physician with experience taking and administering LSD. Abramson was known for throwing LSD parties that got "wild and crazy, right along with all the sex and what have you," one participant said. Abramson was also a cleared consultant for the CIA.

Ruwet and Lashbrook accompanied Olson to Abramson's office in New York City. Olson behaved normally, at least until Ruwet and Lashbrook left the room. "As soon as these gentlemen left," Abramson wrote in his notes, "he showed greater anxiety about his sense of inadequacy." He insisted that his memory was poor, "that his work was inadequate, and that he was failing to live up to the expectations of his family and friends."

Abramson gave Olson the sedative Nembutal to calm his nerves, but Olson, overcome with extreme paranoia, found this suspicious. Before he went to bed that night, he confronted Ruwet in conspiratorial tones, "What's behind all this? Give me the low-down; What are they trying to do with me; are they checking me for security?" Ruwet had no idea what he was talking about.

Two days later, Olson, Ruwet, and Lashbrook returned to

Washington to spend Thanksgiving with their families. But Olson had a nervous breakdown when they arrived. Lashbrook agreed to accompany him back to New York while Ruwet stayed behind to notify Alice about the change of plans. Gottlieb picked up Olson and Lashbrook and drove them back to the airport. "It seemed to me that [Olson] was very mentally disturbed at this time," he wrote in a subsequent report.

In New York, Dr. Abramson diagnosed Olson as being in a "psychotic state which seemed to have been crystalized by an experiment in which Mr. Olson participated the preceding week," the LSD experiment at Deep Creek Lake. Olson agreed to commit himself to Chestnut Lodge, a sanitarium in Rockville, Maryland. Abramson made the necessary arrangements, but the sanitarium needed an extra day to prepare a room. Until then, Olson would have to bide his time.

The next day, November 27, Olson and Lashbrook checked into room 1018A of the Statler Hotel, across the street from Madison Square Garden. They spent the evening drinking martinis in the cocktail lounge, then they shared dinner at the Café Rouge. Before they went to sleep, Olson washed his socks in the sink while he and Lashbrook discussed what time that they needed to wake up to catch the morning flight to Maryland. Olson then called Alice to say that he would see her soon.

"Somewhere around 0230 Saturday morning I was awakened by a loud noise," Lashbrook wrote in his report of the incident. "Dr. Olson had crashed through the closed window blind and the closed window and he fell to his death." Armond Pastore, the hotel's night manager, saw Olson's body sprawled out on the Seventh Avenue sidewalk and ran to him. "His right hand clutched my arm and he raised his head slightly, his lips moving," Pastore remembered. "His eyes were wide with desperation. He wanted to tell me something, I leaned down closer to listen, but he took a deep breath and died."

In December 1953, CIA inspector general Lyman Kirkpatrick, a former OSS officer who had since contracted polio and lost the use of his legs, conducted an investigation into the Olson incident. His first action was to send an aide to interview Willis Gibbons, Sidney Gottlieb's immediate supervisor. During the interview, Gibbons explained that the TSS and SOD occasionally held work retreats to exchange information. Furthermore, he said that only three TSS scientists were cleared to enter SOD premises at Camp Detrick: Gottlieb, Lashbrook, and Henry Bortner. The only other outsider with access to the SOD was a New England chemist named Stanley Lovell.

Another connection between Lovell and the Olson incident was made in Kirkpatrick's diary. The entry from December 18, 1953, reads, "[Sheffield] Edwards and [Harris] Chadwell: advised me that Stanley Lovell had considerable information about the Olsen [sic] case." This was the same Chadwell who had led Division 19. After World War II, he became head of the CIA's Office of Scientific Intelligence, which specialized in compiling, analyzing, and interpreting scientific research conducted abroad.

Yet another tantalizing connection between Lovell and the Olson incident appears in a declassified CIA memo that summarizes a cryptic conversation between Chadwell and Willis Gibbons: "Lovell knew about Frank R. Olson. No inhibitions. Baring of inner man. Suicidal tendencies. Offensive usefulness?" Aside from Kirkpatrick's diary entry and this short summary of a conversation, whatever Lovell knew about Olson, his "suicidal tendencies," or his death remains a mystery. Perhaps he knew about the LSD experiment at Deep Creek Lake, knew that the drug removed "inhibitions," knew that it led Olson to bare his "inner man," and knew that it provoked his "suicidal tendencies." If so, then Lovell may have realized that LSD had "offensive usefulness." In other words, he may have thought that the Olson incident proved that LSD could be used to control, or at least alter, someone's behavior: to make them tell the truth in an interrogation, to make them appear foolish in front of others, or even to make them commit suicide.

Aside from Lovell's connection to the Olson incident, there were many other factors linking the OSS R&D Branch and the CIA's MKULTRA program. George White was one of them. White was the "fat slob" Bureau of Narcotics agent who had conducted truth drug experiments on gangster August del Gracio. Incidentally, when MKULTRA got started, Sidney Gottlieb was looking to hire someone to conduct truth drug experiments of his own. White's former work with the OSS served as his résumé.

But White's reputation preceded him, and others within the CIA had their reservations. In a personal diary kept against Agency rules, White wrote that after Gottlieb recruited him, "A couple of crew-cut, pipe-smoking punks had either known me or heard of me during the O.S.S. days and had decided I was 'too rough' for their league and promptly blackballed me. It was only when my sponsors discovered the root of the trouble they were able to bypass the blockade. After all, fellas, I didn't go to Princeton."

Gottlieb later said that Harry Anslinger, the commissioner of the Bureau of Narcotics, "certainly knew about our financial support" to White. "I certainly talked to Mr. Anslinger myself several times," though Gottlieb assumed that Anslinger would "disclaim all knowledge and responsibility in the event of compromise."

At one of their first meetings, Gottlieb accompanied White

on a car ride to Boston so that they could get acquainted. "Most of what we talked about," Gottlieb said, "was his work with the Division 19 truth drug program and other, related matters." Gottlieb grew fond of White, who he said was "always armed to the teeth with all sorts of weapons; he could be gruff and loutish, vulgar even, but then turn urbane to a point of eloquence."

True to form, White dubbed his secret MKULTRA subproject "Operation Midnight Climax." The provocative name hinted at its provocative nature. Beginning in June 1953, White established a "safe house" in Greenwich Village where he surreptitiously dosed his guests with drugs and reported their reactions back to Gottlieb. By now he had graduated from the OSS days of injecting THC into cigarettes. He instead used a hypodermic syringe to inject LSD through the cork of a wine bottle. "That period," recalled one retired CIA officer, "was a wild and woolly time at the CIA. It was the old OSS mentality: 'Go out and do it. Doesn't matter if it's a good or bad idea, go do it. We're at war, so anything is justified.'"

White tested most of the CIA drugs on himself, just as he had done for the OSS. "He always said he never felt a goddamn thing," said his protégé Ike Feldman. "He thought it was all bullshit. White drank so much booze, he couldn't feel his fucking cock."

In 1955, the Bureau of Narcotics transferred White to San Francisco. He quickly established another safe house at a beautiful apartment on Telegraph Hill, overlooking the Golden Gate Bridge. This time, he hired prostitutes to secretly slip the drugs to their clients. In exchange for their services, he paid the prostitutes $100 a night or gave them a veritable get-out-of-jail-free card with his personal phone number on it. All the while, White patrolled the streets of San Francisco by day, locking up junkies for illegal possession.

A declassified CIA inventory of the San Francisco safe house reveals the uncomfortable truth about what White was doing. Along with the furnishings of a typical home—rugs, drapes, lamps, pictures, throw pillows, a typewriter, a waste basket—the inventory includes a tripod, "dynamic microphones," audio and visual recording equipment, and a "handi-dandi portable toilet." Another CIA memo clarifies, "A 'window' was constructed in a bedroom wall to permit visual surveillance techniques." One CIA agent joked that the safe house was so wired for spying on its occupants "that if you spilled a glass of water you'd probably electrocute yourself." A spilled glass, though not containing water, wouldn't be out of place. White often guzzled booze in an apparent attempt to exceed his legendary constitution.

Inside the San Francisco safe house, from the perch of his $25 portable toilet, peering through a one-way mirror, drunk off the liquor that he bought with CIA funds, White secretly recorded his hired prostitutes drugging and bedding their unwitting clients.

Ike Feldman sometimes joined White on these indoor stakeouts. At least the sex, drugs, and surveillance were less violent than some of the other methods that he had used to obtain information in the past. "Sometimes," Feldman said, speaking of his early career at the Bureau of Narcotics, "when people had information, there was only one way you could get it. If it was a girl, you put her tits in a drawer and slammed the drawer. If it was a guy, you took his cock and hit it with a hammer. And they would talk to you. Now, with these drugs, you could get information without having to abuse people."

But the drugs weren't as effective as Feldman let on. The effects of LSD, Gottlieb said, "varied very much along individuals and were dependent upon the individual physiology of the person." He had reached the same conclusion that Lovell had a decade earlier.

When the CIA terminated Operation Midnight Climax in the 1960s, White wrote Gottlieb an appreciative letter of sorts. Gottlieb insisted that it was nothing more than "a flight of poetic license," but it nevertheless reveals White's attitude toward his assignment. "I was a very minor missionary," he wrote, "actually a heretic, but I toiled wholeheartedly in the vineyards because it was fun, fun, fun. Where else could a red-blooded American boy lie, cheat, steal, rape and pillage with the sanction and blessing of the All-Highest?"

Even beyond MKULTRA, Gottlieb engaged in many of the same activities that Lovell had during World War II. For example, throughout the 1960s, he advised the CIA on methods of assassination, just as Lovell had done for the OSS. His main target was Fidel Castro, the Communist revolutionary who had taken control of the Cuban government in 1959. One CIA plot against Castro involved lacing his shoes with thallium salts, a depilatory that would cause his beard to fall out (Lovell had chosen to attack Hitler's mustache with female sex hormones). Another plot involved impregnating Castro's famous Cuban cigars with botulinum toxin, the same substance that Lovell had equipped both Carl Eifler and the Chinese prostitutes with.

In 1960, Gottlieb personally took anthrax to the Congo to assassinate its former prime minister Patrice Lumumba, but the attempt was scrapped at the last minute. Soon afterward, a rival political leader's forces captured, tortured, and beat Lumumba to death. That same year, Gottlieb mailed a handkerchief doused with tuberculosis to Colonel Abd al-Karim Qasim, who had recently seized power in Iraq and established friendly diplomatic relations with the Soviet Union. The handkerchief never reached its target, but like Lumumba, Qasim was soon killed by his political rivals. The CIA's Near East Division reported on his death with a touch of humor: "[Qasim] suffered a terminal illness before a firing squad in Baghdad (an event we had nothing to do with)."

During World War II, Stanley Lovell had primarily overseen the development of devices, documents, and disguises. During the Cold War, in addition to running MKULTRA and advising on assassinations, Sidney Gottlieb did the same thing for the CIA. In 1966, he became the head of the CIA's Technical Services Division (TSD), the successor to the TSS, and transformed it into a doppelgänger of the OSS R&D Branch.

With Gottlieb at the helm, the scientists, engineers, and technicians of the TSD produced a number of cunning tricks for undercover agents, including dead drops, portable key-copying kits, lasers that could pick up audio from windowpane vibrations, and Trojan Horse surveillance systems that were embedded in gifts destined for foreign diplomats—the gift that kept on giving. They also developed a pen that could shoot out Mace or nerve gas, a realization of Vannevar Bush's flippant comment to the R&D Branch about "a fountain pen that does things no self-respecting fountain pen would ever do."

In conjunction with the scientists at Camp Detrick, Gottlieb launched a project to upgrade the R&D Branch K-pills and L-pills. The resulting knockout drug relied on a "neurotropic toxic substance" found in the salivary glands of ticks. The resulting suicide device consisted of a needle coated with deadly shellfish toxin, a substance one thousand times deadlier than sarin nerve agent and fatal within seconds of a finger prick.

Like the R&D Branch Documents Division, the TSD had a Secret Writing Division that developed invisible inks and produced fake bank cards, driver's licenses, and birth certificates.

Like the R&D Branch Camouflage Division, the TSD had a Disguise Operations Division that produced disguises for undercover agents. These two divisions were originally based out of the old OSS headquarters, the same Foggy Bottom complex in Washington, D.C., where Lovell had first met Bill Donovan. Tony Mendez, an artist for the TSD, said that when the CIA commandeered the building, "The remainder of the World War II steel-plate engraving and die-sinking operations were spread haphazardly around the second floor." A sign was put outside that read "U.S. Printing Office," which was supposed to mask the real tenant, though it was inadvertently somewhat accurate.

The careers of Lovell and Gottlieb paralleled each other in remarkable ways. Both men were chemists. Both served in the American intelligence community. Both led the research and development branch of their respective organizations. Both were involved in assassination plots. Both oversaw the creation of devices, documents, and disguises. Both pursued the development of truth drugs and sanctioned unwitting drug experiments.

In fact, so comparable were their careers that when MKULTRA was first revealed to the public in the 1970s, Lovell's neighbor, Erwin Canham, made a direct comparison between the two men in a newspaper article: "In these days when the dirty tricks of the CIA are being exposed, it is worth remembering people like Stanley Lovell. Because, during World War II he was a tireless inventor of dirty tricks."

There were, however, some differences in the careers of Lovell and Gottlieb, the most significant of which was simply the different contexts in which they operated: war and peace. This one difference explains their divergent legacies, as illustrated by Canham's treatment of the two men in his article. Lovell was a patriotic "citizen soldier" while Gottlieb deserved to be "condemned." Even though their work was so similar, the public praised one and vilified the other.

Allen Dulles explained the reasoning behind this phenomenon. "In time of war," he said, "there is a justification for the ruthless methods which I would hardly favor in time of peace." Al Polson, the scientist who had worked on the umbrella gun and Beano grenade for Division 19, reached the same conclusion in a postwar interview: "If I was doing the stuff today that I did during the war, I would be in jail for 56 consecutive life sentences without a chance of parole." In other words, desperate times call for desperate measures; war justifies otherwise criminal acts. Gottlieb believed that he *was* operating in a time of war—a Cold War that could turn hot at any moment—and therefore he believed that he *was* justified in doing the same things that Lovell had done during World War II. But others saw it differently.

If MKULTRA, one of the most shameful sores on the CIA's controversial reputation, had been a World War II operation, it would have garnered as little controversy as Lovell's R&D Branch. And vice versa.

It's not a coincidence that the careers of Stanley Lovell and Sidney Gottlieb were so similar. It was planned.

In the 1980s, Gottlieb gave a series of depositions for several lawsuits that the victims of MKULTRA had launched against the CIA. One of those depositions took place on May 17, 1983, in a small meeting room of the Boxwood House Motel in Culpeper, Virginia. The questioning started at 10:00 A.M. Within the first ten minutes, attorney James Turner handed Gottlieb a memo from the early days of the CIA and told him to read the names listed in it. Gottlieb spent a silent moment studying the memo.

"Who is H. M. Chadwell, Doctor?" Turner asked.

"I think Chadwell was head of a unit in CIA in the early 50's known as the Office of Scientific Information [Intelligence]."

Turner then asked about another name in the memo. "The Lovell referred to is Stanley Lovell?"

"I believe that is who he is," Gottlieb said.

"Who is he?"

"Stanley Lovell was somebody who was active in World War II in OSS in the technical side."

"What was his connection with the Agency?"

"I don't think he had any formal connection. This memorandum certainly implies contact of some kind. I would describe what relation he had with the Agency as ad hoc contact with whom they would talk every once in a while."

"Did his areas of expertise include the use of drugs and similar techniques?"

"I don't know that I would know all his areas of expertise. They were some of the areas he talked about or wrote about when he was in OSS."

"Is he alive?"

"I really don't know."

Lovell had, in fact, died seven years earlier. On January 4, 1976, at the age of eighty-five, he suffered a fatal heart attack while walking his dog.

Over the course of the depositions, Gottlieb gradually revealed his inspiration for MKULTRA. When he had started the program, "I didn't know anything about this." Desperate for guidance, he turned to history to inundate himself with ideas. "I was pulling all of the stops I could, looking at World War II Office of Strategic Services records." Searching through those dilapidated boxes, he found the blueprints for his career at the CIA.

Appendix 1

The following are the code names and descriptions of Division 19's secret projects as listed in a declassified internal history.

Abalone: The problem concerned with attaching limpets and explosive charges.

Adam's Plan: Bats bearing incendiaries for release over Japan.

Adhesive: Materials used for attaching explosive charges above water.

Anerometer: A barometric fuse responding to altitude change of roughly 1,500 feet.

Arson: The problem of instructing personnel in the use of fire.

Aqua Vita: The problem of producing pleasant-tasting, sterile water in the field from contaminated sources.

Aunt Jemima: High-explosive flour.

Balsam: A paper readily destroyed by mastication but resistant to natural humidity.

Barney: A glass cloth jacket for covering outboard motors.

Bat: An alternative name for the Adam's Plan.

Beano: A baseball hand grenade, both high explosive and white phosphorous.

Belcher: Chemicals which when introduced into water supplies in parts per billion render the water nauseating and undrinkable without being poisonous.

Bigot: The adaption of the spigot mortar principle to a .45-caliber automatic.

Big Joe: The rifle-size Penetrometer.

Black Joe: High explosive camouflaged as coal.

Blackout: High-explosive electric light bulb initiated by the passage of electricity.

Brimstone: The general name for incendiary problems.

Bulls Eye: The application of scientific and special devices to specific targets named by OSS.

BURP or BRP: British Urgent Railway Plan for the derailment of locomotives.

Bushmaster: The types of time-delay rifle and machine-gun simulators.

Caccolube: The destruction of motor vehicles by the introduction of chemicals into the oil or fuel supply.

Camel: The code name for camouflage.

Campbell: A method of quickly sinking and firing an explosive-laden boat.

Canister Locater: A device to enable reception parties to locate at night stores dropped by air with parachutes.

Cannon: An assassin's pistol.

Casey Jones: Attack on railroads in general.

Clam: A magnetic explosive charge equipped with time delays for attacking steel targets.

Clockwork: Precise waterproof clockwork delays.

Cluck: A communication device.

Cricket: A compact radio receiver-transmitter.

Dog Drag: A device for throwing bloodhounds off the trail of an agent.

Dragon: A gun firing a dart by means of gas pressure.

Dropping: The term usually used in reference to supply by air of ground forces.

Emily Post: Dealing with poisons.

Facsimile: A method of transmitting by wire reproductions of documents.

Fantasia: Psychological ideas for the purpose of frightening the enemy.

Firefly: An explosive hand-size delay-action grenade which when introduced in the fuel tank of a motor vehicle, explodes the tank and ignites the contents.

Fountain: A shaped charge and accompanying equipment placed in the roadbed of a railroad with the object of destroying the boiler or cylinders of a locomotive.

Hedy: A device to create panic in a crowd.

Honeymoon: Work on time delays.

Hooter: An underwater noise maker.

IFT: Induction Field Transmitter—an electromagnetic device for short-range secret communication.

IFL: Induction Field Locator—an electromagnetic transmitter on which men equipped with IFT can home.

Impact Testing Machine: A silent weapon throwing a dart propelled by a spring.

Joe Louis: The largest-size Penetrometer capable of throwing grenades or small mortar cells.

Lacrima Tojo: The use of liquid explosives disguised as innocent materials such as lubricating oil.

Limpetry: The problem of underwater attack on steel and wooden ships.

Little Joe: A pistol model of the Penetrometer.

Locust: Sabotage of high-precision machinery by contamination with small amounts of chemicals.

Lost Chord: The problem of communication, homing, and identification of agents.

Lulu: A disperser-igniter for inflammable dust.

Matchhead: A waterproof ending to the Pencil giving silent ignition to incendiary devices.

Maude Muller: Concerned with the destruction of tropical foliage.

Mitchell Device: An early name used to refer to a radio switch activated by a frequency of 100 kc.

Mark II Pencil: An electrolyte time delay based on the general design of the Mark I Pencil.

Mole: A photo-sensitive electronic switch for attacking trains in tunnels.

Moth: Readily destroyed briefcases and notebooks based on incendiary or explosive principles.

MWT: Microwave transmitter—a device for secure communication over short distances.

Nemo: Attack on submarines in general.

Odometer: A distance switch developed to trigger charges placed on a train at a pre-selected spot.

Paul Revere: An incendiary working both on land and on water and capable of igniting crude oil as well as more combustible materials.

Pencil: A chemical time-delay standard with the British.

Penetrometer: A silent, flashless weapon throwing a dart and utilizing rubber as the propelling force.

PEP: The transmission of secret messages utilizing existing facilities.

Pin-up: A device to attach limpets to either steel or wooden ships.

Pocket Incendiary: A celluloid case filled with gelled solvent and equipped with time pencils and matchheads.

Popeye: An electric alarm system depending on trip wire to give warning of the presence of marauders.

Postell: Dealing with a method for the utilization of enemy-controlled telephone wires.

Pneumonia: On causing death without detectable traces.

Rainbow: On ultraviolet and infrared communication.

Rocket: The three-and-a-half-inch spin-stabilized rocket for which a rocket launcher was developed.

Saint Michael: A magnetic recorder together with microphone and telephone line input and playback.

Salex: A slow-burning explosive composed of sulfur, aluminum, and TNT.

Sandeman Club: The original code name of Division 19.

Shell: Attack on motor vehicles by using cashew nut shell oil.

Shortstop: On the attack of electrical equipment by subtle means.

Silencer: A device to eliminate muzzle noise from standard weapons.

Simultaneous Events: A radio switch to respond to a selected signal but to be safe from accidental triggering.

Sky Wave: A method of radio transmission in which the antenna is located on the ground.

Sleeping Beauty: A one-man underwater craft developed by the British and used in attacks on harbors and ships.

Slima: A model of the Penetrometer.

Snail: An alternative name for Pin-up.

Speedometer: A switch developed for attack on railway equipment mounted on an axle and activated by centrifugal force.

Spigot Mortar: A silent, flashless weapon developed by the British.

SRA: Signal Relay American—the American time pencil.

SRI: Signal Relay Incendiary—the time pencil equipped with matchhead.

Suction Cup: The attachment of limpets by means of rubber suction cups.

Sutherland Bulb: A method of preventing accidental triggering and depending on evolution of gas by electrolysis in a closed bulb containing dilute sulfuric acid.

Switack: A model of the Penetrometer.

Sympathetic Fuse: A device for activating one explosive charge underwater by the firing of another.

Teak: Methods of attacking wooden ships and bridges.

Thwaites Device: An alternative name for Firefly.

Turtle Eggs: A device for attacking automotive equipment by introducing into the oil system materials which destroy the bearings without arousing suspicion.

TVA: The code name under which the services of NDRC in performing large-scale experiments in North Carolina were provided.

UWT: Underwater Telephone—a device for communicating between Sleeping Beauties.

Varga: A shaped charge to open and set fire to storage tanks of oil.

Veritas: A device giving delayed-action firing of signal flares to be dropped by air.

Vitamin Pills: Capsules of a chemical soluble in water, undetected by standard methods of analysis and capable of destroying storage batteries.

Wandering Boys: Concerned with homing devices and the location and pickup of agents on hostile shores.

Well: A self-tapping crucible containing thermite for attack on machinery and metal targets.

Who Me?: A harassing device for annoying the enemy by contaminating his person with foul-smelling liquids.

William Tell: The final model of the Penetrometer of the rifle type.

Wire: An alloy of aluminum having fair electrical and mechanical properties but rapidly soluble in salt water.

Woodchuck: A device to wreck a train on a bridge.

Woolworth Gun: A cheap, impermanent pistol for distribution among conquered peoples.

X-Ray: The code name for the Adam's Plan and more specifically for the time delay developed under the program.

Zephyr: The code name for the silencing of outboard motors.

Appendix 2

The disappointing reality about researching and writing history is that many of the incredible sources from the archives don't neatly fit within the scope of the story and are left on the cutting-room floor. That's what almost happened to the following source, a firsthand survival account of a downed American pilot in Burma, but its content is too gripping not to be published somewhere, and so it appears here. The account is minimally edited for spelling.

Narrative by 1st. Lt. Freeling H. Clower, Given in Hosp. January 1944

As we came into the targeted area 2 Japs off left little above. Called Major Smith but evidently no contact made. Dropped bomb and turned into first one which was coming in on his tail and fired about 45 degrees and it broke away with some smoke trailing. At same time his wing men pulled straight up rolled and came down and we met head on but I was in a near stall attitude. After the exchange of fire I saw my engine on fire and pieces of metal and oil were flying in all directions. I pointed the nose straight down and went as far away from the target area until heat and smoke became intense. At approximately 1000 feet I had to leave the ship. I floated down and hit the ground rather rapidly only a few hundred yards north of the railway. I pulled my chute down out of the trees and thought about burying it but could hear trampling in the brush so I knew there was a patrol nearby. My leg was burned and had two large holes in it which were gushing profusely. I salvaged what I could from my pack and started North. Once the patrol passed very nearby and I hid under a pile of dead branches and leaves. It was nearly dark when I started out again. The first night found me curled up inside a hollow tree trunk nervous and cold. Sleep was impossible or my mind was muddled at my prospects. I had no map and only a meager remembrance of how the hills ran. I did get my compass so the early morning I started north and west when possible. I thought the brush and tangles were impossible but they were simple to what came later. Trails were not too easy to follow for they seemed to go in one direction and then reverse entirely. One day I walked quite easily through swamp grass but then I came to a clearing, then hills all around. I headed west and got on a good path. The path was very steep and my leg bled a lot whenever I strained. The heat was intense at first but I soon became accustomed and also my ears picked up the sound of streams more readily.

About the third night I lit a fire and tried to dry out. At the same time I washed my wounds and applied iodine to the open holes. I had 12 tablets of sulfanilamide of which I took some by mouth, the remainder I crushed to use as a powder in the deep holes. I put the boric salve on my burns and they were healing nicely. The whole leg and foot were very black and blue with much distortion from swelling.

The remainder of the twelve days alone was a series of disappointments and in one word HELL. It seemed as if I was running in circles. At one point I waded for a day in grass above my head. It was matted and tangled. Occasionally an animal track would help progress but invariably it wound up going in the direction from which I had come. After a very tedious day in this bewildering, cutting mess I emerged on the bank of the stream. I saw smoke in the distance but it was nearly dark so I stopped. My bar of chocolate was holding up swell and I knew I could last for 20 days if needs be.

It was well I didn't reach the smoke because as I decided later it was

Japs burning bushes from the road. It seemed as if I had been successful for as I was wading up the shallow river I came to a small bamboo bridge. It looked too well made to be of a native type but there was a road going north. I started up this trail and all the way expected to run into a Jap patrol. Occasionally I came to a cold camp. From scraps of paper, etc., I knew it must be an enemy trail, the same which had been burnt off the night before. Close! I stayed on this through many high hills but the pace was telling. I then encountered a gruesome thing. Coming around a bend I saw a deserted village. The huts were partially burned and old wreckage of autos littered the roadside. In one hut was a human charred pile of bones with the skull as sort of a symbol for me to get out. I needed little persuasion. I decided then and there that I would rather die alone in the jungle than be captured.

For the next week I was never on a beaten path again. I was hopelessly wandering one minute in a swampy tangled hole and then I would struggle for hours trying to reach a peak. The hills seemed to get steeper and steeper and more dense as the days went by. I knew I was getting weaker and decided I must find some other way. One morning I came to a mountain stream. It was about a foot wide and I determined to follow it. It was rocky and my shoes were fast beginning to wear. I thought I had hit a good plan because the stream eventually became a river with smaller streams running into it. The water became too deep to wade so I started climbing the banks instead. This was well for only a short time. The river became a bottomless swirling mass. There were no sides to cling to for they had become vertical rock piles forming a gorge. I was hemmed in. No way to go forward and the walls were impossible. Then the rains came. I sat on the 45 degree rock pile from 4 P.M. to 7 A.M. with the rain beating down in torrents. That was the most hopeless and dismal time I have ever encountered in my short life. I didn't see how I could stand it much more.

With the cold gray morning I hoped for at least the sun to dry myself. No soap. It stayed dark and misty. All wood was wet so a fire was out of the question. I sat and pondered and then tried to build a raft. This resulted in my hitting a rock and swimming the rest of the way to a falls. I didn't know whether to keep swimming and hope I drowned or turn back. I made my way up the river experiencing a couple of duckings from slipping and falling down the rocky slopes back into the river. Once I slid and rolled about 25 feet coming to a jarring jolt when I collided with a boulder coming sharply into my ribs. I was stunned for a short time and continued on when I realized I had broken no bones. All of the time my leg was hurting more because of the wet clothes and terrific beating it had taken.

The bend in the river was a godsend. I took the fork and started wading up stream. As the day went on I saw that the hills were getting smaller and I hoped I would emerge into a valley soon.

On the 12th day my hopes arose. I came to a bamboo structure across the stream. It was hand made so I knew the people had been there at some time. I finally spotted a trail leading into the bamboo forest where I could see signs of freshly cut wood, so I knew I must be getting some place. Was it friendly? Was I coming to a Jap camp? Those thoughts tortured me to no end, I came to the top of a hill and the sun was beaming down. It was glorious to stretch out and feel that warmth. I opened my wounds and let the sun play on them. At the same time I took off my soggy shoes and clothes and de-leeched and de-ticked myself. It was about 2 o'clock. I debated whether to stay there and hope some planes would come over. In that case I could light some grass. The only drawback my matches were too wet to fire. I struck down on the trail and walked for about two hours. I was weak, my head ached and I was just ready to stop for the night when I saw some huts at the top of a hill. I guess I fairly ran the rest of the way.

I must have passed out for as I came to I saw a pair of eyes peeking at me from one corner and chickens and pigs were running in all directions. I was sprawled in the midst of this on my face. I motioned for the dark fellow to come to me but he only ducked out of sight. Eventually I spotted a strong husky lad and persuaded him to come. He stood at a distance with his knife and gun pointing very distastefully down my famished gullet. And then I heard someone say, "Do you speak English?" A little brown fellow with grey shorts, handlebar moustache, and stocking cap was coming toward me. Of course I started rambling at once on who I was and what I wanted. I showed him my wounds and miracle of all he said "I am a doctor." That was too much. I was skeptical and wondered if he was a native medicine man or what. As soon as he started working I knew different. His hands worked with skill and tenderness, he had some supplies. As he worked he explained he had run away from Myitkyina with his family leaving his home and all of his years supply of instruments behind. He was of Indian birth but spoke to the people fluently in their native tongue. He said they were Kachin Hill people and would help me. He also sent a runner with a note to the Boss. The boss was unknown to me but must have been a chief of something.

Clower's narrative ends there. A note appended to the back explains, "Lt. Clower leaves his story unfinished because of the Security that has been drummed into these pilots to disclose nothing that would connect their rescue with the efforts of Detachment 101. Actually Lt. Clower was delivered to 'Pat' whom he refers to as 'The Boss' in his story. 'Pat' is one of our key operatives who is looked up to by the Kachins as 'The Boss.'"

Acknowledgments

It takes a village. I couldn't have done it without mine.

I want to thank the following institutions and organizations for their support: the American Institute of Physics, Austin Community College, the California Institute of Technology, the Clements Center for National Security, the Lone Star Historians of Science, Louisiana Tech University, the National Academy of Sciences, Texas A&M University, the University of Texas, the Waggonner Center for Civic Engagement and Public Policy. Thanks also to the many archivists and librarians who helped me find sources.

Thank you to my agent, Scott Miller, and my editor at St. Martin's Press, Marc Resnick, for making this book possible.

I want to thank the teachers, professors, and colleagues who taught me about scholarship, especially H. W. Brands, Bruce Hunt, Mark Lawrence, Alberto Martínez, Jeremy Mhire, Abena Osseo-Asare, Megan Raby, Anthony Stranges, and Sherman Wall. My advisor, Alberto Martínez, deserves a special thank-you for his help and guidance.

Lastly, I owe the largest debt of gratitude to my friends and family. Thank you to the Bonds, Lisles, and Stocktons. Thank you to Max and Sarah, Blair and Marty, and my nephews Jack, Quinn, Peter, Nolan, and Oslo. Thank you to my wife, Osiris, for your love, support, humor, insight, and kindness. Most of all, thank you to my parents, Mike and Lanette Lisle, for everything. This book is dedicated to you.

References

Interviews

Jonathan Lovell (September 26, 2018)

Merrily Lovell (October 9, 2018)

Databases

Ancestry: ancestry.com

Black Vault: theblackvault.com

Frank Olson Project: frankolsonproject.org

HathiTrust Digital Library: hathitrust.org

Internet Archive: archive.org

Mary Ferrell Foundation: maryferrell.org

National Security Archive: nsarchive.gwu.edu

Science History Institute: sciencehistory.org

Periodicals

The Baltimore Sun

The Boston Globe

Bucks County Courier Times

Bulletin of the Atomic Scientists
Collier's
Counterpunch
The Dallas Morning News
Federal News Service
Genii Magazine
The Guardian (London)
Harper's Magazine
The Independent (London)
Indiana Gazette
Minneapolis Morning Tribune
The National Interest
The New York Times
OSS Society Journal
Popular Science
Prologue
The Saturday Evening Post
Shoe and Leather Facts
Spin Magazine
Sunday Tribune
Time Magazine
The Washington Post

Reports

Aalmans, William. *A Booklet with a Brief History of the "Dora"-Nordhausen Labor-Concentration Camps and Information on the Nordhausen War Crimes Case of the United States of America versus Arthur Kurt Andrae et al.* 1947.

Borden Institute. *Military Medical Ethics.* Vol. 2. 2003.

Chambers, John. *OSS Training in the National Parks and Service Abroad in World War II.* U.S. National Park Service, 2008.

CIA. *Kubark Counterintelligence Interrogation.* 1963.

Civil Defense Liaison Office. *Fire Effects of Bombing Attacks.* 1950.

Commission on CIA Activities Within the United States. *The Nelson Rockefeller Report to the President.* 1975.

Department of Commerce. *Administrative History of the National Inventors Council.* 1947.

Murray, Henry. *An Analysis of the Personality of Adolf Hitler with Predictions of His Future Behavior and Suggestions for Dealing with Him Now and After Germany's Surrender.* 1943.

NDRC. *Summary Technical Report of Division 19.* 1946.

OSRD. *Chemistry: A History of the Chemistry Components of the National Defense Research Committee, 1940–1946.* Little, Brown and Company, 1948.

OSS. *Area F Reallocation Booklet.*

OSS. *Personal Disguise.* 1944.

OSS. *Simple Sabotage Field Manual.* 1944.

OSS. *Special Operation Field Manual.* 1944.

Presidential Commission for the Study of Bioethical Issues. *Ethically Impossible: STD Research in Guatemala from 1946 to 1948.* 2011.

Roosevelt, Kermit. *The Overseas Targets: War Report of the OSS.* Vol. 2. Walker and Company, 1976.

Roosevelt, Kermit. *War Report of the OSS.* Walker and Company, 1976.

Select Committee to Study Governmental Operations. *Alleged Assassination Plots Involving Foreign Leaders,* S. Rep. No. 94–94–465, 1st Sess. 1975.

Articles

Bailey, Roderick. "The Secret Scalpel: Plastic Surgery for Wartime Disguise." *The Lancet* 384, no. 9952 (October 18, 2014).

Bailey, Roderick. "Special Operations: A Hidden Chapter in the Histories of Facial Surgery and Human Enhancement." *Medical Humanities* 46, no. 2 (July 6, 2020).

Bimmerle, George. "'Truth' Drugs in Interrogation." *Studies in Intelligence* 5, no. 2 (Spring 1961).

Bloom, Murray. "Uncle Sam: Bashful Counterfeiter." *International Journal of Intelligence and Counterintelligence* 2, no. 3 (1988).

Crane, Conrad. "Chemical and Biological Warfare during the Korean War: Rhetoric and Reality." *Asian Perspective* 25, no. 3 (2001).

Fearer, Christian. "The Lordly Pilot and Lowly Saboteur: The Army Air Forces, Office of Strategic Services, and Project Campbell/Javaman."

U.S. Special Operations Command History and Research Office (October 2015).

Fischer, Benjamin. "Dirty Tricks and Deadly Devices: OSS, SOE, NDRC and the Development of Special Weapons and Equipment." *Journal of Intelligence History* 2 (Summer 2002).

Frischknecht, Friedrich. "The History of Biological Warfare: Human Experimentation, Modern Nightmares and Lone Madmen in the Twentieth Century." *EMBO Reports* 4, no. 1 (June 2003).

Gaillard, Yvan, Philippe Regenstreif, and Laurent Fanton. "Modern Toxic Antipersonnel Projectiles." *American Journal of Forensic Medicine and Pathology* 35, no. 4 (December 2014).

House, Robert. "The Use of Scopolamine in Criminology." *The American Journal of Police Science* 2, no. 4 (1931).

Knollenberg, Bernhard. "General Amherst and Germ Warfare." *Journal of American History* 41, no. 3 (December 1954).

Madsen, Chris. "Strategy, Fleet Logistics, and the Lethbridge Mission to the Pacific and Indian Oceans 1943–1944." *The Journal of Strategic Studies* 31, no. 6 (December 2008).

Murphy, John. "Secret Weapons of the Secret War." *International Journal of Intelligence and Counterintelligence* 14 (2001).

Murphy, Mark. "The Exploits of Agent 110: Allen Dulles in Wartime." *Studies in Intelligence* (1994).

Passie, Torsten, and Udo Benzenhöfer. "MDA, MDMA, and Other 'Mescaline-like' Substances in the US Military's Search for a Truth Drug (1940s to 1960s)." *Drug Test and Analysis* 10, no. 1 (January 2018).

Torrey, Gordon, and Donald Avery. "Postal Forgeries in Two World Wars." *Studies in Intelligence* 4, no. 3 (Summer 1960).

Trimble, William, and David Lewis. "Lytle S. Adams: The Apostle of Non-stop Airmail Pickup." *Technology and Culture* 29, no. 2 (April 1988).

Books

Albarelli, H. *A Terrible Mistake: The Murder of Frank Olson and the CIA's Secret Cold War Experiments.* Springfield, OR: Trine Day, 2009.

Alcorn, Robert. *No Bugles for Spies: Tales of the OSS.* New York: David McKay Company, 1962.

Aldrich, Richard. *Intelligence and the War against Japan: Britain, America and the Politics of Secret Service.* Cambridge: Cambridge University Press, 2000.

Andrews, Christopher. *For the President's Eyes Only: Secret Intelligence and the American Presidency from Washington to Bush.* New York: Harper, 1995.

Applegate, Rex, and Chuck Melson. *The Close-Combat Files of Colonel Rex Applegate.* Boulder, CO: Paladin Press, 1998.

Berg, Ethel. *My Brother Morris Berg: The Real Moe.* New York: Schulsinger Brothers, 1976.

Bloom, Murray. *Money of Their Own: The Great Counterfeiters.* New York: Charles Scribner's Sons, 1957.

Blum, Howard. *The Last Goodnight: A World War II Story of Espionage, Adventure, and Betrayal.* New York: Harper, 2016.

Boyce, Frederic, and Douglas Everett. *SOE: The Scientific Secrets.* Sparkford, UK: Sutton, 2003.

Brown, Anthony. *The Last Hero: Wild Bill Donovan.* New York: Times Books, 1982.

Bruce, David. *OSS against the Reich: The World War II Diaries of Colonel David K. E. Bruce.* Kent, OH: Kent State University Press, 1991.

Brunner, John. *OSS Weapons.* Williamstown, NJ: Phillips Publications, 1994.

Bush, Vannevar. *Pieces of the Action.* New York: William Morrow, 1970.

Byrnes, James. *All in One Lifetime.* New York: Harper and Brothers, 1958.

Carroll, Rebecca. "Under the Influence: Harry Anslinger's Role in Shaping America's Drug Policy." In *Federal Drug Control: The Evolution of Policy and Practice,* edited by Jonathon Erlin and Joseph Spillane. Binghamton, NY: Pharmaceutical Products Press, 2004.

Clark, Ronald. *The Greatest Power on Earth: The Story of Nuclear Fission.* London: Sidgwick and Jackson, 1980.

Clarke, Donald. *Wishing on the Moon: The Life and Times of Billie Holiday.* New York: Viking, 1994.

Coon, Carleton. *Adventures and Discoveries: The Autobiography of Carleton S. Coon.* Englewood Cliffs, NJ: Prentice-Hall, 1981.

Coon, Carleton. *A North Africa Story: The Anthropologist as OSS Agent, 1941–1943.* Ipswich, MA: Gambit, 1980.

Cornish, Paul. "Weapons and Equipment of the Special Operations Executive." In *Special Operations Executive: A New Instrument of War*, edited by Mark Seaman. Abingdon: Routledge, 2006.

Cornwell, John. *Hitler's Scientists: Science, War and the Devil's Pact*. New York: Viking, 2003.

Couffer, Jack. *Bat Bomb: World War II's Other Secret Weapon*. Austin: University of Texas Press, 1992.

Covert, Norman. *Cutting Edge: A History of Fort Detrick, Maryland 1943–1993*. Fort Detrick, MD: Headquarters U.S. Army Garrison, 1993.

Daniels, Jonathan. *White House Witness, 1942–1945*. New York: Doubleday, 1975.

Dawidoff, Nicholas. *The Catcher Was a Spy: The Mysterious Life of Moe Berg*. New York: Pantheon Books, 1994.

De River, Joseph. *The Sexual Criminal: A Psychoanalytical Study*. Springfield, IL: Charles C. Thomas, 1950.

Dreux, William. *No Bridges Blown: With the OSS Jedburghs in Nazi-Occupied France*. Notre Dame, IN: University of Notre Dame Press, 2020.

Duffy, Francis. *Father Duffy's Story: A Tale of Humor and Heroism, of Life and Death with the Fighting Sixty-Ninth*. New York: George H. Doran Company, 1919.

Dulles, Allen. *From Hitler's Doorstep: The Wartime Intelligence Reports of Allen Dulles, 1942–1945*. Edited by Neal Petersen. University Park: Pennsylvania State University Press, 1996.

Dunlop, Richard. *Donovan: America's Master Spy*. Chicago: Rand McNally and Company, 1982.

Fairbairn, William. *Scientific Self-Defence*. New York: D. Appleton-Century, 1931.

Fieser, Louis. *The Scientific Method: A Personal Account of Unusual Projects in War and Peace*. New York: Reinhold, 1964.

Foot, M. *SOE: An Outline History of the Special Operations Executive, 1940–46*. Frederick, MD: University Publications of America, 1986.

Ford, Corey. *Donovan of OSS*. Boston: Little, Brown, 1970.

Ford, Corey, and Alastair MacBain. *Cloak and Dagger: The Secret Story of the OSS*. New York: Random House, 1946.

Fraser-Smith, Charles, Gerald McKnight, and Sandy Lesberg. *The Secret*

War of Charles Fraser-Smith: The "Q" Gadget Wizard of World War II. Exeter: Paternoster Press, 1981.

Geißler, Erhard. *Biologische Waffen—Nicht in Hitlers Arsenalen: Biologische und Toxin-Kampfmittel in Deutchland von 1915 bis 1945.* Münster: Lit Verlag, 1999.

Glaser, Lynn. *Counterfeiting in America: The History of an American Way to Wealth.* New York: Clarkson N. Potter, 1968.

Gold, Hal. *Unit 731 Testimony: Japan's Wartime Human Experimentation Program.* Boston: Tuttle, 2003.

Guiet, Jean Claude. *Dead on Time: The Memoir of an SOE and OSS Agent in Occupied France.* Stroud, UK: History Press, 2016.

Hall, Roger. *You're Stepping on My Cloak and Dagger.* Annapolis, MD: Naval Institute Press, 2004.

Harris, Stephen. *Duffy's War: Fr. Francis Duffy, Wild Bill Donovan, and the Irish Fighting 69th in World War I.* Washington, DC: Potomac Books, 2006.

Haukelid, Knut. *Skis Against the Atom.* Minot, ND: North American Heritage Press, 1989.

Hayden, Sterling. *Wanderer.* Dobbs Ferry, NY: Sheridan House, 2000.

Heisenberg, Elizabeth. *Inner Exile: Recollections of a Life with Werner Heisenberg.* Boston: Birkhauser, 1984.

Helms, Richard, and William Wood. *A Look Over My Shoulder: A Life in the Central Intelligence Agency.* New York: Random House, 2003.

Hershberg, James. *James B. Conant: Harvard to Hiroshima and the Making of the Nuclear Age.* New York: Knopf, 1993.

Hilmas, Corey, Jeffery Smart, and Benjamin Hill. "History of Chemical Warfare." In *Medical Aspects of Chemical Warfare*, edited by Shirley Tuorinsky. Washington, DC: Borden Institute, 2008.

Hofmann, Albert. *LSD: My Problem Child.* Translated by Jonathan Ott. San Jose, CA: MAPS 2009.

Holloway, David. *Stalin and the Bomb: The Soviet Union and Atomic Energy 1939–56.* New Haven, CT: Yale University Press, 1994.

Houghton, Vince. *Nuking the Moon: And Other Intelligence Schemes and Military Plots Left on the Drawing Board.* New York: Penguin Books, 2019.

Hymoff, Edward. *The OSS in World War II*. New York: Richardson and Steirman, 1986.

Jacobsen, Annie. *Operation Paperclip: The Secret Intelligence Program That Brought Nazi Scientists to America*. Boston: Little, Brown and Company, 2014.

Jakub, Jay. *Spies and Saboteurs: Anglo-American Collaboration and Rivalry in Human Intelligence Collection and Special Operations, 1940–45*. New York: St. Martin's Press, 1999.

Junge, Traudl. *Until the Final Hour: Hitler's Last Secretary*. New York: Arcade Publishing, 2004.

Kahn, Jeffrey. *Mrs. Shipley's Ghost: The Right to Travel and Terrorist Watchlists*. Ann Arbor: University of Michigan Press, 2016.

Kennedy, Gregory. *Vengeance Weapon 2: The V-2 Guided Missile*. Washington, DC: Smithsonian Institution Press, 1983.

Kinzer, Stephen. *Poisoner in Chief: Sidney Gottlieb and the CIA Search for Mind Control*. New York: Henry Holt and Company, 2019.

Kirkpatrick, Lyman. *The Real CIA*. New York: Macmillan, 1968.

Kodosky, Robert. *Psychological Operations American Style: The Joint United States Public Affairs Office, Vietnam and Beyond*. Lanham, MD: Lexington Books, 2007.

Kruzman, Dan. *Blood and Water: Sabotaging Hitler's Bomb*. New York: Henry Holt and Company, 1997.

Langelaan, George. *Knights of the Floating Silk*. London: Hutchinson and Company, 1959.

Lanouette, William, and Bela Szilard. *Genius in the Shadows: A Biography of Leo Szilard*. Chicago: University of Chicago Press, 1994.

Leahy, William. *I Was There: The Personal Story of the Chief of Staff to Presidents Roosevelt and Truman Based on His Notes and Diaries Made at the Time*. London: Victor Gollancz, 1950.

Lee, Martin. *Smoke Signals: A Social History of Marijuana—Medical, Recreational, and Scientific*. New York: Scribner, 2012.

Lee, Martin, and Bruce Shlain. *Acid Dreams: The CIA, LSD, and the Sixties Rebellion*. New York: Grove Press, 1985.

Lehr, Dick, and Gerard O'Neill. *Whitey: The Life of America's Most Notorious Mob Boss*. New York: Crown Publishers, 2013.

Lilienthal, David. *The Journals of David Lilienthal: The Atomic Energy Years: 1945–1950*. New York: Harper and Row, 1964.

Lockwood, Jeffrey. *Six-Legged Soldiers: Using Insects as Weapons of War*. New York: Oxford University Press, 2009.

Lovell, Stanley. *Of Spies and Stratagems*. Englewood Cliffs, NJ: Prentice-Hall, 1963.

MacDonald, Elizabeth. *Undercover Girl*. New York: Macmillan, 1947.

Marks, John. *The Search for the Manchurian Candidate: The CIA and Mind Control*. New York: Times Books, 1979.

Mattingly, Robert. *Herringbone Cloak–GI Dagger: Marines of the OSS*. Washington, DC: U.S. Marine Corps History and Museums Division, 1989.

McIntosh, Elizabeth. *Sisterhood of Spies: The Women of the OSS*. Annapolis, MD: Naval Institute Press, 1998.

McLean, Donald. *The Spy's Workshop: America's Clandestine Weapons*. Boulder, CO: Paladin Press, 1989.

Mears, Ray. *The Real Heroes of Telemark: The True Story of the Secret Mission to Stop Hitler's Atomic Bomb*. London: Coronet Books, 2004.

Melton, H. Keith, and Robert Wallace. *The Official CIA Manual of Trickery and Deception*. New York: HarperCollins, 2009.

Mendez, Antonio. *The Master of Disguise: My Secret Life in the CIA*. New York: William Morrow, 1999.

Moon, Tom. *This Grim and Savage Game: OSS and the Beginning of U.S. Covert Operations in World War II*. Cambridge, MA: Da Capo Press, 2000.

Moon, Tom, and Carl Eifler. *The Deadliest Colonel*. New York: Vantage Press, 1975.

Moore, Kate. *The Radium Girls: The Dark Story of America's Shining Women*. Naperville, IL: Sourcebooks, 2017.

Moorhouse, Roger. *Killing Hitler: The Plots, the Assassins, and the Dictator Who Cheated Death*. New York: Bantam Books, 2006.

Morgan, William. *The OSS and I*. New York: Norton, 1957.

Neer, Robert. *Napalm: An American Biography*. Cambridge, MA: Belknap Press, 2013.

Nelson, Wayne. *A Spy's Diary of World War II: Inside the OSS with an*

American Agent in Europe. Jefferson, NC: McFarland and Company, 2009.

Neustatter, Walter. *Psychological Disorder and Crime*. New York: Philosophical Library, 1957.

Newcomb, Richard. *Iwo Jima: The Dramatic Account of the Epic Battle That Turned the Tide of War*. New York: Henry Holt and Company, 1965.

O'Donnell, Patrick. *Operatives, Spies, and Saboteurs: The Unknown Story of the Men and Women of WWII's OSS*. New York: Free Press, 2004.

Osada, Arata. *Children of the A-Bomb: The Testament of the Boys and Girls of Hiroshima*. Ann Arbor, MI: Midwest, 1982.

Peers, William, and Dean Brelis. *Behind the Burma Road: The Story of America's Most Successful Guerrilla Force*. Boston: Little, Brown and Company, 1963.

Perisco, Joseph. *Casey: From the OSS to the CIA*. New York: Viking, 1990.

Perisco, Joseph. "Casey's German Gamble." In *Experience of War: An Anthology of Articles from MHQ, the Quarterly Journal of Military History*, edited by Robert Cowley. New York: Laurel, 1992.

Perisco, Joesph. *Nuremberg: Infamy on Trial*. New York: Viking, 1994.

Perisco, Joseph. *Piercing the Reich: The Penetration of Nazi Germany by American Secret Agents during World War II*. New York: Viking, 1979.

Perisco, Joseph. *Roosevelt's Secret War: FDR and World War II Espionage*. New York: Random House, 2001.

Powers, Francis. *The Trial of the U2: Exclusive Authorized Account of the Court Proceedings of the Case of Francis Gary Powers Heard before the Military Division of the Supreme Court of the USSR*. Chicago: Translation World, 1960.

Powers, Thomas. *Heisenberg's War: The Secret History of the German Bomb*. New York: Knopf, 1993.

Powers, Thomas. *The Man Who Kept the Secrets: Richard Helms and the CIA*. New York: Knopf, 1979.

Purnell, Sonia, *A Woman of No Importance: The Untold Story of the American Spy Who Helped Win World War II*. New York: Viking, 2019.

Regis, Ed. *The Biology of Doom: The History of America's Secret Germ Warfare Project*. New York: Henry Holt and Company, 1999.

Rhodes, May, and T. D. Rhodes. *A Biographical Genealogy of the Lovell Family in England and America.* Asheville, NC: Biltmore Press, 1924.

Richelson, Jeffrey. *Spying on the Bomb: American Nuclear Intelligence from Nazi Germany to Iran and North Korea.* New York: Norton, 2006.

Richelson, Jeffrey. *The Wizards of Langley: Inside the CIA's Directorate of Science and Technology.* Boulder, CO: Westview, 2001.

Robins, Peter. *The Legend of W. E. Fairbairn: Gentleman and Warrior, the Shanghai Years.* London: CQB Publications, 2005.

Rogers, James. *Wartime Washington: The Secret OSS Journal of James Grafton Rogers, 1942–1943.* Edited by Thomas Troy. Frederick, MD: University Publications of America, 1987.

Roosevelt, James. *My Parents: A Differing View.* Chicago: Playboy Press, 1976.

Sacquety, Troy. *The OSS in Burma: Jungle War against the Japanese.* Lawrence: University Press of Kansas, 2013.

Sanderson, James. *Behind Enemy Lines.* Princeton, NJ: D. Van Nostrand Company, 1959.

Schaffer, Ronald. *Wings of Judgment: American Bombing in World War II.* New York: Oxford University Press, 1985.

Smith, Bradley. *The Shadow Warriors: O.S.S. and the Origins of the C.I.A.* New York: Basic Books, 1983.

Smith, R. Harris. *OSS: The Secret History of America's First Central Intelligence Agency.* Berkeley: University of California Press, 1972.

Srodes, James. *Allen Dulles: Master of Spies.* Washington, DC: Regnery, 1999.

Stafford, David. *Camp X.* Toronto: Lester and Orpen Dennys, 1986.

Stahl, Bob. *You're No Good to Me Dead: Behind Japanese Lines in the Philippines.* Annapolis, MD: Naval Institute Press, 1995.

Stourton, Edward. *Cruel Crossing: Escaping Hitler Across the Pyrenees.* London: Doubleday, 2013.

Streatfeild, Dominic. *Brainwash: The Secret History of Mind Control.* New York: Picador, 2007.

Tuchman, Barbara. *Stilwell and the American Experience in China, 1911–45.* New York: Macmillan, 1971.

Turkel, Studs. *The Good War: An Oral History of World War II*. New York: Free Press, 1997.

Valentine, Douglas. *The Strength of the Wolf: The Secret History of America's War on Drugs*. London: Verso, 2004.

Vigurs, Kate. *Mission France: The True History of the Women of SOE*. New Haven, CT: Yale University Press, 2021.

Wakeman, Frederic. *Spymaster: Dai Li and the Chinese Secret Service*. Berkeley: University of California Press, 2003.

Wallace, Robert, and Keith Melton. *Spycraft: The Secret History of the CIA's Spytechs, from Communism to Al-Qaeda*. New York: Plume, 2009.

Waller, Douglas. *Wild Bill Donovan: The Spymaster Who Created the OSS and Modern American Espionage*. New York: Free Press, 2011.

Weiner, Tim. *Legacy of Ashes: The History of the CIA*. New York: Doubleday, 2007.

Weissman, Stephen. *American Foreign Policy in the Congo 1960–1964*. Ithaca, NY: Cornell University Press, 1974.

Werth, Alexander. *Russia at War: 1941–1945*. New York: Skyhorse, 2017.

Wiggan, Richard. *Operation Freshman: The Rjukan Heavy Water Raid, 1942*. London: William Kimber, 1986.

Winter, Alison. *Memory: Fragments of a Modern History*. Chicago: University of Chicago Press, 2012.

Yang, Yan-Jun, and Yue-Him Tam. *Unit 731: Laboratory of the Devil, Auschwitz of the East*. Stroud, UK: Fonthill Media, 2018.

Zachary, G. Pascal. *Endless Frontier: Vannevar Bush, Engineer of the American Century*. New York: Free Press, 1997.

Notes

Archives

AHEC   United States Army Heritage and Education Center, Carlisle, Pennsylvania

BL   Bancroft Library, Berkeley, California

CIT   California Institute of Technology Archives, Pasadena, California

DBC   Dolph Briscoe Center for American History, Austin, Texas

GUA   Georgetown University Archives, Washington, D.C.

HSTL Harry S. Truman Presidential Library, Independence, Missouri

LOC   Library of Congress, Washington, D.C.

MIT   Massachusetts Institute of Technology Libraries, Cambridge, Massachusetts

NARA National Archives and Records Administration, College Park, Maryland

NAS   National Academy of Sciences Archives, Washington, D.C.

UIA   University of Illinois Archives, Urbana, Illinois

YSML Yale Sterling Memorial Library, New Haven, Connecticut

Abbreviations

B	Box
CIA	Central Intelligence Agency
COI	Coordinator of Information
CREST	CIA Records Search Tool
DSG	Deposition of Sidney Gottlieb
E	Entry
F	Folder
FBI	Federal Bureau of Investigation
FOPD	Frank Olson Project Documents
JRP	Joseph Rauh Papers
LSD	Lysergic acid diethylamide
MORI	Management of Officially Released Information Identification
NASA	National Aeronautics and Space Administration
NDRC	National Defense Research Committee
OSI	Office of Scientific Intelligence
OSS	Office of Strategic Services
POW	Prisoner of war
R&A	Research and Analysis
R&D	Research and Development
RG	Record Group
SOD	Special Operations Division
SOE	Special Operations Executive
TSD	Technical Services Division
TSS	Technical Services Staff
VBP	Vannevar Bush Papers

1. Donovan's Dragoons

1 "like a youngster at Halloween": Waller, *Wild Bill Donovan*, 22. Donovan earned the nickname "Wild Bill" from an exhausted young soldier who fell behind him on a forced march. How, the soldier wondered, could a commander in his mid-thirties outpace his teenage recruits unless he was wild to his core?

1 "felt as if somebody": Brown, *The Last Hero*, 62.

2 He was known to sock them: McIntosh, *Sisterhood of Spies*, 1–2.

2 "showered with the remnants": Brown, *The Last Hero*, 62–63.

2 They arrived to find a harrowing scene: Brown, *The Last Hero*, 63–64.

3 "It doesn't belong with me": Waller, *Wild Bill Donovan*, 35.

3 from a tough, working-class neighborhood: Donovan married into the upper class. Hs wife, Ruth Rumsey, was a slim, platinum blonde, aristocratic heiress to one of Buffalo's wealthiest families. He was Catholic, she was Protestant. Their religious differences occasionally tested their marriage, though not incurably.

3 "The law is the law": Brown, *The Last Hero*, 86.

3 "Nor did he smoke": Coon, *Adventures and Discoveries*, 161.

4 "Modern war operates": Chambers, *OSS Training in the National Parks*, 16.

5 a fourth domain: McIntosh, *Sisterhood of Spies*, 5.

5 "Bill Donovan is an old friend": Perisco, *Roosevelt's Secret War*, 64.

5 The emotional toll: Brown, *The Last Hero*, 142.

5 "great influence with the President": Brown, *The Last Hero*, 153.

6 "supplementary activities": Waller, *Wild Bill Donovan*, 71–77.

6 Donovan moved COI headquarters: Ford, *Donovan of OSS*, 121.

6 "fifty professors, twenty monkeys": Brown, *The Last Hero*, 174.

6 "as unromantic as their surroundings": Ford and MacBain, *Cloak and Dagger*, 4.

7 "meat grinder turned by a maniac": James Aswell to Joseph Scribner, personal collection of Jeff Rogg. Aswell gave an example of the organization's chaotic environment: "I was told to go to the Area with Mr. Kloman for one day as he set up the first so-called 'Finishing School'—which, God forgive me, I helped formulate under orders although it has always seemed to me pure Alice-in-Wonderland stuff. No, I was not to do that. I was to go to an Army camp with Colonel Potter. No, I was not, on second thought, to do that. I was to go with Mr. Kloman to the Area . . ."

7 "closely resembled a cat house": Brown, *The Last Hero*, 174.

7 "a secret bureau": Brown, *The Last Hero*, 166.

8 "dismal cellar tenants": Arthur Daley, "Giants Rule Favorites at 5

to 6 in Encounter with Dodgers Today," *The New York Times* (December 7, 1941): S1; Arthur Daley, "Manders Excels in 21–7 Triumph," *The New York Times* (December 8, 1941): 32.

8   "Attention, please!": Brown, *The Last Hero*, 3.

9   "They caught our ships": Brown, *The Last Hero*, 6–7.

9   slew of additional epithets: Alcorn, *No Bugles for Spies*, 75; Smith, *OSS*, 8, 16; Waller, *Wild Bill Donovan*, 93, 150. Donovan often said that he would "rather have a young lieutenant with guts enough to disobey than a colonel too regimented to think and act for himself," not the kind of culture that won admirers among the traditional military branches. Alcorn, *No Bugles for Spies*, 81–82.

10 "a Tinker Toy outfit": Dunlop, *Donovan*, 348.

11 Despite the name change: Donovan similarly received a new nickname, "The Wizard of OSS" (*The Wizard of Oz* movie having been released in 1939), though it never replaced "Wild Bill." He took much of the name-calling in stride, but personal attacks on his character were another matter. Once, when an Army intelligence officer insulted him, he responded, "Unless the general apologizes at once, I shall have to tear him to pieces physically and throw his remains through these windows." The offending party made an immediate and deferential apology. Smith, *OSS*, 172–73.

11 "If you should by chance": Brown, *The Last Hero*, 301.

11 "brewed a slow poison": Ford and MacBain, *Cloak and Dagger*, 7.

12 The Research and Analysis Branch: Many of the members of the R&A Branch were Ph.Ds. who insisted on being called "doctor," leading others to jokingly nickname the branch "the medical school."

12 Roger Hall never forgot: Hall, *You're Stepping on My Cloak and Dagger*, 82–97. For related stories, see Jim Bishop, "Cloak and Daggering," *Indiana Gazette* (April 16, 1971): 10; Erwin Canham, "Some Fond Memories of a Dirty Trickster," *Buck County Courier Times* (January 15, 1976): 14.

2. Professor Moriarty

16 "salty little Yankee inventor": Rogers, *Wartime Washington*, 156.

16 "The glorification of war": Lovell, *Of Spies and Stratagems*, 138–43.

16 "that great German savant": Stanley Lovell, "Spengler Warns U.S.," *The Boston Globe* (September 17, 1934): 14.

16 "Military motorcycles screeched": Lovell, *Of Spies and Stratagems*, 138–43.

17 Lovell pledged to defend: Lovell, *Of Spies and Stratagems*, 144–45.

17 Stanley Lovell thought that his ancestors: Lovell's distant uncle, James Lovell, was a member of the Continental Congress and a renowned codebreaker for the Americans in the Revolutionary War.

17 They had sailed: Stanley Lovell's grandson Jonathan said in an interview, "These are the tales that we were introduced to as young children and which spread with great abandonment among all our friends." Author interview with Jonathan Lovell.

17 Gustavus Lovell: Author interview with Jonathan Lovell.

18 "No, no, I don't want them": Author interview with Jonathan Lovell.

19 "a strong belief": Hymoff, *The OSS in World War II*, 155.

19 The Cornell yearbook: *The Cornell Class Book* (1912): 173. Franklin Roosevelt would later say of Lovell, "You're either a Down East Yankee or you've got a case of the adenoids." Dunlop, *Donovan*, 377.

19 "The practice of 'shifting'": "'The Era' Muckraking," *Cornell Alumni News* 13 (September 1, 1910–August 31, 1911): 99–100; "Ask Clean Eating Places," *The New York Times* (November 21, 1910): 8.

20 he openly criticized organized religion: Perhaps this suited a native of Brockton, Massachusetts. In 1929, the city became one of the last in the country to charge someone with blasphemy—using a blasphemy law that had been passed during the time of the Salem Witch Trials some two and a half centuries earlier.

21 Mabel adored Lovell: Author interview with Jonathan Lovell. Mabel's twin sisters, Blanche and Mildred, married a pair of twin brothers, Stanley and Albert White, who happened to have been Lovell's classmates at Cornell. Stanley and Albert White were brothers of E. B. White, the author of *Stuart Little* and *Charlotte's Web*.

21 four different shoe and leather: OSS, "Request for Service Record," November 6, 1942, RG 226, E A1 224, B 464, F "Lovell, Stanley P.," NARA.

21 "The Moth Ball King": "Company Makes Camphor," *Shoe and Leather Facts* 34, no. 1 (January 1922): 37.

21 Lovell was walking across Boston Common: Lovell, *Of Spies and Stratagems*, 13.

22 His stated reason: OSS, "Request for Service Record," November 6, 1942, RG 226 E A1 224, B 464, F "Lovell, Stanley P.," NARA.

22 In the hullabaloo: "To Advise on Quartermaster Matters," *Army and Navy Journal* 79, no. 39 (May 30, 1942): 1077.

22 "How to make a grommet": Lovell, *Of Spies and Stratagems*, 14.

22 Vannevar Bush saved Lovell: "Vannevar" rhymes with "beaver."

23 "probably had the highest regard": Author interview with Jonathan Lovell.

23 "pioneering spirit": Vannevar Bush, MIT Oral History Interviews, 98A–99.

24 "You are about to land": Lovell, *Of Spies and Stratagems*, 15.

24 The sun was setting: Lovell, *Of Spies and Stratagems*, 15–17.

26 "for the invention": "History of the Office of Research and Development," RG 226, E A1 210, B 108, F 7, NARA. On Lovell's philosophy of intelligence gathering, see Stanley Lovell, "December 1944 Memorandum," William J. Donovan Papers, B 80, AHEC.

27 "The American people": Lovell, *Of Spies and Stratagems*, 21.

27 "go out and set Europe ablaze!": Wallace and Melton, *Spycraft*, 5.

27 While abroad for their lessons: "History of the Office of Research and Development," RG 226, E A1 210, B 108, F 7, NARA. On OSS and SOE collaboration, see Jakub, *Spies and Saboteurs*, 50–51.

27 "Ah, those first OSS arrivals": Brown, *The Last Hero*, 185.

28 "What they teach you": O'Donnell, *Operatives, Spies, and Saboteurs*, 7. In a section titled "Sabotage by Destruction," the OSS *Special Operation Field Manual* says, "Thousands of destructive methods are available including explosions, fires, floods, wrecks, accidents, leaks, breaks, overwork of machinery, maladjustment of machinery, and the adulteration of lubricants, fuels and products."

28 "a bundle of playboys": Rogers, *Wartime Washington*, 156.

28 "highly undisciplined": Vannevar Bush, MIT Oral History Interviews, 685.

29 "Stanley, I'm so glad": Lovell, *Of Spies and Stratagems*, 59–61.

29 "If they want to make": Vannevar Bush, MIT Oral History Interviews, 684–86. Bush came to view the "OSS wild men" running around his shop as "a damn nuisance." They butted into things that didn't concern them and interfered with Bush's other contractors. Bush almost cut off the aid until he and Donovan came to an agreement that all requests for help would come directly from Lovell and nobody else. Donovan also agreed to let Bush remove anyone who stepped out of line. "It worked alright," Bush later said of the arrangement. "Stan had a way about him and kept things in order. I think we stopped all sorts of possible leaks by the kind of thing that we did there." Vannevar Bush, MIT Oral History Interviews, 685–86.

29 "Throw all your normal": Lovell, *Of Spies and Stratagems*, 22.

29 "Sandeman Club": NDRC, *Summary Technical Report of Division 19*. Before the NDRC adopted a numerical ordering system, the division was known as Division B-9-C, with Lovell, Chadwell, Warren Lothrop, Roger Adams, and George Kistiakowsky serving as technical aides. OSRD, *Chemistry*, 433.

30 "one of the last chaps": Vannevar Bush, MIT Oral History Interviews, 684–86.

30 "should be brought to the attention": Harris Chadwell to Vannevar Bush, January 1, 1946, RG 226, E A1 210, B 84, F 6, NARA. These documents even provide insight into discussions that weren't originally written down. For example, one R&D Branch notes, "This information has been passed on only verbally by Mr. Lovell and Dr. Chadwell allegedly from Dr. Van Bush." A. Gregg Noble "Status Summary of Projects Special Assistance Division," January 22, 1945, RG 226, E 211, B 20, NARA.

3. The Sandeman Club

31 the Congressional's picturesque golf course: "History of the Office of Research and Development," RG 226, E A1 210, B 108, F 7, NARA; Warren Lothrop, "History of Division 19," June 30, 1945, RG 226, E A1 210, B 84, F 6, NARA, 5; Warren Lothrop, "History of Division 19," June 30, 1945, RG 226, E A1 210, B 84, F 12, NARA, 301.

32 crawled on their bellies: One recruit was killed while crawling under the machine-gun fire. He came face to face with a snake and jumped. Chambers, *OSS Training in the National Parks*, 260.

32 "We literally just blew the place up": Bill Pennington, "When the Rounds were Ammo," *The New York Times* (June 12, 2011).

32 a short welcome booklet: OSS, *Area F Reallocation Booklet*.

33 the scientists of Division 19 installed: "Establishment and Operation of Maryland Research Laboratories," Kenneth Pitzer Papers, B 2, F 2, BL.

33 "Just what is my job?": Lovell, *Of Spies and Stratagems*, 19.

33 Better to ask for forgiveness: William Casey, the head of the OSS Secret Intelligence Branch, later made the same point: "You didn't wait six months for a feasibility study to prove that an idea could work. You didn't tie up the organization with red tape designed mostly to cover someone's ass. You took the initiative and the responsibility. You went around end, you went over somebody's head if you had to. But you acted. That's what drove the regular military and the State Department chair-warmers crazy about the OSS." Perisco, *Casey*, 57.

33 "cloak and dagger boys": Joe Harrington, "Newton Agent Bares O.S.S. Secrets," *The Boston Globe* (November 12, 1963).

33 "a pianist, improvising": Lovell, *Of Spies and Stratagems*, 7.

34 One day while touring: Hall, *You're Stepping on My Cloak and Dagger*, 25.

34 "made my hair stand on end": Wallace and Melton, *Spycraft*, 14.

34 With a time pencil: "History of the Office of Research and Development," RG 226, E A1 210, B 108, F 7, NARA.

35 "one of the great universities": "Minutes of the Meeting of the Sandeman Club," October 23, 1942, RG 226, E A1 210, B 81, F 3, NARA.

35 it was Columbia University: OSRD, *Chemistry*, 433.

35 the limpet mine: On the limpet, see "Maryland Research Laboratories Report No. 4," September 15, 1943, Kenneth Pitzer Papers, B 2, F 2, BL; "Maryland Research Laboratories Report No. 15," Kenneth Pitzer Papers, B 2, F 2, BL; "Maryland Research Laboratories Report No. 93," June 6, 1944, Kenneth Pitzer Papers, B 2, F 1, BL.

35 On one maritime mission: Sanderson, *Behind Enemy Lines*, 108–11.

36 Some of his first detonation tests: Fieser, *The Scientific Method*, 41–42.

37 "looking like a blackface comedian": Neer, *Napalm*, 26. Some quotes in this book are insensitive, but they're nevertheless important because they reflect historical attitudes.

37 His first product for Division 19: "History of the Office of Research and Development," RG 226, E A1 210, B 108, F 7, NARA.

37 Fieser nearly got into big trouble: Fieser, *The Scientific Method*, 75. A Federal Express station porter once picked up one of Fieser's parcels and said, "It feels heavy enough to be a bomb." Neer, *Napalm*, 31.

38 Lovell named it the "City Slicker": A similar device that worked on both land and sea was dubbed "Paul Revere."

38 "Everyone was happy": Fieser, *The Scientific Method*, 96–99. Given Fieser's success with Division 19, the OSS asked him to write an instruction manual for saboteurs on the art of arson. The final product, *Arson: An Instruction Manual*, drew from a series of experiments that he had conducted in Bryson City, North Carolina. The Tennessee Valley Authority was planning to flood the region, but before it did, it gave the OSS permission to conduct weapons tests on the ill-fated buildings, bridges, and railroad tracks. Fieser led the incendiary group. By strategically placing pocket incendiaries in one of the condemned houses, he was able to collapse it in just over fifteen minutes.

38 Bill Donovan led a crowdsourcing effort: Thomas Edison had launched a similar campaign during World War I and concluded, "The soldier of the future will not be a sabre-bearing, blood thirsty savage. He will be a machinist." "Machine Fighting is Edison's Idea," *The New York Times* (October 16,1915): 4.

38 "many of these, although extremely amusing": Department of Commerce, *Administrative History of the National Inventors Council*, 15; "Crackpot Holiday," *Time Magazine* (August 25, 1941). The National Inventors Council recommended 106 out of 208,975 submissions for production.

39 "I ignore nothing": Smith, *OSS*, 3; "Minutes of the Meeting of the Sandeman Club," October 23, 1942, RG 226, E A1 210, B 81, F 3, NARA.

39 "chaps out in the woods somewhere": Vannevar Bush, MIT Oral History Interviews, 227–29.

39 "death ray": Adam Kline and Robyn Dexter, "Secret Weapons, Forgotten Sacrifices," *Prologue* (Spring 2016): 29–30.

39 "just a simple-minded fellow": Vannevar Bush, MIT Oral History Interviews, 227–29.

39 "Now look. You must understand": Vannevar Bush, MIT Oral History Interviews, 229–29A.

40 "Everyone knows that a cat": Lovell, *Of Spies and Stratagems*, 63.

40 air mail delivery system: Trimble and Lewis, "Lytle S. Adams: The Apostle of Nonstop Airmail Pickup." The OSS, in conjunction with the Army Air Forces, later developed a similar "Man Pick-Up" system for exfiltrating agents on the ground. During the first live test of the system, a sheep had its neck broken. Soon afterward, successful tests were made with humans. One of them said that it was "less severe than a parachute jump." "Man Pick-Up," November 15, 1943, RG 226, E A1 134, B 52, F "Pick-up Equipment," NARA.

41 "The millions of bats": "Proposal for Surprise Attack," January 12, 1942, Jack Couffer Bat Bomb Research Papers, B 4C758, F "Government Documents 1," DBC.

42 "This man is *not* a nut": Franklin Roosevelt to William Donovan, February 9, 1942, Jack Couffer Bat Bomb Research Papers, B 4C758, F "Government Documents 1," DBC.

42 "it is suicidal folly": Couffer, *Bat Bomb*, 11–12.

43 Griffin set about answering: Couffer, *Bat Bomb*, 35.

43 "The project seems silly": Fieser, *The Scientific Method*, 121.

43 "Female red bats": Couffer, *Bat Bomb*, 45.

44 "the damnedest thing": Couffer, *Bat Bomb*, 61.

44 The first test of the Bat Bomb: Fieser, *The Scientific Method*, 124–27.

45 another test was scheduled: Couffer, *Bat Bomb*, 114–18.

48 "a mesh of twisted steel girders": Fieser, *The Scientific Method*, 129.

48 "Upon receipt of your letter": Couffer, *Bat Bomb*, 145.

48 "I was very glad": Couffer, *Bat Bomb*, 208–9.

49 Fieser concluded that 3,720 pounds: Fieser, *The Scientific Method*, 130–31.

49   "uncertainties involved in the behavior": Couffer, *Bat Bomb*, 226.

49   Chadwell admitted that he didn't think: Couffer, *Bat Bomb*, 218.

4. Division 19 Destruction

50   He walked over to the White House: Lovell, *Of Spies and Strata-gems*, 40–41.

51   Lovell joined him in the back seat: Lovell, *Of Spies and Strata-gems*, 182–83.

52   "loaded and brandished": "Memorandum of the First Meeting of Division 19," May 3, 1943, RG 226, E A1 210, B 81, F 3, NARA.

52   "more like a giant typewriter": "History of the Office of Research and Development," RG 226, E A1 210, B 108, F 7, NARA.

52   "This is emphatically not a weapon": "Fortnightly Report No. 17," February 1, 1945, RG 226, E A1 154, B 129, F 2262, NARA.

52   "was sent off to assassinate people": O'Donnell, *Operatives, Spies, and Saboteurs*, 18.

53   "Wait a minute": Morgan, *The OSS and I*, 74–76.

53   Lovell had been eager: Lovell, *Of Spies and Stratagems*, 36–37.

54   "The way it killed people": O'Donnell, *Operatives, Spies, and Sab-oteurs*, 17.

54   "To the horror of us all": Lovell, *Of Spies and Stratagems*, 37–38. During additional field trials in Europe, Beanos injured forty-four people and killed two others, causing the Army to lose interest. In Burma, however, Detachment 101 R&D section chief Sam Lucy called the Beano "a honey" in a letter to Lovell, and in another letter to R&D Branch officer John Jeffries, he said, "What has happened to the Beanos which were supposed to have come to this theater by air during February? Have they definitely left the states? Operational people are crying for these units." McLean, *The Spy's Workshop*, 192; Sam Lucy to Stanley Lovell, June 28, 1944, RG 226, E A1 154, B 129, F 2263, NARA; Sam Lucy to J. Jeffries, March 26, 1945, RG 226, E A1 154, B 129, F 2263, NARA.

54   "He was blown apart": O'Donnell, *Operatives, Spies, and Sabo-teurs*, 17.

54   "You sit down": Lovell, *Of Spies and Stratagems*, 47.

54 "You're sure this stuff": Hymoff, *The OSS in World War II*, 1.

55 "and ate them in front": Marks, *The Search for the Manchurian Candidate*, 14. OSS officer Frank Gleason once told a Chinese cook to make a batch of Aunt Jemima muffins. He emphasized, "Do not eat those muffins! They are poison. Do not eat them!" The chef produced a gorgeous batch and concluded that Gleason had told him not to eat them because he selfishly wanted them all for himself. The temptation proved irresistible. The chef stuffed himself with the forbidden muffins. Gleason matter-of-factly recalled, "He almost died," though that's probably an exaggeration. O'Donnell, *Operatives, Spies, and Saboteurs*, 7–8.

55 "The Disappearing Donkey": Moon, *This Grim and Savage Game*, 53.

55 "Aunt Jemima doughs": "Evaluation of Aunt Jemima," May 2, 1944, RG 226, E A1 210, B 108, F 7, NARA.

55 He dumped one hundred pounds: "Evaluation of Aunt Jemima," May 2, 1944, RG 226, E A1 210, B 108, F 7, NARA.

56 Stanley Lovell's own troubles: Lovell, *Of Spies and Stratagems*, 49–50.

57 Lovell experienced another close call: Lovell, *Of Spies and Stratagems*, 187–88.

58 "were covered from collarbone": Dunlop, *Donovan*, 394.

58 "would have given anything": Lovell, *Of Spies and Stratagems*, 34. Hedy Lamarr, an inventor in her own right, helped develop a mechanism to prevent radio-operated torpedoes from jamming.

58 "interrupted me by suddenly shrieking": Lovell, *Of Spies and Stratagems*, 34.

59 Lovell's presentations: During another weapons demonstration, there was a "slight accident" that "marred the enjoyment of the new weapons." According to the minutes of a meeting of Division 19, Commander T. R. Bird accidentally broke a crossbow gun. "The group was most solicitous of [Bird] but were assured that he was not injured and he declined a glass of water." "Memorandum of the First Meeting of Division 19," May 3, 1943, RG 226, E A1 210, B 81, F 3, NARA.

59 "The group had gone back": MacDonald, *Undercover Girl*, 31. Also see Rogers, *Wartime Washington*, 175.

59 John Jeffries was tasked: "History of the Office of Research and Development," RG 226, E A1 210, B 108, F 7, NARA.

60 The OSS was unaware: Nazi occupation officials in Belgium said that the "most effective" form of sabotage against them was "that directed against the French railroads." Between June 1943 and May 1944, "a total of 1,822 locomotives was [*sic*] damaged, 200 passenger cars destroyed, 1,500 cars damaged, 2,500 freight cars destroyed and 8,000 damaged." Hymoff, *The OSS in World War II*, 242.

60 "which scored a direct hit": O'Donnell, *Operatives, Spies, and Saboteurs*, 113.

61 "This is a Car Movement Control Device": Lovell, *Of Spies and Stratagems*, 38–39.

61 "We guessed, the German soldier": Rudolf Hoess, commandant of the Auschwitz concentration camp, later confirmed Lovell's suspicion, saying, "We were all so trained to obey orders without thinking that the thought of disobeying never occurred to anybody." Perisco, *Nuremberg*, 319.

61 "The Joe exploded": "Coal Explosive," RG 226 E A1 210, B 108, F 7, NARA. Also see "Maryland Research Laboratories Report No. 94," June 24, 1944, Kenneth Pitzer Papers, B 2, F 1, BL.

62 "I was just the one": McIntosh, *Sisterhood of Spies*, 234; Adam Bernstein, "Elizabeth McIntosh, Journalist Who Became an Agent for the Office of Strategic Services Whose Efforts were Crucial in the War in the East," *Independent* (June 16, 2015).

62 The "Anerometer": Lovell later heard a rumor that an Anerometer had brought down the plane carrying Chinese general Dai Li, the so-called Himmler of China, but the rumor was false. Dai's plane crashed during a massive rainstorm. The pilot had been reluctant to fly in the first place, but Dai pressured him to go. Once in the air, the pilot communicated with the ground several times about the inclement weather. The Chinese Air Force scrambled four planes to guide the plane down, but they never found it in the storm. The pilot's last communication indicated that he was *descending* in altitude

to attempt an emergency landing, not ascending as the Anerometer would have required.

62 "would be sitting over": Lovell, *Of Spies and Stratagems*, 42–43.

62 "Along the highways": Lovell, *Of Spies and Stratagems*, 43.

63 "Mail!": Hall, *You're Stepping on My Cloak and Dagger*, 9.

63 Depending on the target: "Contaminant, Oil, Abrasive," August 29, 1945, RG 226, E A1 210, B 108, F 7, NARA. On August 8, 1945, one sabotage team in China reported that they had "received word that our sabotage embryo was at last blossoming. Between the 1st and the 5th, ten trucks were cacklubed at Lingling by us and in addition, many trucks were breaking down along the highway as a result of our work." "Cacklube Anyone?" *OSS Society Journal* 2, no. 1 (Spring–Summer 2009): 38.

63 In fact, one American mechanic: McLean, *The Spy's Workshop*, 76–79.

63 "We got submarines": "Interview with John Pitts Spence," Veterans History Project, LOC (online).

64 "Using the Lambertsen Units": O'Donnell, *Operatives, Spies, and Saboteurs*, 129.

64 "human mine suicide swimmers": Hymoff, *The OSS in World War II*, 335.

64 "A concussion from the mortar": O'Donnell, *Operatives, Spies, and Saboteurs*, 138–41.

64 "Javaman": Javaman was originally code-named "Campbell."

64 Traditional air raids: RG 226, E UD 140, B 18, F 147, NARA.

65 "technical development be carried out": Fearer, "The Lordly Pilot and Lowly Saboteur," 12.

65 The resulting motorboat "missiles": "Campbell Project," RG 226, E UD 140, B 18, F 147, NARA.

65 The first full test: "Monthly Report," September 11, 1944, RG 226, E UD 140, B 18, F 147, NARA; "Campbell Project," RG 226, E UD 140, B 18, F 147, NARA; Fearer, "The Lordly Pilot and Lowly Saboteur," 18–19. In 2014, Abd al-Rahim al-Nashiri, one of the terrorists accused of planning the bombing of the USS *Cole*, cited Javaman as a defense in his military tribunal.

66   "I am grateful": Fearer, "The Lordly Pilot and Lowly Saboteur," 36.

66   "Any means which hastens": "New O.S.S. Weapons," RG 226, E 211, B 20, NARA.

5. Kill or Be Killed

67   invisible inks: On invisible inks, see RG 226, E A1 211, B 20, F "WN24152–24154," NARA; OSRD, *Chemistry,* 439.

67   "Simple Sabotage": OSS, *Simple Sabotage Field Manual.*

68   "Our British associates": "Camouflage Intelligence Summary," October 30, 1944, RG 226, E A1 134, B 54, F 469, NARA.

68   One item that the SOE developed: Boyce and Everett, *SOE,* 73–74; Fraser-Smith, *The Secret War,* 85–86. SOE agents in Norway laced sardine cans with croton oil, a well-known purgative. McLean, *The Spy's Workshop,* 225.

69   "The trouble caused": Richard Norton-Taylor, "How Exploding Rats Went Down a Bomb," *The Guardian* (October 27, 1999); Boyce and Everett, *SOE,* 67.

69   "I'd put Stalin": Alcorn, *No Bugles for Spies,* 134.

69   "Not at all": Perisco, *Roosevelt's Secret War,* 101.

70   "They mumbled some Russian": Lovell, *Of Spies and Stratagems,* 185–86.

70   specialty pills: Roosevelt, *War Report of the OSS,* 159; Brunner, *OSS Weapons,* 91; Boyce and Everett, *SOE,* 78–79. On K-pills, see "Final Summary Report of K Tablet," September 5, 1945, RG 226, E 211, B 20, NARA.

70   "produce extreme illness": "Monthly Report—July 1945," August 3, 1945, RG 226, E 211, B 20, NARA. The report also mentions that the R&D Branch had been asked to examine a pellet that had been recovered from a European battlefield and was suspected of containing poison. After a careful analysis, the pellet was found to be a "harmless, sugar-coated laxative pill."

70   "If you're ever in a position": "Interview with Alfred Borgman," Veterans History Project, LOC (online).

71   "butter of almonds": "Final Summary Report of 'L' Tablet," September 4, 1945, RG 226, E 211, B 20, NARA.

71   One time, a helpless agent: Roosevelt, *War Report of the OSS*, 159.

71   The OSS often exaggerated: Boyce and Everett, *SOE*, 79.

71   "I don't know which is the L tablet": Waller, *Wild Bill Donovan*, 102.

72   "What better end": Smith, *OSS*, 184–85.

72   "Bilious yellow clouds": Bruce, *OSS against the Reich*, 60.

72   Once near the shore: Bruce, *OSS against the Reich*, 64–65.

72   "David, you've got": Brown, *The Last Hero*, 548. Years earlier, a soldier under Donovan's command had called him "a son of a bitch," but reluctantly admitted, "He's a game one." When Donovan was told the story, he said, "Write that as my epitaph." Duffy, *Father Duffy's Story*, 220.

73   "Now it will be like this": Brown, *The Last Hero*, 548.

73   "Excitement made him snort": Dunlop, *Donovan*, 336–37.

73   "David, we mustn't be captured": Smith, *OSS*, 184–85. Also see Bruce, *OSS against the Reich*, 220 n. 29.

74   "the feeding of sodium metal": "Memorandum of the Meeting of the Sandeman Club," November 6, 1942, RG 226, E A1 210, B 81, F 3, NARA.

75   Lovell chose botulinum toxin: Lovell, *Of Spies and Stratagems*, 86–88. According to Lovell, the Navy personnel tested the botulinum toxin on donkeys to gauge its potency. It had no effect and the Navy lost interest. Lovell later claimed that "donkeys are one of the few living creatures immune to botulism." More recent studies have shown that botulism outbreaks have occurred in donkeys.

75   "One can never tell": Vannevar Bush to Harvey Bundy, April 2, 1945, RG 227, E NC-138 1, B 10, NARA.

75   "Toxic Materials": "Final Summary Report of Toxic Materials," September 17, 1945, RG 226, E 211, B 20, NARA. Also see Gaillard, Regenstreif, and Fanton, "Modern Toxic Antipersonnel Projectiles."

75   "protested Lovell's interest in poisons": Rogers, *Wartime Washington*, 157–60.

76   "foodstuffs like sugar": Donald Summers, "Suggestions for Possible Sabotage Items to Be Investigated by a Future Organization Taking Such Responsibility," September 28, 1945, RG 226, E 211, B 20, F 4, NARA.

76 "a large feminine component": Murray, *An Analysis of the Personality of Adolf Hitler*, 4–5.

76 "Either that": Lovell, *Of Spies and Stratagems*, 84–85.

77 "a very Hard School of Learning": Robins, *The Legend of W. E. Fairbairn*, 89–91.

78 "gouging, biting": Dreux, *No Bridges Blown*, 34.

78 "It's a simple matter": "Gutter Fighting Training by OSS at Catoctin," posted on YouTube by Catoctin NPS: https://www.youtube.com/watch?v=rkvHoOH9I3w&ab_channel=CatoctinMountainPark.

79 "It was like watching": Dreux, *No Bridges Blown*, 34.

79 "It was like a huge carnival": Applegate and Melson, *The Close-Combat Files*, 346.

79 "circus stuff": Byrnes, *All in One Lifetime*, 195.

80 "Lieutenant Applegate": Applegate and Melson, *The Close-Combat Files*, 3.

80 "Off duty his conversation": Langelaan, *Knights of the Floating Silk*, 66.

81 "Now indeed": Langelaan, *Knights of the Floating Silk*, 70–71.

81 "Jerk your hands": Fairbairn, *Scientific Self-Defence*, 3–5.

81 "grab my privates": Helms and Wood, *A Look Over My Shoulder*, 32.

81 Fairbairn gave the recruits: Langelaan, *Knights of the Floating Silk*, 66; Morgan, *The OSS and I*, 128–29; Fairbairn, *Scientific Self-Defence*, 102.

82 He also taught the recruits: Regarding falls, Fairbairn couldn't resist quoting in his book an article from the 1916 *North China Daily News*. Along with studying physically crippling combat and monitoring red-light districts in Shanghai, he was also a thespian. He was once shot dead while acting in the play *The Breed of the Treshams*. His limp body falling down the stairs "was such as we have never seen equaled," the newspaper lauded. Fairbairn, *Scientific Self-Defence*, 136.

82 "gave us more and more": Foot, *SOE*, 64.

6. Psychological Warfare

83 "were of the opinion": Persico, *Roosevelt's Secret War*, 190–91.

84 In Operation Cornflakes: Torrey and Avery, "Postal Forgeries in Two World Wars," 63–67. The OSS exploited the German mail sys-

tem in other ways. As part of Operation Cornflakes, two million envelopes were packed with propaganda and addressed to random names found in a German phone book. Once the envelopes were ready for delivery, they were bound together in parcels (Americans interrogated German mail carriers for the correct method of packaging) and an Army Air Forces fighter group dropped them onto a destroyed German mail train. In theory, the Germans would collect the parcels, assume that they had belonged on the train, and send them on their way.

84 League of Lonely War Women: McIntosh, *Sisterhood of Spies*, 65–66. For a similar operation in Japan, see MacDonald, *Undercover Girl*, 178.

84 A group of psychoanalysts: Smith, *OSS*, 222–23.

85 "produce unmistakable evidence": Adam Kline and Robyn Dexter, "Secret Weapons, Forgotten Sacrifices," *Prologue* (Spring 2016): 26.

85 Crocker had gotten his start: Christina Couch, "The Stench of War," *MIT Technology Review* (June 27, 2018), www.technologyreview.com/2018/06/27/141948/the-stench-of-war.

85 But a Navy doctor: Adam Kline and Robyn Dexter, "Secret Weapons, Forgotten Sacrifices," *Prologue* (Spring 2016): 27.

86 "comic relief": Lovell, *Of Spies and Stratagems*, 56.

86 "which was not at all surprising": Lovell, *Of Spies and Stratagems*, 57.

86 "pleasant man": MacDonald, *Undercover Girl*, 11.

86 Between 1903 and 1914: "Edgar Salinger, 83, Aided War Victims," *The New York Times* (February 26, 1971): 36.

87 In one psychological scheme: Ed Salinger, "Psychological Warfare Proposals Against the Japanese," March 13 (no year), William J. Donovan Papers, B 119, AHEC.

87 Operation Fantasia: The name "Fantasia" probably derived from Walt Disney's whimsical 1940 animated film of the same name.

87 "The foundation for the proposal": Ed Salinger, "Psychological Warfare Proposals Against the Japanese," March 13 (no year), William J. Donovan Papers, B 119, AHEC.

87 "These whistles": Ed Salinger, "Psychological Warfare Proposals Against the Japanese," March 13 (no year), William J. Donovan Papers, B 119, AHEC. Also see "OSS Plan to Fox Japs with Ghost Foxes Recalled," *Sunday Tribune* (March 21, 1948): 1; Kodosky, *Psychological Operations American Style*, 73.

88 The health risks: See Moore, *The Radium Girls.*

88 In his tenure at the zoo: "Dr. Harry Nimphius, Park Zoo Director," *The New York Times* (September 28, 1944): 19.

89 "Horrified citizens": "U.S. Bares Plan to Frighten Japs with Luminous Foxes," *Minneapolis Morning Tribune* (March 12, 1948): 1.

89 Under the cloak: Ed Salinger, "Psychological Warfare Proposals Against the Japanese," March 13 (no year), William J. Donovan Papers, B 119, AHEC; Houghton, *Nuking the Moon*, 48.

90 "If enough foxes": Ed Salinger, "Psychological Warfare Proposals Against the Japanese," March 13 (no year), William J. Donovan Papers, B 119, AHEC.

90 "a peculiarly potent manifestation": Ed Salinger, "Psychological Warfare Proposals Against the Japanese," March 13 (no year), William J. Donovan Papers, B 119, AHEC. According to Elizabeth MacDonald, during a demonstration in the woods, Salinger wore "a phosphorescent skeleton costume" and "rose in the darkness like a phoenix," scaring the attendees. MacDonald, *Undercover Girl*, 12.

91 At best, he thought: Richard Dunlop, "Interview with Stanley Lovell," 1961, AHEC.

91 "I trust that this will serve": "Division 19 Meeting of August 5th," August 6, 1943, RG 226, E A1 210, B 81, F 2, NARA.

91 "This problem of Fantasia": "Minutes of the Sixth Meeting of Division 19," November 5, 1943, RG 226, E A1 210, B 81, F 2, NARA; Lovell, *Of Spies and Stratagems*, 21.

7. Detachment 101

92 "amusing murder nonsense": Rogers, *Wartime Washington*, 42.

92 "deadliest hombre": Lovell, *Of Spies and Stratagems*, 108.

93 "You'd better get up here": Moon and Eifler, *The Deadliest Colonel*, 19–21.

94 "Glad you are joining": Moon and Eifler, *The Deadliest Colonel*, 31.

94 "We are sending a group": Moon and Eifler, *The Deadliest Colonel*, 36.

94 "It has merit": Moon and Eifler, *The Deadliest Colonel*, 41.

95 "From behind the desk": Moon and Eifler, *The Deadliest Colonel*, 44.

95 "Hit me in the stomach": Eifler enjoyed impressing people with his physical feats. The only time that anyone ever knocked him unconscious was when he taught his secretary self-defense and she delivered a blow to his massive neck, dropping him on the spot.

95 "as if it were entirely habitual": Peers and Brelis, *Behind the Burma Road*, 29.

96 "You have ninety days": Sacquety, *The OSS in Burma*, 2.

96 "will develop rust pits": "Report Covering Period June 1 to June 30, 1943," July 1, 1943, RG 226, E 99, B 65, F 1, NARA.

96 "[Jim] Tilly got lost": "Captain Tilly with the Knothead Group," December 9, 1942, RG 226, E 190, B 38, F 48, NARA.

96 For fun, and for protection: Moon and Eifler, *The Deadliest Colonel*, 139. Food was hard to come by in Nazira. On occasion, the Americans resorted to eating insects, crows, and monkeys. One sergeant from the Bronx described his experience catching a monkey: "I knocked this big black son-of-a-gun out of a tree and when I ran up to him he was lying on his back with his arms stretched out, opening and clenching his fists and moaning, 'Oooh, Oooh,' with tears running down his cheeks. And the way he looked up at me." The sergeant shook his head in empathy. "From now on the only monkeys I kill will be Japs." Ford and MacBain, *Cloak and Dagger*, 92.

96 One night while Captain Red Maddox: Peers and Brelis, *Behind the Burma Road*, 95.

97 In one popular rendition: Peers and Brelis, *Behind the Burma Road*, 123. Detachment 101, and the OSS in general, apparently

had a number of dark comics in its ranks. During one firefight across
a river at Walawbum, Burma, the Japanese yelled at the Americans
in broken English, "To hell with Roosevelt." A joke circulated among
the Americans. "Did you kill him?" one would ask. "No," another
would say, "I couldn't shoot a Republican." Moon and Eifler, *The
Deadliest Colonel*, 197.

97 the Kachins: The Kachins were reluctant to jump from planes. On
one occasion, a Kachin stood at the edge of a plane with eyes like a
"wild stallion," said Jim Tilly, a member of the crew. When the Kachin
finally jumped, he "turned in mid-air and grabbed the static line before
it had reached its length. The slipstream slammed him against the side
of the ship. He hung on for dear life, rat-tat-tatting against the aluminum side of the C-47. With pursed lips, wild eyes and a determination
that I think I can call admirable, he inched his way up the static line,
little hand over little hand." Tilly reached out and pulled the Kachin
back inside the plane. "You never saw such a happy smile." Until, that
is, Tilly "dusted him off, turned him around and while both of us were
still ecstatic, I booted him ten feet straight out." Sacquety, *The OSS in
Burma*, 70.

97 The plan was for twelve saboteurs: Sacquety, *The OSS in Burma*,
33–41.

98 "We could see a discomforting sight": Peers and Brelis, *Behind the
Burma Road*, 102.

98 During the next mission, Eifler planned: Moon and Eifler, *The
Deadliest Colonel*, 117–18; Peers and Brelis, *Behind the Burma Road*,
116.

99 The rafts had been retrieved: Despite these early setbacks, Detachment 101 soon successfully ambushed a column of Japanese soldiers. A group of saboteurs placed a camouflaged string of grenades
along a rugged trail that the Japanese frequented. After setting the
trap, the saboteurs hid in the nearby brush, careful not to create any
unnecessary noise. The Japanese column approached in the distance.
Before they arrived, a scout dog scampered up the trail. To the relief
of the saboteurs, the dog let them pet it and left without barking.

Then came the Japanese soldiers. The scene went from silent calm to deafening mayhem. The grenades exploded, killing more than one hundred soldiers. The saboteurs opened fire on the remaining members of the column. Detachment 101 suffered not a single casualty. Sacquety, *The OSS in Burma*, 208.

99 "Same type of government": Moon and Eifler, *The Deadliest Colonel*, 78. Also see Tuchman, *Stilwell and the American Experience in China*, ch. 13.

99 Without hesitation: Moon and Eifler, *The Deadliest Colonel*, 194.

99 "There were many situations": Sacquety, *The OSS in Burma*, 68.

100 To placate Detachment 101's demand: "Inventory," June 1, 1945, RG 226, E A1 154, B 129, F 2255, NARA; "Arson Manual," June 30, 1945, RG 226, E A1 154, B 129, F 2261, NARA.

100 Stanley Lovell personally invented: "Firing Device, Auto Weapons," August 28, 1945," RG 226, E A1 210, B 108, F 8, NARA.

100 "caused untold apprehension": Peers and Brelis, *Behind the Burma Road*, 147.

100 Now that Eifler had learned: Carl Eifler to Stanley Lovell, April 8, 1944, RG 226, E A1 146, B 173, F "Eifler," NARA; Carl Eifler to Stanley Lovell, March 28, 1944, RG 226, E A1 146, B 175, F "Far East," NARA; McLean, *The Spy's Workshop*, 204–7.

101 "absolutely impossible": McLean, *The Spy's Workshop*, 166.

101 "keep the engineers": Sam Lucy to Commanding Officer, May 2, 1945, RG 226, E A1 154, B 129, F 2255, NARA.

101 "Colonel Peers, Major Lucy": Newton Jones to E. Kellogg, February 14, 1945, RG 226, E A1 154, B 129, F 2260, NARA. On War Paint, see RG 226, E A1 134, B 52, F "Personal Disguise/Makeup Kits," NARA.

101 In Nazira, the members: Sam Lucy to Commanding Officer, July 26, 1945, RG 226, E A1 154, B 129, F 2255, NARA; Moon and Eifler, *The Deadliest Colonel*, 142; T. Pittman to Watts Hills, December 11, 1944, RG 226, E A1 154, B 129, F 2260, NARA; [Untitled and undated "top secret" report], RG 226, E A1 134, B 54, F 596A, NARA; "Concealement (Camouflage) Items," September 24, 1944, RG 226, E A1 134, B 54, F 601.

101 "There is a definite question": "Camouflage Intelligence Summary," October 30, 1944, RG 226, E A1 134, B 54, F 469, NARA.

102 "Dear Sam": Thomas Daugherty to Sam Lucy, April 9, 1945, RG 226, E A1 154, B 129, F 2255, NARA.

102 "Won't they be surprised!": Sacquety, *The OSS in Burma*, 141.

102 "like eggshells": Sacquety, *The OSS in Burma*, 141–42.

103 "natural instinct": Carl Eifler to Stanley Lovell, March 28, 1944, RG 226, E A1 146, B 175, F "Far East," NARA.

103 but Ray Peers argued against it: Peers and Brelis, *Behind the Burma Road*, 145.

8. Target Heavy Water

104 Still other tidbits: Richelson, *Spying on the Bomb*, 29.

104 "Met Niels and Margrethe": Clark, *The Greatest Power on Earth*, 95. The threat of a German atomic bomb was considered so serious that in 1939, Leo Szilard, the first person to have conceived of a nuclear chain reaction, decided to warn President Roosevelt. Szilard wasn't famous enough to get Roosevelt's attention, so he enlisted the help of someone who was. In July 1939, Szilard visited Albert Einstein at his Long Island cottage and explained to him the concept of a nuclear chain reaction, which Einstein hadn't considered before. Einstein agreed that if Szilard drafted a letter to Roosevelt, he would sign it and lend his credibility to the cause. The letter ultimately had little impact. It wasn't until Vannevar Bush explained to Roosevelt the conclusions of the British MAUD Committee—named after "Maud Ray" in Meitner's letter—that the American government took serious steps toward the Manhattan Project. Lanouette and Szilard, *Genius in the Shadows*, 198–202.

105 "One of my men": Lovell, *Of Spies and Stratagems*, 126–27. Also see Dulles, *From Hitler's Doorstep*, 37–38.

106 This new plutonium: Uranium can also be used to make an atomic bomb, but the necessary isotope, uranium-235, must be separated from the more abundant uranium-238. This separation is costly and time-consuming because the two isotopes are chemically identical.

Creating plutonium circumvents that cumbersome process because it can be chemically separated from uranium.

106 The OSS considered information: McIntosh, *Sisterhood of Spies*, 43.

106 In Dulles's report: Lovell, *Of Spies and Stratagems*, 127.

106 Lovell wasn't the first: Powers, *Heisenberg's War*, 75–76.

107 Both gliders crashed: Mears, *The Real Heroes of Telemark*; Wiggan, *Operation Freshman*.

107 Lastly, in Operation Gunnerside: Kruzman, *Blood and Water*.

108 "must be launching sites": Lovell, *Of Spies and Stratagems*, 128–29. In a 2003 interview, Donovan's aide Edwin Putzell confirmed that there was intelligence indicating that heavy water was being sent to Peenemünde. "Interview with Edwin P. Putzell," Veterans History Project, LOC (online).

109 The bombing raid seriously delayed: The Germans quickly built a new complex for assembling the rockets by forcing sixty thousand malnourished prisoners from the Buchenwald and Mittelbau-Dora concentration camps to dig tunnel shafts in an abandoned gypsum mine with their bare hands. Half of them died before the underground complex was completed. The resulting caves, devoid of fresh air, water, or sanitation, became the V-2 assembly site known as Mittelwerk. After the war, a British reconnaissance party called the Fedden Mission toured the remnants of Mittelwerk with "revulsion and disgust." The Fedden Mission's final report describes the stark scene in contrast to the natural beauty of Germany: "This factory is the epitome of megalomaniac production. . . . Everything was ruthlessly executed with utter disregard for humanitarian conditions. . . . We were told that 250 of the slave workers perished every day, due to overwork and malnutrition." There were "stretchers heavily saturated in blood, a room in which there was a slab on which the bodies were drained of blood, and the incinerators in which the bodies were burnt. These are all facts which require to be seen to be fully appreciated." Aalmans, *A Booklet with a Brief History of the "Dora"-Nordhausen Labor-Concentration Camps*.

109 If Haukelid could sink: While Haukelid was planning the operation, he learned that his friend's mother was scheduled to travel

aboard the *Hydro* on the portentous day. Haukelid begged him to keep her at home, "even if it meant knocking her down and locking her in a closet." Haukelid, *Skis Against the Atom*, 165.

109 On a freezing February 20, 1944: Haukelid, *Skis Against the Atom*, 192–94.

110 Halvard Asskildt and his fiancée: "Hitler's Sunken Secret," *PBS NOVA*, www.pbs.org/wgbh/nova/transcripts/3216_hydro.html.

111 Haukelid's sabotage mission succeeded: Fifty years later, two local Norwegians, Thor Olav Sperre and Johny Skogtad, located the sunken barrels at the bottom of Lake Tinn. In 2004, the underwater archaeology firm ProMare recovered one barrel. It still contained heavy water. "Artifact Spotlight: German Heavy Water Barrel," *National World War II Museum* (August 13, 2012), www.nww2m.com/2012/08/artifact-spotlight-german-heavy-water-barrel.

9. Pursuit of the Mastodon

112 "got behind my light machine gun": Dunlop, *Donovan*, 399.

112 "foolish guts": Turkel, *The Good War*, 494.

113 "a fellow spirit": Lovell, *Of Spies and Stratagems*, 110.

113 "Would the General": Moon and Eifler, *The Deadliest Colonel*, 147.

113 OSS agent Nicol Smith: Dunlop, *Donovan*, 423.

114 "That damned plane": Moon and Eifler, *The Deadliest Colonel*, 171.

114 The plane somehow managed: Moon and Eifler, *The Deadliest Colonel*, 169–73. Also see Sacquety, *The OSS in Burma*, 56, 72.

115 During their meeting: Powers, *Heisenberg's War*, 125–27.

115 Heisenberg had recently stopped publishing: In 1942, Soviet physicist Georgy Flerov noticed a curious absence of journal articles by top Americans physicists and reached the same conclusion about the United States. "This silence is not the result of an absence of research," he wrote. "In a word, the seal of silence has been imposed, and this is the best proof of the vigorous work that is going on now abroad." Holloway, *Stalin and the Bomb*, 78.

116 Eifler cut to the chase: Powers, *Heisenberg's War*, 263.

116 The details of the kidnapping: Moon and Eifler, *The Deadliest Colonel*, 181–84.

117 "Strategic Trial Unit": Stanley Lovell to William Donovan, February 23, 1944, RG 226, E A1 146, B 173, F "Eifler," NARA. Also see "Eifler Mission," RG 226, E A1 146, B 173, F "Eifler," NARA; Powers, *Heisenberg's War*, 267.

118 The strangest plot: Lovell, *Of Spies and Stratagems*, 89–91.

119 Lovell devised another assassination plot: Lovell, *Of Spies and Stratagems*, 81–84. Anthropologist and OSS agent Carleton Coon once suggested to Donovan that the OSS create a secret assassination squad "to judge the needs of our world society and to take whatever steps are necessary to prevent this society from a permanent collapse." Brown, *The Last Hero*, 270.

121 Carl Eifler didn't require: Moon and Eifler, *The Deadliest Colonel*, 184.

121 "When can we secure this equipment?": Carl Eifler to William Donovan, June 12, 1944, RG 226, E A1 146, B 173, F "Eifler," NARA.

121 "Mark this day": Moon, *This Grim and Savage Game*, 216. Stilwell later came to regret the decision not to kill Chiang Kai-shek. He confessed to Eifler, "You know, I was wrong in calling you off that Chiang job. If you had bumped him it would have changed the whole course of world history." Moon and Eifler, *The Deadliest Colonel*, 242.

122 "We've cracked the atom": Powers, *Heisenberg's War*, 312.

122 "voice that would dwarf": Sacquety, *The OSS in Burma*, 71.

10. The Heisenberg Uncertainty

123 "Europe is in flames": Arthur Daley, "Moe Berg, A Man of Many Facets," *The New York Times* (June 1, 1971): 55.

123 "I don't care how many": Arthur Daley, "Moe Berg, A Man of Many Facets," *The New York Times* (June 1, 1971): 55.

124 Back in 1934, Berg had joined: Dawidoff, *The Catcher Was a Spy*, 133. At a geisha house, Babe Ruth repeatedly groped a visibly shaken girl. Berg jotted down some katakana script and handed it to her. When Ruth grabbed her again, she turned, bowed, and sounded out the note: "Fuck you, Babe Ruth." Dawidoff, *The Catcher Was a Spy*, 90.

124 Two months later, the OSS assigned Berg: Powers, *Heisenberg's War*, 292; RG 226, E UD 137, B 20, F "Berg—Italy," NARA; RG 226, E UD 140, B 19, F "Larson Project Miscellaneous," NARA. Berg's code name during his mission to Rome was Remus (another agent was Romulus).

124 On the eve of Berg's departure: Powers, *Heisenberg's War*, 297.

125 In Italy, Berg set his sights: Powers, *Heisenberg's War*, 307; RG 226, E A1 146, B 169, F "Nuclear Physics (Intelligence)," NARA.

125 "a great love for": Howard Dix to Stanley Lovell, June 19, 1944, RG 226, E A1 146, B 169, F "Nuclear Physics (Intelligence)," NARA.

126 "At one time during the war": Powers, *Heisenberg's War*, 257.

126 "It probably would have cost Berg": Powers, *Heisenberg's War*, 393.

126 Disguised as Swiss physics students: Dawidoff, *The Catcher Was a Spy*, 201–4; Powers, *Heisenberg's War*, 397–99.

127 "Now you have to admit": Powers, *Heisenberg's War*, 402.

128 When Heisenberg left the diner party: Heisenberg's widow later wrote about the dinner party: "Later that night, a young man, whom [Heisenberg] had noticed throughout the evening and whom he had found exceptionally agreeable, accompanied him back to his hotel. On their way, their conversation was relaxed and animated. He told me about this encounter. Years later we received a book with the title *Moe Berg, Athlete, Scholar, Spy*. While leafing through the book, Heisenberg recognized Moe Berg as his young Swiss acquaintance, who had accompanied him to the hotel, who had listened so attentively in the first row during his lecture, and who had participated in the discussion at Scherrer's with such interest and interested questions." Heisenberg, *Inner Exile*, 97.

128 "[German] separation of U235": Dawidoff, *The Catcher Was a Spy*, 206–7; O'Donnell, *Operatives, Spies, and Saboteurs*, 71–72.

128 "Moe Berg how are you?": Dawidoff, *The Catcher Was a Spy*, 317.

129 "Carl, what's the matter?": Moon and Eifler, *The Deadliest Colonel*, 251–52.

129 "I hereby warn": Lovell, *Of Spies and Stratagems*, 110–11.

129 Detachment 101 has since been credited: "Rep. Latta Introduces Office of Strategic Services Congressional Gold Medal Act," *Federal*

News Service (December 1, 2015); Sacquety, *The OSS in Burma*, 222; Peers and Brelis, *Behind the Burma Road*, 220.

130 "You know": Moon and Eifler, *The Deadliest Colonel*, 263, 266. Eifler told author Thomas Powers, "We were all criminals." Powers, who wrote a book about Heisenberg's role in the German effort to build an atomic bomb, said that Eifler was the only person whom he interviewed who spoke "without reservation." Powers, *Heisenberg's War*, 540 n. 38.

11. The Documents Division

131 During an OSS staff meeting: Lovell, *Of Spies and Stratagems*, 23–24; "Interview with Stanley P. Lovell," June 24, 1966, CREST.

132 "It was very easy": John Steinbeck, "The Secret Weapon We Were Afraid to Use," *Collier's* (January 10, 1953). Also see Bloom, "Uncle Sam."

133 To Lovell's delight: The closest that Morgenthau had previously come to the world of intrigue was when he agreed to lend 14,700 tons of the Treasury's silver to the Manhattan Project to aid in the electromagnetic separation of uranium isotopes. And even then, President Roosevelt never told Morgenthau exactly what the silver was for because he thought that Morgenthau would oppose the atomic bomb and withhold the silver. Perisco, *Roosevelt's Secret War*, 407.

133 "the President has a cold": Lovell, *Of Spies and Stratagems*, 23–25; "Interview with Stanley P. Lovell," June 24, 1966, CREST.

134 Morgenthau had cleverly verbalized: On Morgenthau, Roosevelt, and plausible deniability, see the transcript of Morgenthau's telephone conversation with Milo Perkins, a member of the Board of Economic Warfare, in Morgenthau's diaries, volume 551, document 58, available online through the FDR Library: www.fdrlibrary.marist .edu/_resources/images/morg/md0797.pdf.

134 "Jim the Penman": Lovell, *Of Spies and Stratagems*, 103. The appellation "Jim the Penman" derived from a notorious forger from the nineteenth century named Emanuel Ninger, whom authorities labeled "Jim the Penman" before learning his true identity. Ninger

was a Prussian artist and sign painter. He began forging American currency in 1878, starting with a ten-dollar bill and gradually progressing to the twenty, fifty, and one hundred.

134 At the Documents Division: Lovell, *Of Spies and Stratagems*, 104.

134 "Any interference with their vital mission": Lovell, *Of Spies and Stratagems*, 52–53. Also see Stanley Lovell to C. M. Sears, April 28, 1944, RG 226, E A1 146, B 173, F "Eifler," NARA.

135 At a training camp on the Scottish coast: Langelaan, *Knights of the Floating Silk*, 62–64.

136 "Thanks to an understanding boss": Lovell, *Of Spies and Stratagems*, 105.

137 In April 1944, seven members: "Summary of Organization, R&D Branch, London," January 1, 1945, RG 226, E A1 210, B 199, F 4, NARA; Perisco, *Piercing the Reich*, 27. A survey trip to France scouted out the possibility of moving the entire office to continental Europe to reduce the time that it took to get products to agents in the field, but because of security and supply problems, the office remained in London. In November 1944, a small part of the Documents Division moved to Strasbourg when the city fell to Allied forces.

137 Among the most commonly forged documents: Over a single two-week period in March 1945, the workers in the Documents Division forged 177 signatures, manufactured 130 rubber stamps in duplicate, made 264 identification photographs for 27 individuals (they took so many photographs that they had to convert one of the bathrooms into a makeshift darkroom to meet the demand), and created 10 counterfeit document templates, which served as the basis for more than 800 additional counterfeit documents. "Progress Report, 15 March to 31 March, 1945," April 2, 1945, RG 226, E A1 154, B 129, F 2262, NARA; H. J. Anderson to William Donovan, November 13, 1944, William J. Donovan Papers, B 66, AHEC.

137 Even the photographs: Brown, *The Last Hero*, 763. Forged rubber stamps similarly had to match the style of their alleged town of origin. Creating authentic-looking stamps was a particular challenge because every town had its own unique seal. Whenever an

agent needed a stamp on a document from a new town, an expert artist had to recreate the seal. When the Allies liberated Strasbourg in 1944, a "Madame Issler" who owned a stamp factory there was recruited to make the rubber stamps for the Documents Division. "Report on the Cover and Documents Branch," May 8, 1945, RG 226, E A1 210, B 3, F 1, NARA.

137 "a chemical of his own invention": "Report on the Cover and Documents Branch," May 8, 1945, RG 226, E A1 210, B 3, F 1, NARA.

137 Another method involved: Roosevelt, *The Overseas Targets*, 185; Alcorn, *No Bugles for Spies*, 55; McIntosh, *Sisterhood of Spies*, 110.

137 Passports were among the most difficult: For a short time, one German-issued identity card stumped the Documents Division. Each card had a unique nine-digit number that the police could examine and instantly know if it was legitimate. But the workers in the Documents Division discovered its secret before long. The first three digits represented the city where the person was from, the next five gave the day, month, and year of their birthdate, and whether the last digit was even or odd indicated whether they were male or female. Roosevelt, *The Overseas Targets*, 185.

138 For the best results: Untitled Document, RG 226, E A1 210, B 3, F 1, NARA; Karl Krause Ausweis, February 26, 1945, RG 226, E A1 210, B 18, F 12, NARA. The workers also impregnated documents with invisible ink. First, they washed the paper to be written on in a solution of a "stable organic compound," one memo says. Next, they pressed the paper with a hot iron and wrote an invisible message with an alcohol solution of phenolphthalein. When it dried, they covered the surface of the paper in a solution of diluted starch. Lastly, they wrote a visible decoy letter between the lines of invisible ink. To reveal the secret text, the receiver would rub the surface with a designated reagent. "Alcohol Solution of Phenolphthalein Used as Secret Ink," June 19, 1944, RG 226, E A1 210, B 3, F 1, NARA.

138 Obtaining fake American passports: Kahn, *Mrs. Shipley's Ghost*, 12; Waller, *Wild Bill Donovan*, 99; Perisco, *Piercing the Reich*, 24.

138 Donovan once visited: Perisco, *Piercing the Reich*, 28–29.

139 "The enemy forges identity papers": "Report on the Cover and Documents Branch," May 8, 1945, RG 226, E A1 210, B 3, F 1, NARA.

139 "differed greatly when examined": Roosevelt, *The Overseas Targets*, 162. There was only so much that the Documents Division could do. The personality of a particular agent was just as important in deceiving the enemy as the quality of their documents. "A self-assured agent with no papers has a better chance than a timid one with excellent papers," concludes a report by the Documents Division, "for timidity only invites investigation, and no cover is good enough to stand up under a thorough control." "Report on the Cover and Documents Branch," May 8, 1945, RG 226, E A1 210, B 3, F 1, NARA.

139 The R&D Branch therefore developed: McLean, *The Spy's Workshop*, 233, 242; Fieser, *The Scientific Method*, 138.

139 "These sad sacks": Bloom, "Uncle Sam," 354; Perisco, "Casey's German Gamble," 498.

140 Unlike Lovell, Reddick put little faith: When Ellic Howe (a.k.a. Armin Hull), the director of a British forging operation, was asked in a postwar interview whether he hired convicts, he said, "Heavens no. My staff was entirely respectable. We wouldn't have known how to act around that sort." Herbert Friedman, "Conversations with a Master Forger," http://www.psywarrior.com/ConversationwithaForger.html.

140 "He was the boss": Bloom, "Uncle Sam," 353.

140 Eifler sent samples: Sacquety, *The OSS in Burma*, 62.

140 "Major, don't you know": Bloom, "Uncle Sam," 353.

141 "The guy was horrified": Bloom, "Uncle Sam," 354–55.

141 "Suppose these guys decide": Perisco, "Casey's German Gamble," 498.

141 Eifler had also sent samples: Moon and Eifler, *The Deadliest Colonel*, 144.

142 "It was the most honest job": Lovell, *Of Spies and Stratagems*, 26–29. Also see Stanley Lovell, "Deadly Gadgets of the OSS," *Popular Science* (July 1963): 57–58; Glaser, *Counterfeiting in America*, 251. Other countries similarly forged currency during the war. In

Operation Bernhard, the Germans forged British bank notes, which they planned to drop over Britain to collapse the economy.

143 "How he did it, I'll never know": Lovell, *Of Spies and Stratagems*, 26.

143 The Philippine bills were a rush order: Reddick later explained how he otherwise aged the bills: "We tried a mixture of lanolin to make it greasy and added black dye and dry sienna powder. We put it all in a washing machine. First time we just got pulp. Then we found if you left it in only two/three minutes it would come out just right. And we added coffee which gave it the fluorescence the Japanese notes had. The final step was littering the floor with the completed notes and trampling them during our lunch break. We'd simply toss thousands of them on the floor which wasn't too clean to begin with and we'd just walk all over them." Bloom, "Uncle Sam," 355–56.

143 "Finance Forms": Lovell, *Of Spies and Stratagems*, 27.

143 "which seemed to be all the time": Stahl, *You're No Good to Me Dead*, 27.

143 "Well done, Professor Moriarty": Lovell, *Of Spies and Stratagems*, 27.

12. The Camouflage Division

144 In 1944, the R&D Branch opened: On the establishment of the Camouflage Division, see Stanley Lovell to Strategic Services Officers, August 5, 1944, RG 226, E A1 134, B 54, F 596A, NARA.

144 It occupied four small rooms: "Summary of Organization, R&D Branch, London," January 1, 1945, RG 226, E A1 210, B 199, F 4, NARA.

144 The Camouflage Division supplied: "Camouflage Intelligence Summary," October 30, 1944, RG 226, E 99, B 14, F 469, NARA; G. Hawthorne to Chief, R&D Branch, January 22, 1945, RG 226, E A1 134, B 54, F 596B, NARA. The Camouflage Division quickly found an enlisted OSS man who had previously worked as a tailor. Polish Intelligence furnished a cobbler. Roosevelt, *The Overseas Targets*, 161.

145 The workers often scoured: Perisco, *Piercing the Reich*, 4. Everything that the Camouflage Division produced was as authentic as

possible. For example, to obtain authentic German military uniforms, workers visited POW camps and took what they needed from the prisoners. The terms of the Geneva Convention were strictly observed. If an item was taken from a prisoner, a replacement item was given, though it didn't necessarily fit. "Functions of Clothing and Equipment Office," December 29, 1944, RG 226, E A1 210, B 199, F 4, NARA; Perisco, *Casey*, 74. Also see Bruce, *OSS against the Reich*, 84, 107.

145 "people as a whole": OSS, *Personal Disguise*, 2.

145 Evangeline Bell was one: Antony Beevor and Artemis Cooper, "Obituary: Evangeline Bruce," *Independent* (December 15, 1995); James Barron, "Evangeline Bruce, 77, Hostess Known for Washington Soirées," *The New York Times* (December 14, 1995): B18.

146 "burst into tears": McIntosh, *Sisterhood of Spies*, 109–10.

146 During its first six months: "Report of Clothing & Equipment Officer," January 1, 1945, RG 226, E A1 210, B 199, F 4, NARA. Sometimes the workers in the Camouflage Division would supply an agent with two disguises to enable a "quick change." In this case, the agent had to be mindful of which disguise to wear first. A manual from the Camouflage Division warned, "It will be much easier to switch from a bank clerk to a tramp, for example, than vice versa." OSS, *Personal Disguise*, 4.

146 "needed to get cracking": "Interview with Robert B. Springsteen," Veterans History Project, LOC (online).

147 These included a Volkswagen: [List of items supplied by the Camouflage Division], RG 226, E A1 134, B 54, F 596A, NARA.

147 "If an individual is thoroughly confident": William Turnbull to M. Morgan, October 3, 1944, RG 226, E A1 134, B 54, F 596B, NARA.

147 "When it comes to clothes": "Body Search," posted on YouTube by realmilitaryflix: https://www.youtube.com/watch?v=j7we3M-rN7w&ab_channel=realmilitaryflix. Also see "SI Detachment, 'Melanie' Mission," October 1944, RG 226, E 99, B 14, F 469, NARA.

148 "Right up to Germany's surrender": Lovell, *Of Spies and Stratagems*, 64–65.

148 molded messages into suppositories: "Message Suppositories," RG 226, E A1 210, B 199, F 4, NARA. On concealment methods, see "Organization, July, August, September 1944," RG 226, E A1 211, B 20, F "WN24136–24140," NARA.

148 Aided by Hollywood makeup artists: "Camouflage Intelligence Summary," October 30, 1944, RG 226, E A1 134, B 54, F 469, NARA; OSS, *Personal Disguise.*

149 "At a conference in London": Lovell, *Of Spies and Stratagems*, 67.

150 "Complete baldness with a persistence": Bailey, "Special Operations."

150 In 1933, at the age of twenty-seven: Purnell, *A Woman of No Importance*, 14–15.

150 "The woman who limps": McIntosh, *Sisterhood of Spies*, 114.

151 "a bitch of bitches": Stourton, *Cruel Crossing*, 250.

151 "Cuthbert is giving me trouble": McIntosh, *Sisterhood of Spies*, 118.

151 Nevertheless, with the assistance: Purnell, *A Woman of No Importance*, 197–98.

151 "tart friends": Purnell, *A Woman of No Importance*, 61–62.

152 "You have every reason": Purnell, *A Woman of No Importance*, 254.

152 "permanent make-up": Bailey, "Special Operations." Also see OSS, *Personal Disguise*, 33; "British SOE Camouflage Stations XV and XV-A," October 30, 1944, RG 226, E 99, B 14, F 469, NARA. The motivations for facial surgery were sometimes complicated. Frederick Lowenbach, a Romanian Jew working with the SOE, wanted "an Aryan look" that would give him and his family a "fresh start" after the war. Bailey, "Special Operations."

152 George Langelaan, the agent: Langelaan, *Knights of the Floating Silk*, 80–88.

153 For complete authenticity: Langelaan, *Knights of the Floating Silk*, 91–119.

155 On one sunny weekday afternoon: Langelaan, *Knights of the Floating Silk*, 135–43.

158 Langelaan's situation: Langelaan, *Knights of the Floating Silk*, 152–232.

13. Undercover Missions

161 *"Know* the character": OSS, *Personal Disguise*, 1. The manual was written by Newton Jones. In a letter outlining his initial thoughts on the topic, he wrote, "An appointment has been made for early next week for us to go through the Rogue's Gallery at Scotland Yard where I expect to pick up some ideas from things criminals have done to change their appearance." Newton Jones to Major Hill, RG 226, E A1 134, B 52, F "Personal Disguise/Makeup Kits," NARA.

161 The British once uncovered: Alcorn, *No Bugles for Spies*, 2.

162 "One walked into a pub": Fraser-Smith, *The Secret War*, 139.

162 American agents in Europe: On cultural distinctions and mannerisms, see OSS, *Personal Disguise*, 1.

162 "Darling": Hymoff, *The OSS in World War II*, 103.

163 At the OSS office in London: Perisco, *Casey*, 73; Perisco, *Piercing the Reich*, 31–33.

163 "I was born on": Perisco, *Piercing the Reich*, 176. Also see "Cover Story for the Time After 1.1.44.," RG 226, E A1 210, B 19, F 3, NARA.

165 "that the man who was questioned": Roosevelt, *The Overseas Targets*, 186.

165 To recruit them: Perisco, *Casey*, 73.

165 Agent "Louis" parachuted: "Report on the Cover and Documents Branch," May 8, 1945, RG 226, E A1 210, B 3, F 1, NARA.

165 In the greatest testament: Ford and MacBain, *Cloak and Dagger*, 53.

165 The Army soon developed: Kirkpatrick, *The Real CIA*, 56–57.

166 Women made particularly effective agents: See McIntosh, *Sisterhood of Spies*; Vigurs, *Mission France*.

167 During the German occupation: Perisco, *Piercing the Reich*, 261–62.

167 "We used the name": "Report on the Cover and Documents Branch," May 8, 1945, RG 226, E A1 210, B 3, F 1, NARA.

167 Just before takeoff: Perisco, *Piercing the Reich*, 262–63.

167 "controlled many times": "Report on the Cover and Documents Branch," May 8, 1945, RG 226, E A1 210, B 3, F 1, NARA.

168 *"pour la belle France"*: Perisco, *Piercing the Reich*, 263.

168 Small but consequential errors: "Report on the Cover and Documents Branch," May 8, 1945, RG 226, E A1 210, B 3, F 1, NARA.

169 "Adrian" parachuted into Germany: Perisco, *Piercing the Reich*, 250–52.

170 Other OSS agents: "Report on the Cover and Documents Branch," May 8, 1945, RG 226, E A1 210, B 3, F 1, NARA.

170 Sometimes death offered: O'Donnell, *Operatives, Spies, and Saboteurs*, 154–59. Another form of Gestapo torture and execution was described by a member of the OSS: "The Gestapo torture team rammed the point of a meathook under the jaw of their victim. The meathook was fastened to a rope strung from a tree limb. The truck was driven out from under the victim leaving the partisan wriggling his life away at the end of the rope, his toes barely touching the ground." Hymoff, *The OSS in World War II*, 228.

171 "Adrienne" was one of the few: Alcorn, *No Bugles for Spies*, 148–69.

14. Biological Warfare

176 "plume of what appeared": Borden Institute, *Military Medical Ethics*, 485.

176 Unbeknownst to the Chinese villagers: The plague at Ningbo wasn't the first time that biological weapons had been used in war. Eight hundred years earlier, in 1155, Holy Roman emperor Frederick Barbarossa poisoned Italian water wells with the bodies of dead soldiers. In 1495, the Spanish laced batches of wine destined for their French foes with the blood of leprosy patients. In 1763, Jeffrey Amherst, a British commander in North America, asked fellow commander Henry Bouquet, "Could it not be contrived to send the smallpox among the disaffected tribes of Indians?" Bouquet seized the blankets of infected soldiers and distributed them to the Natives. Frischknecht, "The History of Biological Warfare"; Knollenberg, "General Amherst and Germ Warfare."

177 "Trails of Sulphur": Borden Institute, *Military Medical Ethics*, 485.

177 "Typhoid could be introduced": Regis, *The Biology of Doom*, 20–21.

177 "dirty business": Regis, *The Biology of Doom*, 25.

177 The British had already: Regis, *The Biology of Doom*, 28–31.

178 "I feel that you were responsible": Albarelli, *A Terrible Mistake*, 46–47. On the origins of Camp Detrick, see Covert, *Cutting Edge*.

178 "pandemic organisms": Lovell, *Of Spies and Stratagems*, 132.

178 In its first two and a half years: Regis, *The Biology of Doom*, 57, 80. The Naval Research Unit at the University of California, Berkeley, conducted controlled bubonic plague experiments on human volunteers at San Quentin State Prison. Some of the convict test subjects developed soreness and headaches, but they reported no other serious side effects.

179 General Donovan "despised" the idea: Lovell, *Of Spies and Stratagems*, 131–33.

179 "I am studying biological warfare": Rogers, *Wartime Washington*, 6.

179 "aimless, political, and socialite": Rogers, *Wartime Washington*, 157–58.

180 "infinitely less barbarous": Lovell, *Of Spies and Stratagems*, 134.

180 Among the distinguished group: When the meeting adjourned, the group took a tour of Camp Detrick, where Marquand gave it the nickname "The Health Farm." Through no coincidence, Marquand would later name two characters in his book *Point of No Return* Francis Stanley and Lawrence Lovell. Lovell, *Of Spies and Stratagems*, 131.

181 "a new front": "Conference of 31 December 1943," December 31, 1943, Committees on Biological Warfare, F "Chemical Warfare Service," NAS.

181 "peach fuzz": "Report of a Subcommittee of the ABC Committee," May 15, 1944, Committees on Biological Warfare, F "ABC Committee," NAS; O'Donnell, *Operatives, Spies, and Saboteurs*, 21.

181 "There is no question": Kinzer, *Poisoner in Chief*, 16.

182 One method involved: "Summary of Activities of Special Assistants Division, R&D," January 1, 1945, to August 15, 1945, RG 226, E 211, B 20, NARA. Lovell's plan to poison crops wasn't substantially different from a plan by Robert Oppenheimer, the head of the Los Alamos Laboratory where the atomic bombs were built, to destroy enemy food with radioactivity. In a letter to Enrico Fermi, Oppenheimer

advised him to continue working on this secret project as long as "we can poison food sufficient to kill half a million men." Powers, *Heisenberg's War,* 354. Also see Alex Wellerstein, "Fears of a German Dirty Bomb," *Restricted Data,* blog.nuclearsecrecy.com/2013/09/06 /fears-of-a-german-dirty-bomb/#footnote_4_4517.

182 "the stalks fall over": "Final Summary Report of BW," September 28, 1945, RG 226, E 211, B 20, NARA. In an April 1945 experiment, the Army crop-dusted fields in Texas and Indiana with a compound named Vegetable Killer Acid. Joseph Trevithick, "Revealed: America Nearly Attacked Japan with Chemical Weapons in 1945," *National Interest* (June 10, 2016).

182 "There was a spirited discussion": Leahy, *I Was There,* 512.

182 "the Joint Chiefs of Staff have given": "Monthly Report—July 1945," August 3, 1945, RG 226, E 211, B 20, NARA.

183 "The flames which blaze": Osada, *Children of the A-Bomb,* 234.

183 "What about nuclear waste?": Author interview with Jonathan Lovell.

183 "It is a poisonous thing": Leahy, *I Was There,* 514.

184 "carried out by B.W. aircraft sprays": "German B.W. Intelligence of Russian Activity," RG 165, E NM84 187, B 137, F "BW," NARA. Also see Geißler, *Biologische Waffen,* 353 n. 4.

184 During his interrogation: "Interrogation of Blome," July 30, 1945, RG 319, E A1 134-B, B 79, F "Kurt Blome 3," NARA.

185 "a liar and a medical charlatan": E.W.B. Gill, "Interrogation of Doctor Kurt Blome," July 1, 1945, RG 319, E A1 134-B, B 79, F "Kurt Blome 3," NARA.

185 "experiments were carried out": *Nuremberg Trial Proceedings* 21 (August 26, 1946): avalon.law.yale.edu/imt/08-26-46.asp.

186 Operation Paperclip: Jacobsen, *Operation Paperclip,* 344.

186 "Our God-given mission": Regis, *Biology of Doom,* 40–41.

186 The unit's depraved experiments: Gold, *Unit 731 Testimony.* According to an Army major and pharmacist attached to Unit 731, "One *maruta* was a sixty-eight-year-old man. Back at Unit 731, he had been injected with plague germs but did not die. He was put through the

phosgene gas test and survived. An army doctor injected air into his veins, and he still did not die. The doctor then used an extra-heavy needle, and again injected air into the vein, but the man still survived. Finally, the doctors killed him by hanging him by the neck from a tree."

187 "greatly supplemented and amplified": Yang and Tam, *Unit 731*.

187 "At that time, the general thinking": Gold, *Unit 731 Testimony*.

15. Chemical Warfare

190 "the Luftwaffe will prepare": "Gas Warfare," June 4, 1943, RG 226, E A1 146, B 169, F "General (Intelligence)," NARA.

190 "very much afraid": Vannevar Bush, MIT Oral History Interviews, 165. Also see Henry Stimson, "Diaries," December 18, 1943, Henry Stimson Papers, B 59, YSML. German prisoners of war had told David Bruce that the Nazis were going to "scatter virulent germs" with their rockets. Bruce, *OSS against the Reich*, 64–65.

190 "Well, you've scared the hell": Vannevar Bush, MIT Oral History Interviews, 164; Henry Stimson, "Diaries," January 12, 1944, Henry Stimson Papers, B 59, YSML. Also see "Gas Warfare," June 16, 1943, RG 226, E A1 146, B 169, F "General (Intelligence)," NARA.

190 "About this V-1 business": Vannevar Bush, MIT Oral History Interviews, 166.

191 "It was like 4th of July": "Interview with Charles Dee," Veterans History Project, LOC (online).

191 "was not great": Vannevar Bush, MIT Oral History Interviews, 166. As part of Operation Paperclip, the United States hired several German rocket scientists, including Wernher von Braun, to kick-start an American rocket program. Von Braun would later lead the development team for the Saturn V rocket that put men on the Moon during NASA's Apollo program. The night before the first Apollo launch, a smug reporter asked von Braun if he could guarantee that the rocket wouldn't land on London, as his V-2s had during the war. Kennedy, *Vengeance Weapon 2*, 29; Cornwell, *Hitler's Scientists*, 423.

191 "It is absurd to consider": Hilmas, Smart, and Platoff, "History of Chemical Warfare," 52.

192 Between 1940 and 1945: "History of United States' Involvement in Chemical Warfare," *DENIX*, https://denix.osd.mil/rcwmprogram /history/.

192 While Donovan and Louis Fieser: Fieser, *The Scientific Method*, 14.

192 "probably more persons": Civil Defense Liaison Office, *Fire Effects of Bombing Attacks*, 22.

192 Lovell specifically wanted: Lovell, *Of Spies and Stratagems*, 70.

193 The task of responding: Newcomb, *Iwo Jima*, 240; Madsen, "Strategy, Fleet Logistics."

193 "Jam the Iwo Jima radio transmitter": Lovell, *Of Spies and Stratagems*, 70–71.

193 "must be administered": John Ellis van Courtland Moon, "Chemical Warfare: A Forgotten Lesson," *Bulletin of the Atomic Scientists* 45, no. 6 (July 1989): 40.

193 According to Lovell: Lovell, *Of Spies and Stratagems*, 72–77. Lovell's personnel records show that he traveled to Hawaii in July 1944. Joseph Grant to James Kirk, July 29, 1944, RG 226, E A1 224, B 464, F "Lovell, Stanley P.," NARA.

195 In fact, Lovell had briefly experimented: "Final Summary Report of TB.," August 27, 1945, RG 226, E 211, B 20, NARA; "Final Summary Report of VG," August 31, 1945, RG 226, E 211, B 20, NARA. Regarding TB, an internal report says that it "causes the individual to feel only as if he were seeing in a dense fog or white smoke. The individual is capable of perceiving only between light and dark. The value of this agent in sabotage of air crews will be seen if a few small crystals were placed either in the oxygen manifolds or in the individual oxygen outlets for the various crew members of a bomber." "New O.S.S. Weapons," RG 226, E 211, B 20, NARA.

196 Corporal Melford Jarstad: "Interview with Melford K. Jarstad," Veterans History Project, LOC (online).

197 "After the terrible losses": Lilienthal, *The Journals of David Lilienthal*, 199.

197 During the postwar Nuremberg trials: Lovell, *Of Spies and Stratagems*, 77–78.

198 "a Professor Moriarty is as un-American": Lovell, *Of Spies and Stratagems*, 21.

16. Truth Drugs

199 "apparently sound asleep": House, "The Use of Scopolamine in Criminology."

200 The idea that drugs: In 1753, a twenty-one-year-old George Washington dined with French officers in the Ohio wilderness and wrote that the accompanying wine "soon banished the restraint which at first appeared in their Conversation, & gave license to their Tongues to reveal their Sentiments more freely. They told me it was their absolute Design to take Possession of the Ohio, & by G— they wou'd do it." Andrews, *For the President's Eyes Only*, 6.

200 In 1922, House conducted: House, "The Use of Scopolamine in Criminology."

200 He was found guilty: The ruling was a blow to House, but he was vindicated in the long run. Years later, Scrivener admitted to robbing another store in Dallas, but never the pharmacy. The original prosecuting attorney looked into the matter and reversed his initial opinion. He became convinced that Scrivener was in Fort Worth, not Dallas, on the day that Guy's Pharmacy was robbed.

200 As for Ed Smith: "Negro Questioned Under 'Twilight Sleep' Freed of Charge of Murder," *Dallas Morning News* (February 21, 1922). Also see "Truth Drugging," *The New York Times* (March 9, 1947): E9; "Husband Sentenced; Told, Under Drug, of Killing Wife," *The New York Times* (January 3, 1968): 45.

200 "test of twilight serum": House, "The Use of Scopolamine in Criminology."

201 *Frye v. United States:* The *Frye* standard was later superseded by the Federal Rules of Evidence.

201 "We are not told": Winter, *Memory*, 42.

202 "Experiments to date": Torsten and Benzenhöfer, "MDA, MDMA, and Other Mescaline-like Substances."

202 "Within the context of Auschwitz": Streatfeild, *Brainwash*, 37–38.

202 "eliminate the will": Streatfeild, *Brainwash*, 38; Lee and Shlain, *Acid Dreams*, 6.

203 "Truth drugs were discontinued": Fry, *The London Cage*, 90; "Use of Special Interrogation Techniques by Foreign Countries," June 22, 1948, MORI 184372.

203 "very crude torture mechanisms": "Use of Special Interrogation Techniques by Foreign Countries," June 22, 1948, MORI 184372.

203 CIA contractors Harold Wolff and Lawrence Hinkle: Lawrence Hinkle and Harold Wolff, "Communist Control Techniques," April 2, 1956, CREST.

203 "considered fantastic by the realists": Brown, *The Last Hero*, 745–46.

204 Truth Drug Committee: The members of the Truth Drug Committee were Roger Adams, Harry Anslinger, E. P. Coffy, Watson Eldridge, R. D. Halloran, James Hamilton, Lawrence Kubie, R. E. Looker, Winfred Overholser, Charles Stephenson, Edward Stricker, and John Whitehorn.

204 None of these drugs: "Report of T. D.," June 2, 1943, CREST.

204 "If the hideous monster": Lee, *Smoke Signals*, 49.

205 In a subsequent report: "Truth Drug," April 5, 1946, MORI 144773.

206 "I guess we were safer": Marks, *The Search for the Manchurian Candidate*, 6; "Report of T. D.," June 2, 1943, CREST.

206 "The subject gradually becomes relaxed": Brown, *The Last Hero*, 746.

207 "fat slob": Douglas Valentine, "Sex, Drugs and the CIA," *Counterpunch* (June 19, 2002); White and his ex-wife, Albertine Calef, apparently had much in common. When journalist Douglas Valentine interviewed Calef about White's CIA activities, she "descended into a string of expletives that would have embarrassed a sailor. Her tirade left this writer with the firm impression that she was thoroughly capable of having been White's accomplice in his dirty work."

207 "roly-poly": Lovell, *Of Spies and Stratagems*, 57.

208 "interfered terminally": Moon and Eifler, *The Deadliest Colonel*, 157.

208 "He used to keep": Richard Stratton, "Altered States of America," *Spin Magazine* (March 1994).

208 "I was one of the best": Clarke, *Wishing on the Moon*, 304.

208 "White was a son of a bitch": Richard Stratton, "Altered States of America," *Spin Magazine* (March 1994).

208 White happily experimented on himself: Marks, *The Search for the Manchurian Candidate*, 6.

209 White wrote in an intelligence report: "Memorandum on T.D.," June 2, 1943, MORI 184373.

211 "Before we went in": Marks, *The Search for the Manchurian Candidate*, 7–8.

211 They once interrogated forty: "Investigation of Use of TD in Interrogation," MORI 144773.

211 "highly dangerous": Carroll, "Under the Influence: Harry Anslinger's Role in Shaping America's Drug Policy," 75.

212 The interrogator wanted to extract: "Truth Drug," April 5, 1946, MORI 144773. Lovell claimed that the truth drug was administered in alcohol, but all other evidence suggests that it was given in a cigarette. One declassified report of the incident says that the Americans had tried giving the German alcohol, but he was suspicious of their motives and refused. "Investigation of Use of TD in Interrogation," MORI 144773.

212 "I'm going to tell you something": Lovell, *Of Spies and Stratagems*, 58–59.

213 "did not want to know": Brown, *The Last Hero*, 751.

213 "If you have a blowtorch": Marks, *The Search for the Manchurian Candidate*, 44.

214 "Indications are that uninhibited": "Final Summary Report of T.D.," September 6, 1945, RG 226, E 211, B 20, NARA. During World War II, psychiatrist Walter Neustatter experimented with pentothal at his private practice and reached the same disappointing conclusion. The "truth" in "truth drug" is a misnomer, he said. "Not only can they [the recipients] lie, but they can fabricate very effectively under the influence." Neustatter, *Psychological Disorder and Crime*, 82–83. Also see De River, *The Sexual Criminal*, ch. 20.

214 Eifler devised a plan: Moon and Eifler, *The Deadliest Colonel*, 122–27. Also see Sacquety, *The OSS in Burma*, 55–56; Peers and Brelis, *Behind the Burma Road*, 106–9.

216 The performance had worked: A 1963 CIA manual on interrogations describes a similar technique: "The interrogatee is given a placebo (a harmless sugar pill). Later he is told that he has imbibed a drug, a truth serum, which will make him want to talk and which will also prevent his lying. The subject's desire to find an excuse for the compliance that represents his sole avenue of escape from his distressing predicament may make him want to believe that he has been drugged and that no one could blame him for telling his story now." CIA, *Kubark Counterintelligence Interrogation*.

216 "He'd come to me": Vannevar Bush, MIT Oral History Interviews, 686.

217 "affected by a remarkable restlessness": Hofmann, "LSD," 43–47.

217 "Tasteless, odorless": OSI, "Development of Research in Connection with Project Artichoke," November 21, 1951, MORI 147406.

217 "of all substances now known": "Subject: Attached," MORI 148093; "Potential New Agent for Unconventional Warfare," August 5, 1954, MORI 148381.

217 "An infinitesimally small dose": Harris Chadwell, "Briefing for the Psychological Strategy Board," May 13, 1953, CREST.

218 "would give a man symptoms": Vannevar Bush, MIT Oral History Interviews. During the interview, Bush said that he had "talked to Stimson about the handling of this." Secretary of War Henry Stimson died in 1950.

218 "At the end of the war": The pages containing this quote only appear in one of the two existing copies of the interview. The second copy is located at the Carnegie Institution for Science.

17. Lovell's Twilight

219 Those who found their bodies: Junge, *Until the Final Hour*.

219 "I consider that the disruption": Roosevelt, *The Overseas Targets*, 222.

219 "has surpassed all our expectation": Chambers, *OSS Training in the National Parks,* 377.

220 "fantastic damn organization": Hayden, *Wanderer,* 330. Also see Perisco, *Roosevelt's Secret War,* 166.

220 "The main purpose of this school": "Colonel Park's Comments on OSS," March 12, 1945, HSTL.

221 "seemed to become a mausoleum": MacDonald, *Undercover Girl,* 294.

221 "We have come to the end": Dunlop, *Donovan,* 473–74.

222 "What a man!": Brown, *The Last Hero,* 833.

222 "very greatly disappointed": Howard Dix to Moe Berg, October 3, 1944, RG 226, E A1 146, B 245, F "Reading File," NARA.

223 "the physicists have known sin": Robert Oppenheimer, "Physics in the Contemporary World," *Bulletin of the Atomic Scientists* 4, no. 3 (March 1948): 66.

223 No doubt influencing: Donovan and Roosevelt had been in similar situations. Donovan's son David was a captain in the Navy and would have participated in an invasion of Japan. Roosevelt told his son James, a Marine Corps colonel stationed in the Pacific, not to fear death because the United States had developed a secret weapon that "we will certainly use before you or any of our sons die in an invasion of Japan." Roosevelt, *My Parents,* 170.

224 "By the Turkman Gate": Stanley Lovell to Roger Adams, December 29, 1946, Roger Adams Papers, B 8, F "Poems," UIA.

224 Lovell was initially interested: "Interview with Stanley P. Lovell," June 24, 1966, CREST. At a White House ceremony inaugurating Admiral Sidney Souers as the first director of the CIG, Truman jokingly presented him with a black cloak and a wooden dagger. Powers, *The Man Who Kept the Secrets,* 27.

225 "certainly sticks out your chin": Vannevar Bush to Stanley Lovell, July 7, 1947, VBP, B 66, F 1610, LOC.

225 His other patents: For example, see patents US3002650A, US2677646A, US2218844A, US2251252A, and US2415391A.

225 "intellectual reparations": See Gimbel, *Science, Technology, and Reparations.*

225 He then sold the rights: Donald White, "Firm's Product 82% Nothing," *The Boston Globe* (February 12, 1964): 14; Arthur Riley, "Bedford-Built Filter Helps Feed, Protect Astronauts," *The Boston Globe* (February 2, 1969): 8A. Also see patent application US2783894A.

225 "A person whom I know very well": Stanley Lovell to Vannevar Bush, April 11, 1947, VBP, B 66, F 1610, LOC.

226 "never forgot with what fascination": Erwin Canham, "Some Fond Memories of a Dirty Trickster," *Buck County Courier Times* (January 15, 1976): 14.

226 "To the best of my belief": Lovell, *Of Spies and Stratagems*, 8.

226 "Not one word": "FDR Halted Gas Attack," *Wisconsin State Journal* (March 24, 1963).

227 Operation Capricious: Lovell, *Of Spies and Stratagems*, 134–37.

227 Russian children used frozen German corpses: Werth, *Russia at War*.

228 "spilled the whole affair": Vannevar Bush, MIT Oral History Interviews, 684.

228 "in a light vein": Stanley Lovell to Richard Helms, July 25, 1963, Richard Helms Papers, B 1, F 87, GUA.

228 Helms responded the following week: A journalist noted that Lovell was "understandably relieved when he received commendable letters from the high officials of the CIA, not only praising his literary efforts but stating some fine young recruits had been influenced to serve in this secret branch after reading the volume." Joe Harrington, "Newton Agent Bares O.S.S. Secrets," *The Boston Globe* (November 12, 1963).

228 Dulles even fed plots: Powers, *The Man Who Kept the Secrets*, 54.

229 "a senior officer now intimately concerned": Richard Helms to Stanley Lovell, July 31, 1963, Richard Helms Papers, B 1, F 87, GUA.

229 Lovell instead subscribed to the Oxfordian theory: This theory was first proposed in 1920 by the aptly named J. Thomas Looney (publishers tried to convince him to adopt a pseudonym).

229 "A Mystery Beyond Words": Stanley Lovell, "A Mystery Beyond Words," Roger Adams Papers, B 36, F "L, 1968–71," UIA.

230 Bush once asked Lovell: Vannevar Bush to Stanley Lovell, October 6, 1953, VBP, B 66, F 1610, LOC.

230 "I do a whole lot better": Stanley Lovell to Vannevar Bush, May 27, 1949, VBP, B 66, F 1610, LOC; Stanley Lovell to Vannevar Bush, October 23, 1947, VBP, B 66, F 1610, LOC.

230 "Dear Stan": Vannevar Bush to Stanley Lovell, November 20, 1947, VBP, B 66, F 1610, LOC. Bush once began another letter, "I do not think that you are probably interested in trick storage batteries, but then you may be, for you are interested in all sorts of things that have chemicals in them." He then proceeded to describe the battery in front of him. Vannevar Bush to Stanley Lovell, September 15, 1947, VBP, B 66, F 1610, LOC.

230 "get one of your youngsters": Vannevar Bush to Stanley Lovell, May 20, 1947, VBP, B 66, F 1610, LOC.

230 "has provoked as much trial": Stanley Lovell to Vannevar Bush, July 7, 1947, VBP, B 66, F 1610, LOC.

230 "O! What a tangled web we weave": Stanley Lovell to Vannevar Bush, July 3, 1947, VBP, B 66, F 1610, LOC.

231 "which will completely remove": Stanley Lovell to Vannevar Bush, May 27, 1949, VBP, B 66, F 1610, LOC.

231 "Some were undramatic": Stanley Lovell, "Cloak-and-Dagger Behind the Scenes," *The Saturday Evening Post* (March 3, 1962): 30.

232 "Demon Photographer": Stanley Lovell to Richard Dunlop, March 19, 1962, AHEC.

232 "Doctor Moriarty": Stanley Lovell, "Cloak-and-Dagger Behind the Scenes," *The Saturday Evening Post* (March 3, 1962): 35.

18. A Legacy of Lessons

233 "Warfare is no longer a matter": Wallace and Melton, *Spycraft*, 53.

233 "Did it produce the gadgets": DSG, September 25, 1980, JRP, B 243, F 7, LOC, 8–9.

234 "more classical application": DSG, April 19, 1983, JRP, B 222, F 7, LOC, 10.

234 "Mr. Gottlieb is a very high type": Kinzer, *Poisoner in Chief*, 7.

235 "felt that the Soviet Union": DSG, September 25, 1980, JRP, B 243, F 7, LOC, 10.

235 Several downed American pilots: "Depositions by Captured US Airmen Concerning Their Participation in Germ Warfare," September 16, 1952, Joseph Koepfli Papers, B 2, F "Korean War Germ Warfare," CIT.

236 Many of the experiments: "Hypnotic Experimentation and Research," February 10, 1954, MORI 190691.

236 Gottlieb even hired renowned magician: Melton and Wallace, *The CIA Manual of Trickery and Deception*; Michael Edwards, "The Sphinx and the Spy: The Clandestine World of John Mulholland," *Genii Magazine* (April 2001).

237 "Is that LSD you're drinking?": Nicholas Horrock, "Destruction of LSD Data Laid to C.I.A. Aide in '73," *The New York Times* (July 18, 1975).

237 "was very much like the earlier Division 19": Albarelli, *A Terrible Mistake*, 66.

238 "a totally different person": Deposition of Alice Olson, September 16, 1988, JRP, B 226, F 4, LOC, 12.

238 "I can't eat this food": Deposition of Alice Olson, September 16, 1988, JRP, B 226, F 4, LOC, 16.

238 "wild and crazy": Albarelli, *A Terrible Mistake*, 286.

238 "As soon as these gentlemen left": Harold Abramson, "Observations on Mr. Frank Olson," December 4, 1953, FOPD.

238 "What's behind all this?": Vincent Ruwet on Frank Olson, FOPD.

239 "It seemed to me": Sidney Gottlieb, "Observation on Dr. Frank Olson," FOPD.

239 "psychotic state": Harold Abramson, "Observations on Mr. Frank Olson," December 4, 1953, FOPD.

239 "Somewhere around 0230 Saturday morning": Robert Lashbrook, "Observations on Frank Olson," FOPD.

239 "His right hand clutched my arm": Armond Pastore to Alice Olson, July 13, 1975, FOPD.

240 His first action was to send: Albarelli, *A Terrible Mistake*, 101.

240 "[Sheffield] Edwards and [Harris] Chadwell": "Kirkpatrick Diary," FOPD.

240 Office of Scientific Intelligence: The OSI had also initiated Project Bluebird, the precursor to MKULTRA.

240 "Lovell knew about Frank R. Olson": "Conversation with Gibbons," December 14, 1953, FOPD.

241 "A couple of crew-cut": John Crewdson, "Abuses in Testing of Drugs by C.I.A. to be Panel Focus," *The New York Times* (September 20, 1977): 85.

241 "certainly knew about our financial support": DSG, May 17, 1983, JRP, B 223, F 2, LOC, 393; John Earman, "Report of Inspection of MKULTRA/TSD," July 26, 1963, MORI 17748, 11.

242 "Most of what we talked about": Albarelli, *A Terrible Mistake*, 217.

242 "That period": Kinzer, *Poisoner in Chief*, 80.

242 "He always said he never felt": Richard Stratton, "Altered States of America," *Spin Magazine* (March 1994).

242 In exchange for their services: "Accountability for Certain Expenditures under Subproject 42 of MKULTRA," August 17, 1956, MORI 17440.

242 A declassified CIA inventory: "Inventory of [*redacted*]," MORI 17440.

243 "A 'window' was constructed": "Discussion with [*redacted*] Concerning Past and Future Accounting for Funds," August 1, 1955, MORI 17440.

243 "that if you spilled a glass of water": Streatfeild, *Brainwash*, 84.

243 "If it was a girl": Richard Stratton, "Altered States of America," *Spin Magazine* (March 1994).

243 "varied very much along individuals": DSG, September 25, 1980, JRP, B 243, F 7, LOC, 77.

243 He had reached the same conclusion: During World War II, Vannevar Bush oversaw similarly unpalatable experiments in the name of wartime necessity, including one that infected volunteers at Indiana's Terre Haute prison with gonorrhea in an effort to better understand how venereal diseases spread among servicemen. To ease his conscience about the experiment, Bush consulted with the president of the National Academy of Sciences and the chairman of the National

Research Council. In a letter to Bush, both men considered the experiment "desirable and necessary," but they warned him that on matters of legality, "We are of course not competent to advise." The experiment proceeded anyway. The 241 prisoners involved were infected with gonorrhea that had been collected from local sex workers. For their participation, the prisoners received $100, a certificate of merit, and a positive letter for the parole board. Frank Jewett and Ross Harrison to Vannevar Bush, March 5, 1943, RG 227, E NC-138 1, B 26, F "Venereal Diseases," NARA; Presidential Commission for the Study of Bioethical Issues, *Ethically Impossible*, 20–21.

244 "a flight of poetic license": DSG, June 28, 1983, JRP, B 223, F 3, LOC, 523.

244 "I was a very minor missionary": Marks, *The Search for the Manchurian Candidate*, 101.

245 "[Qasim] suffered a terminal illness": Select Committee to Study Governmental Operations, *Alleged Assassination Plots Involving Foreign Leaders*, 181.

245 With Gottlieb at the helm: Wallace and Melton, *Spycraft*, 95.

245 "a fountain pen that does things": Vannevar Bush, MIT Oral History Interviews, 684–86.

245 "neurotropic toxic substance": "The 'K' Problem," MORI 17471.

245 The resulting suicide device: Pilot Francis Gary Powers carried one of these needles with him when he was shot down over the Soviet Union. The Soviets caught him, confiscated the needle, and pricked a dog with it. The results of the experiment were revealed at Powers's trial for espionage: "Within one minute after the prick the dog fell on his side, and a sharp slackening of the respiratory movements of the chest was observed, a cyanosis of the tongue and visible mucous membranes was noted." Powers, *The Trial of the U2*, 102.

245 Secret Writing Division: Commission on CIA Activities Within the United States, *The Nelson Rockefeller Report to the President*, 229; Richelson, *The Wizards of Langley*, 164. The TSD provided the per-

petrators of the Watergate break-in with disguises, false identification papers, and a voice-altering device.

246 "The remainder of the World War II": Mendez, *The Master of Disguise*, 44.

246 "In these days when the dirty tricks": Erwin Canham, "Some Fond Memories of a Dirty Trickster," *Buck County Courier Times* (January 15, 1976): 14.

247 "In time of war": Srodes, *Allen Dulles*, 385. "We felt an aggressive attack by the Soviet Union could not be ruled out," Gottlieb said in defense of MKULTRA, "and I will only make the analogy that, you know, in a wartime situation, things are done that you would never do in some other situation. People get killed. People kill other people." Albarelli, *A Terrible Mistake*, 187.

247 "If I was doing the stuff today": O'Donnell, *Operatives, Spies, and Saboteurs*, 18.

248 "Who is H. M. Chadwell": DSG, May 17, 1983, JRP, B 223, F 1, LOC, 248–49.

248 Lovell had, in fact, died: "Stanley Lovell," *The Boston Globe* (January 6, 1976): 34; Author interview with Jonathan Lovell.

248 "I didn't know anything about this": DSG, September 25, 1980, JRP, B 243, F 7, LOC, 11, 82.

248 Searching through those dilapidated boxes: A 1954 memo by Morse Allen confirms that the CIA held OSS files: "Back in 1954, OSS was attempting to study drugs which might be useful in the interrogation of prisoners of war. Connected with the experiments was one Major George H. White, an Army officer and probably a G-2 man. White conducted experiments particularly using Marijuana, and made some reports on these which we have in our files under DRUGS-OSS Research." Albarelli, *A Terrible Mistake*, 177.

Appendix 1

249 The following are the code names: Warren Lothrop, "History of Division 19," June 30, 1945, RG 226, E A1 210, B 84, F 6, NARA.

For a separate listing, see "Technical Branch Projects & Assignments," RG 226, E A1 154, B 131, F 2281, NARA.

Appendix 2

255 "As we came into the targeted area": "Narrative by 1st. Lt. Freeling H. Clower, Given in Hosp. January 1944," August 1, 1944, RG 226, E 190, B 34, F 15, NARA.

Index